WHO CHANGES?

WHO CHANGES?

Institutionalizing participation in development

Edited by
JAMES BLACKBURN with JEREMY HOLLAND
with a Foreword by ROBERT CHAMBERS

INTERMEDIATE TECHNOLOGY PUBLICATIONS 1998

Intermediate Technology Publications Ltd
103–105 Southampton Row, London WC1B 4HH, UK

A CIP catalogue record for this book is available from the
British Library

ISBN 1 85339 420 3

Typeset by J&L Composition Ltd, Filey, North Yorkshire
Printed in the UK by SRP, Exeter

Contents

v

List of figures, tables and boxes

Abbreviations

AEW	agricultural extension worker
AGRITEX	Agricultural Extension Service (Zimbabwe)
ASD	Agrarian Services Department (Sri Lanka)
ASP	*Asamblea para la Soberania de los Pueblos* (Assembly for the Sovereignty of Communities – Bolivia)
AWS	annual working plan
BMZ	Federal Ministry of Economic Cooperation and Development (Germany)
CAA	Community Aid Abroad (Australia)
CERES	Centre for Studies on Economic and Social Reality (Cochabamba, Bolivia)
CMDA	Calcutta Metropolitan Development Authority
CIDOB	Confederation of Eastern Bolivian Indigenous Peoples (Bolivia)
CONTILL	Conservation Tillage for Sustainable Crop Production System (Zimbabwe)
CORDES	*Corporaciones Regionales de Desarrollo* (Regional Development Corporations – Bolivia)
CSIP	Calcutta Slum-improvement Project (India)
CV	*Comités de Vigilancia* (Vigilance Committees – Bolivia)
DANIDA	Danish Agency for International Development
DAS	Department of Agrarian Services (Sri Lanka)
DVP	Doon Valley Project (Uttar Pradesh, India)
EU	European Union
FAO	Food and Agricultural Organization
FCP	Forestry Cooperation Programme (Sweden–Vietnam)
FDC	*Fondo de Desarrollo Campesino* (Bolivia)
FIS	*Fondo de Inversión Social* (Social Investment Fund – Bolivia)
FIT	Foundation for International Training
FO	farmer organization
GOI	Government of India
GOUP	Government of Uttar Pradesh (India)
GTZ	*Deutsche Gesellschaft für Technische Zusammenarbeit* (Germany)

HQ	headquarters
IC	Intercooperation (Sri Lanka)
IDS	Institute of Development Studies (Sussex, UK)
IFAD	International Fund for Agricultural Development
IIED	International Institute for Environment and Development (UK)
IPDS	*Instituciones Privadas de Desarrollo Social* (Private Institutions for Social Development – Bolivia)
IRDEP	Integrated Rural Development Programme (Zimbabwe)
ITK	indigenous technical knowledge
LPP	*Ley de Participación Popular* (Law of Popular Participation – Bolivia)
LWA	Land and Water Association (Estonia)
M&E	monitoring and evaluation
MNR	*Movimiento Nacional Revolucionario* (National Revolutionary Movement – Bolivia)
MoA	Ministry of Agriculture (Estonia)
NDF	National Development Foundation (Sri Lanka)
NFIGPS	non-farm income-generating programme (OUTREACH, India)
NGO	non-governmental organization
NRM	natural resource management
O&M	Operation and Maintenance
ODA	Overseas Development Administration (UK)
OTB	*Organización Territorial de Base* (Basic Territorial Organisation – Bolivia)
PALM	participatory analysis and learning methods
PAO	*Plan Anual Operativo* (Annual Operative Plan – Bolivia)
PAR	participatory action research
PCM	project cycle management
PDM	*Plan de Desarrollo Municipal* (Municipal Development Plan – Bolivia)
PKK	Family Welfare Movement (Indonesia)
PORP	participatory operational research projects
PRA	partcipatory rural/relaxed appraisal and/or participatory reflection and action
PSA	participatory social assessment
RAP	rapid assessment procedure
RRA	rapid rural appraisal
SCF	Save the Children Fund
SIDA	Swedish International Development Authority
SIP	slum-improvement project (India)
SNPP	*Secretaría Nacional de Participación Popular* (Bolivia)
SSP	Self-help Support Programme (Sri Lanka)
TA	technical assistance

TFT	Training-for-Transformation
TIM	*Territorio Indìgena Multiétnico* (Indigenous Multi-ethnic Territory – Bolivia)
TOT	trainings of trainers
UNICEF	United Nations Children's Fund
UP	Uttar Pradesh (India)
WMC	watershed management committee (OUTREACH, India)
ZOPP	*Zielorientierte Projekt Planung*

Acknowledgements

Putting together this book has been like taking a journey across a full range of climates, continents and altitudes. At times things seemed to come together – the summit appeared close, the sky a bright clear blue. But the journey also had its clouds and cold winds. Getting lost is, I suppose, part of getting there.

I would like to thank the many travelling companions and supporters who made the trip less arduous and more exhilirating. Without their support and encouragement, I am sure I would still be stuck at base camp!

First of all, a big *abrazo* to my most constant of *compañeros*, Jeremy Holland, whose tennis skills, culinary talents (a master at serving fish and chips), quick mind, and cheerful temperament brought much enjoyment to the task. Many thanks too to Robert Chambers for his inimitable bursts of enthusiasm (like filling up with kerosene when all you needed was ordinary fuel) and skilful steering of the process. The authors of the book I thank for their patience and diligence in commenting on edited drafts. Thank you also to Ben Osuga, John Gaventa, Robin Luckam, Kamal Singh, Heidi Atwood, Andy Wilkes and many many others for the enriching discussions held over beers or coffee.

James Blackburn

Foreword

ROBERT CHAMBERS

For us – development professionals in whatever roles, the sort of people who will have a chance to read this book – this is a good time to be alive. Much that we have believed has proved wrong; and a new agenda is fast taking form. As *Who Changes?* shows, this promises, for all of us, whoever we are, whatever our profession or discipline, and wherever we work, the challenge and exhilaration of exploration, innovation, learning, and doing better.

The context

This excitement can be seen in historical context. From the 1950s through the 1960s and 1970s, in the prevailing orthodoxies of development, it was professionals who had the answers. In general we were right and we were the solution. Poor and local people were the problem, and much of the problem was to be solved by education and the transfer of technology. Increasingly, that ideology has been questioned and undermined. The balance has shifted. Development imposed from the top down was often not sustained. More and more we have been recognized as much of the problem, and their participation as the key to sustainability and many of the solutions.

So participation has become a central theme in development. It is new orthodoxy in the World Bank, where it is being mainstreamed: the Bank now has flagship participation projects, and projects are monitored for their degree of participation. An Inter-Agency Learning Group on Participation has been meeting, comprising major multilateral and bilateral donor agencies and some NGOs. In more and more countries and sectors, participation is required in projects and programmes. The lexicon of development has expanded, perhaps irreversibly, to include participation. And as usual with concepts which gain currency, rhetoric has run far, far ahead of understanding, let alone practice.

Requiring participation has preceded a full understanding of its implications. At first, much of the official thinking was that participation was cost-effective: with participation, local people do more; projects cost less; and

xiii

achievements are more sustainable. So participation has been written into project documents, policies, and even, as in Bolivia, laws. There can be, though, a big gap between requirement and reality. For as this book shows, the changes needed extend back up hierarchies to include the cultures, procedures, incentives, rewards, and recruitment and staffing policies, of NGOs and of government and donor agencies.

One source of learning has been experiences with participatory rural appraisal (PRA). This has evolved rapidly as a mindset, a philosophy, and a repertoire of methods. The essence of PRA is changes and reversals – of role, behaviour, relationship and learning. Outsiders do not dominate and lecture; they facilitate, sit down, listen, watch and learn. Outsiders do not transfer technology; instead they share methods which local people can use for their own appraisal, analysis, planning, action, monitoring and evaluation. Outsiders hand over the stick, trusting the capabilities of local people. The methods help: many involve visualizations – mapping, diagramming, estimating, ranking, scoring and the like – by local people. Beyond the methods, and as contributors to this book state again and again, personal behaviour and attitudes are crucial. Nor are new participatory methods and changes in personal behaviour and attitudes enough on their own. Repeatedly, PRA has encountered barriers to good performance, and to spread, which are institutional.

PRA only began to emerge in the late 1980s and early 1990s, but its spread has been exponential, to over 100 countries and into most domains of rural and urban development. It has been adopted by many government agencies and NGOs. As PRA and participation have become popular, they have been demanded and required often at short notice and on a huge scale. The results have often been bad. At the same time, in some cases where introduction has been gradual, with good training, sustained support and institutional change, the results have been profoundly encouraging.

Learning from these experiences has become urgent and vital. Recognizing this, the Institute of Development Studies, Sussex, through support from Swiss Development Co-operation, convened a workshop on Institutionalization of Participatory Approaches. On 16 and 17 May 1996, some 50 people from 26 countries took part. The papers and discussions, with James Blackburn as the main editor, provide the core of this book, updated and augmented by new material from this rapidly evolving field.

Another workshop a few days earlier drew together experience on PRA and policy. A companion volume, *Whose Voice?*, with Jeremy Holland as the main editor, similarly presents and analyses much learning from recent experience in a new field. It finds that PRA and related participatory approaches have opened up new ways in which policy can be influenced by the realities of those who are poor, weak, marginalized and excluded. Thematic studies in a participatory mode, and broader participatory poverty assessments, have revealed new insights with policy implications. *Whose Voice?* and *Who*

Changes? are part of a sequence of publications which draw on PRA-related experience.

Lessons being learnt

The contributions to *Who Changes?* are a rich harvest of experience and judgement. They represent a stage in a process of learning. Most of the authors have been engaged in practical work over at least a decade. Though drawing on experiences from different contexts, countries and continents, they converge strikingly on similar insights and issues. The lessons are convincing but cannot be final. Perhaps there can never be closure on any conventional wisdom in such a dynamic and complex field. In five or ten years' time, more will be known, other lessons will have been learnt, and what we believe we have learnt now will have been qualified and added to by further experience.

All the same, two strong working conclusions stand out as basic and likely to last. They are that:

- sustained participation in development demands transformations in three domains: methods and procedures; institutional cultures; and personal behaviour and attitudes. All three are needed. Each reinforces the others. Each presents points of entry for change.
- of these, personal behaviour and attitudes are crucial. Participation is about how people interact. Dominating behaviour inhibits participation. Democratic behaviour to enable and empower encourages it. For those with power and authority to adopt non-dominating, empowering behaviour almost always entails personal change.

Frontiers now

Many of the frontiers now are practical, about how to make good change happen. They concern methodology – how to do things better, and research – how to learn from experience. The contributors to this book give us a flying start, with readable accounts and practical analysis. Readers of the book may wish to draw up and act on their own lists of priorities. To me, after reading the book, five stand out:

- **Training**. How better to conduct training for attitude and behaviour change, the ABC of PRA (Kumar 1996); how sympathetically to help those threatened by participatory modes of interaction; how best to arrange programmes of total immersion in villages and slums as learning experiences for powerful people (as being implemented for its senior staff by the World Bank), and how to spread this practice; and how to assure continuity of training as part of a long-term process.
- **Going to scale**. How optimally to balance drives to go too fast and brakes to go too slow; how to assess, improve and insert 'benign viruses' in going to scale, elements like behaviour and attitude training, embracing error, reflection and critical self-awareness which have self-improvement built in; and how to insist on small pilots for testing and learning, with only gradual scaling-up at a measured pace.

- **Institutional change**. How to change the cultures and procedures of hierarchical organizations, whether donor agencies, government departments, or larger NGOs; how to overcome the common conflict between low-level corruption and participation; how to avoid the tyranny of targets and drives for disbursements; how to select participatory staff and achieve a gender balance; how to protect and retain good staff and participation when there is a backlash; how to reward participatory work; how to help middle managers who resist change; and how to assure continuity of support at the top.
- **Participatory monitoring and evaluation**. How to complete the participation circle by enabling groups and communities to conduct their own M and E, with their own baselines and indicators; and how to reconcile this with central needs for standard indicators and information.
- **Disempowerment**. How to enable powerful people to recognize that power is not a commodity to be amassed, but a resource to be shared; and how to enable them to gain satisfaction, fulfilment and even fun, from disempowering themselves and empowering others.

To learn how to do these things better will not be easy. It requires more practitioners and researchers to follow contributors to this book in engaging with and learning from field and organizational realities. Combinations of approach may be best, including PRA, participatory action research, process documentation, participatory monitoring and evaluation, and self-critical reflection. Above all, it is vital to make the effort to share experiences and insights openly and without boundaries: in conversations, writing, and workshops, and through words, diagrams, videos, publications, networking and newsletters. This book provides a baseline of rich experience and insight. The challenge is to make the baseline a springboard, to learn more and to do better. May it inspire others to innovate, research, write and share, to help all of us do better in our understanding and actions.

The central message I draw from the contributions to this book is that participation has to be pervasive. In Andrew Shepherd's phrase (this volume) it cannot be bolted on. It cannot be confined to a low-level ghetto. Any belief that induced participation can succeed on any scale without participatory cultures and practices in the initiating organizations, and without personal change, cannot survive this book. Participation has to be lived, and lived at all levels by all concerned.

So the final frontier remains personal. In earlier decades, it was local people who had to change. Now the imperative has been reversed. The finger now points back to us – development professionals, the sort of people most likely to read these words. The experiences presented here drive us to an uncomfortable truth: that the quality of development depends on what sort of people we are and what we do. The title of this book poses the question *Who Changes?* The answer is inescapable. It has to be us.

1

General Introduction

JAMES BLACKBURN AND JEREMY HOLLAND

The use of participatory methodologies in development, particularly participatory reflection and action (PRA),[1] has moved very quickly from relatively marginal NGO-centred experiences in the mid to late 1980s to mainstream development practice and policy in the 1990s. The large international donor agencies, most notably the UN and the World Bank, are today encouraging or even requiring that PRA and other related methodologies be used in increasingly large-scale programmes and projects. Governments in the South are also showing a growing interest in participatory approaches. Such a dramatic 'scaling-up' poses immense conceptual and practical challenges, however. Ideally suited for micro-level development initiatives, approaches such as PRA are now being required to work across entire regions, involving a vast array of different types of organizations, many of which have historically seen the practice of development as an essentially top-down exercise. As participatory approaches become institutionalized, a new set of challenges needs to be addressed.

What is scaling-up?

There are numerous definitions of the term 'scaling up', and conceptual confusion can arise if a precise meaning is not established. Several authors (Clark, 1991; Edwards and Hulme, 1992; Uvin, 1995) have grappled with the term and offered various typologies. Our general understanding of the term is that of an expansion which has a cumulative impact. Scaling-up as so defined is indeed the story of PRA in the period 1988–97. Beginning in small-scale projects in the late 1980s in India and Kenya, the approach has since experienced a massive expansion in both the number and type of organizations which apply and/or promote it. We are now beginning to see how the cumulative impact of the spread of PRA has moved across and up: regional and national policy decisions, and even the strategies of large international donor or regulatory agencies, not just micro, project-level realities, are being (re)formulated at least partly as a result of the scaling-up of the approach.

The growth in the use of methodologies such as PRA has also added fuel to an age-old debate about the meaning of participation. There are those who would like to limit our understanding of the term to little more than a poverty-sensitive policy or project instrument. This view argues that 'participation' is primarily about making policies more sensitive to the needs of the poor, and projects more efficient and effective (in terms of increasing the number of people actively involved in their design, implementation, and evaluation, and thereby reducing overall costs). The 'political' school of participation, in contrast, takes a broader view. Its ultimate goal is not to make policies and projects work better for the poor (although this is considered highly desirable) but to facilitate political change in favour of the dispossessed.

> Beyond PRA, there are other traditions, such as Freireanism, utopian socialism, and Gandhiism which should be explored further and the necessary connections made.
>
> IDS workshop participant, May 1996

Some of those who adhere to this view are concerned that participation is in danger of becoming reduced to a 'technique' which can somehow be separated from its political context.

Indeed for many who use PRA and related methodologies at the grassroots, getting the poor to participate has no meaning unless it simultaneously addresses the power structures that appear to perpetuate poverty. Such a political understanding of participatory development work is precisely what the early pioneers of participatory research have postulated since the 1960s (Fals Borda, 1988; Freire, 1968, 1982; Gaventa, 1980; Illich, 1971). It is also what Korten, Cernea, Uphoff and others have explored in their work on community development and capacity-building from the perspective of grassroots organizational adaptation to development interventions (Cernea, 1991; Korten, 1980, 1990; Uphoff, 1992).

The ideological context of participation may today have shifted significantly since the 1960s, 1970s, and even 1980s, and categories and terminologies in the post-Cold War world have certainly blurred. Yet the heart of Paulo Freire's and others' interpretation of 'participation' – as a way of pressing for and achieving greater social justice – remains pertinent. As readers will see from Chapter 5, on scaling-up in Indonesia, it makes little sense for a government to launch a national village-participatory planning exercise *en masse* unless it is simultaneously prepared to rethink the way power structures operate in the country, particularly Indonesia's top-down style of development planning. The same can be said of the World Bank's recent engagement with participation. Although the Bank's public image has improved over the years, for many of those who work at the grassroots, the social costs of Bank-imposed structural adjustment policies remain a haunting memory. One has to ask: what is the Bank's understanding of participation? Is it prepared to reassess its role and think of creative ways that its systems, procedures, and policy advice might be opened up to facilitate the substantive empowerment of the poor?

Participation is today a sacred cow of the international agencies that control and direct vast intellectual and material resources in the name of 'development'. How does their understanding fit with that of people in southern and northern NGOs, popular organizations, community-based associations, and, increasingly, with government officialdom? All may be engaged in participation-speak, but whether they agree with each other on what they mean by

2

participation is another matter. Even within such organizations, people in different departments, or at different levels in the hierarchy, may be talking at cross-purposes. To some observers, it may then appear strange that a growing number of policies, programmes and projects are now being required to put into practice a concept that remains highly contentious. Whether participation will eventually become hegemonic, and in what form, remains to be seen. These are some of the deeper issues that the reader should draw on as a subtext when confronted with the term 'scaling-up'.

As editors, it is our hope that policymakers will come to understand that what is being scaled up is much more than a 'technique'. Participation is a way of viewing the world and acting in it. It is about a commitment to help create the conditions which can lead to a significant empowerment of those who at present have little control over the forces that condition their lives.

Organizational change: the nitty-gritty of institutionalization?

Taking on an approach such as PRA, introducing it into the project cycle, the policymaking process or the implementation of specific reforms, requires much more than merely training those in the field and leaving everything else untouched. As most of the contributors to this book argue, PRA implies change not only in the way projects are implemented, but also in the procedures and processes by which development decisions are made, resources allocated and policies formulated. Much of the book examines in detail the complex organizational changes required for participatory approaches to become effectively institutionalized.

It is one thing to direct resources to facilitate participatory planning in villages or poor urban districts. It is quite another to question and begin to change the often rigidly hierarchical and risk-averse management structures that exist within institutions and that make participatory approaches difficult to implement over the long term. If participatory approaches are, however, to have a lasting impact, institutions keen to implement them in the field (whatever their nature, be they NGOs, government bodies or donor agencies) must be prepared to examine how their own systems of organization can be made flexible enough to let participation in. Recent literature on business management may provide some of the clearest insights into how development organizations can best manage the inevitable flexibilization that the adoption of participatory approaches requires (Peters, 1987, 1994; Senge, 1990; Senge et al. 1994).

For NGOs that are rapidly expanding in response to the popularity of participatory methodologies, the management of organizational change has become a hot subject (Edwards and Hulme 1992). Jimmy Mascarenhas, Mallika Samaranayake and Sam Joseph describe, in chapters 11, 12 and 13 respectively, the innovative management styles that certain NGOs are using in response to the specific challenges of introducing and sustaining a participatory approach. Key lessons from these and other chapters are summarized in the conclusion.

As for government bureaucracies taking on this challenge, the organizational changes required are even greater given the hierarchism and inflexible procedures that characterize public-sector organizations generally. Thompson

3

in Chapter 16 uses the learning organization (Senge 1990) as a conceptual model to analyse how three large public institutions in Kenya, the Philippines and Sri Lanka have attempted to implement participatory approaches in their programmes. The characteristics of the learning organization thought by the IDS workshop participants to be most relevant to development settings are then outlined in Part 3.

Donors and their implementing agencies are also beginning to review their own *modi operandi* in response to the participation boom. Eylers and Forster, Chapter 15, show how GTZ has set up in-country and regional learning groups to study case-by-case the requirements and impacts of participatory projects. Andrew Shepherd, in Chapter 14, analysing the Doon Valley project in Uttar Pradesh, India, argues that donor pressure, in this case by the European Union, severely constrained the potentially positive results of what was supposed to have been a participatory project. The continuing use of physical targets to measure outcomes, together with the short time frames that pressurize implementing agencies to 'produce' quickly, are shown to be incompatible with the process needs that are inherent to participatory projects.

Governments are also seizing on PRA and related methodologies to assist in the implementation of decentralization policies, as part of a broader shift towards democratization. Decentralization in its various guises (Manor 1995) is now a policy priority in a growing number of countries. As it gathers momentum, the use of participatory methodologies is likely to increase: local authorities will be expected as never before to involve their constituents and partner organizations, such as NGOs, in research, planning and management activities. This is well under way in Bolivia, as Blackburn and De Toma (Chapter 6) discuss in their analysis of the practical challenges facing the implementation of the country's most radical policy of decentralization to date, the Law of Popular Participation in force since April 1994. To make democratic decentralization happen depends in this case largely on the outcomes of processes of participatory municipal planning in which approaches such as PRA are gaining in importance. This can best be described as a scaling-down of government as much as a scaling-up of participatory methodologies, and represents an interesting juncture between those concerned with participation from the grassroots up and those concerned with it from the government down.

The question of behaviour and attitudes

The participants at the IDS workshop were adamant that a fundamental feature of the process of institutionalizing participatory approaches is to explore the behaviour and attitudes of those individuals engaged in such a process. All the chapters of the book touch on this theme, some in more detail than others. Wordofa, for example, shows in Chapter 3 on the spread of PRA in Ethiopia how the question of behaviour and attitudes was not always understood by extension staff undergoing PRA training. He expresses concern about the rapid spread of PRA when its personal and ethical dimensions are overlooked. Equally, Kar and Phillips (Chapter 9) show how community development workers, engineers and health workers in the slums of Calcutta and elsewhere in India quickly grasped the techniques of PRA, but had much more difficulty

4

tackling the behavioural and attitudinal changes needed for the techniques to have any real impact. Hagmann, Chuma and Murwira recommend from experience of participatory extension in Zimbabwe that ongoing training and medium-to-long-term follow up are indispensable to ensure that behaviour and attitudes remain at the centre of any strategy of institutionalization.

It can be argued that, for decades, 'development' was conceived essentially as a problem of structure, something that required resource transfers and/or new forms of management in the fields of technology development, capital accumulation and knowledge dissemination. The role of the individual in this essentially macro world of concepts and solutions was not (and indeed is still not) given sufficient importance (Booth, 1994). The debate on the primacy of agency (the ability and will of individuals to act) as opposed to that of structure (laws, customs, economic forces, environmental factors and so forth, i.e conditions which constrain individual action) in development is now building up. But so far there has been little connection between such a debate and the question of individual behaviour and attitudes. To recognize human agency in development, to place the person at the centre of any intervention, and in participatory development more specifically, also implies exploring individual behaviour and attitudes as a fundamental component of agency. The challenge is to go beyond abstract notions of agency and address the personal aspects of a situation.

Feminist theory and gender studies have contributed enormously to narrowing the gap between the personal and the political. Those interested in participation have much in common with those interested in gender. The exploitation which millions of women suffer in developing countries should be of particular concern to those interested in implementing or promoting more participatory projects. Development interventions have been shown to be more sustainable when women are involved as equal partners.

The participation boom has also called on us to be more self-reflective, and to recognize that if we do not begin with ourselves, we are unlikely to make a real difference to the more abstract economic or social dimensions of development 'out there'. Systems theory (Checkland 1984) has long argued that we are all interconnected. The way we act, and more particularly the behaviour we display and attitudes we hold, have a profound effect on others. Step one of being an agent of change is to accept this obvious fact (Kumar, 1996).

To understand the meaning of participation, then, implies an acceptance that the way we behave and the attitudes we manifest have an effect on those with whom we work, be they poor villagers, office colleagues or funders. Meaningful communication, however, can only begin once common ground has been established, and something is shared, or participated in. To participate, after all, is literally to become a part. The ethical dimension of PRA underlined in the approach's principles, is clear in this respect: the best way to participate, as individuals, is to be humble, and listen, respond to and respect the knowledge, perceptions and feelings of the other, rather than to lecture and impose; but it is easier to advise others to change their behaviour than to do so ourselves! Robert Leurs, in Chapter 18, argues that for the kind of personal change advocated by PRA to last, a system of incentives will need to be devised to reward those individuals who make efforts to 'become a part', to engage in open dialogue with the 'other'. The gap between the grand

5

rhetoric and the day-to-day practice of participation is still far too wide. It will take a great deal of personal effort to narrow it.

The question 'Who changes?' calls us to attention. The point is not what to change as much as how we change ourselves. Participation has little meaning unless we, and particularly those of us in positions of power, allow others to 'take part', to set agendas, take decisions, manage and control resources. To allow the other in means to show him and her trust. People who feel trusted also gain independence; more than participate in their own development, they make it.

Definitional issues

A handful of terms have now become part of the jargon of the people engaged in trying to conceptualise and implement a more participatory form of development. Below we try to clarify our own understanding of some of the book's most common terms, or sets of terms:

- *PRA (participatory reflection and action) and related methodologies.* PRA has been described as a family of approaches, methods and behaviours to enable poor people to express and analyse the realities of their lives and conditions, and themselves to plan, monitor and evaluate their actions (Chambers, 1992). Much has been written on the various disciplinary and methodological streams which have contributed to PRA (Chambers, 1992, 1994c).

  In PRA, outsiders – researchers and/or practitioners who are not members of the community or group with whom they interact – act as catalysts for local people to decide what to do with the information and analysis they generate. Outsiders may also choose to analyse further the findings generated by PRAs, to influence policymaking processes, for example (Holland forthcoming). In either case, there should be a commitment on the part of the facilitating organizations to do their best to support or follow up on those actions that local people have decided on as a result of PRA, if local people feel that such support is needed. The question of what constitutes good, or ethical, PRA practice, and how abuse can be tackled, is explored in some detail in Part 3, in which a summary of the recommendations from the IDS workshop is presented.

  PRA is only one of a growing number of participatory approaches, or methodologies, currently in use. At least 29 such approaches have been developed since the 1970s (Cornwall *et al.*, 1994). The tendency now is not for methodologies to be used on their own but rather in combination with similar or complementary approaches. Hagmann, Chuma and Murwira, for example, in Chapter 8, on the scaling-up of participatory extension approaches in Zimbabwe, make a strong case for broadening the philosophical basis of PRA by combining it with the essentially Freirean approach, training-for-transformation (TFT). There have also been attempts to find umbrella terms to cover the whole gamut of participatory approaches currently in use. One is participatory learning and action (PLA).[2]

It is important to recognise that, technically speaking, PRA is a participatory appraisal, monitoring, and evaluation methodology which has at its core a conviction (i) that local people must be the subjects of their own development, and (ii) that those who facilitate PRAs must pay particular attention to the way they behave when interacting with local people. But PRA is not *per se* a methodology for community-organising or institution-building, although it can be used for these longer-term goals as well. Jimmy Mascarenhas reminds us in his analysis of the work of OUT-REACH (Chapter 11), for example, that PRA on its own will not do. Long-term institution-building requires, in the case of OUTREACH, the training of local people to manage micro-credit or micro-enterprise schemes. There are other approaches which should not be discarded. The long tradition of participatory research that has existed since the 1960s, for example, has spawned an array of approaches, which, when used in combination with PRA, offers exciting new methodological possibilities.

- *Methodologies and approaches to be distinguished from methods, tools and techniques.* In this volume, the terms 'methodology' and 'approach' will be used interchangeably. Both refer to a particular school or current of participatory research. PRA is a methodology (or approach) which can be distinguished from PAR (participatory action research), for example. Often, methodologies will share the same philosophical underpinnings, yet their longer-term goals may differ. PAR sees itself as part of a broader development of helping to shape popular movements pressing for social and political change. PRA is more concerned with the intricacies of recognizing the complex knowledge systems and rationales of local people, and providing them with the tools to design and evaluate their own projects.

Methodology and approach are to be distinguished from method, which is a specific tool or technique. A method is not necessarily restricted to any one methodology. Mapping, for instance, is a particular method (or tool, or technique) which is used in methodologies as diverse as PRA, PAR, agro-ecosystem analysis, farming systems research, RAP (rapid assessment techniques), popular education and others.

Structure of the book

The book is divided into three parts. Each begins with a short introduction presenting summary points of each of the chapters. More detailed synopses are provided at the head of each chapter.

Part 1 explores the opportunities and challenges of scaling-up. It is divided into two sections. Chapters 3, 4, 5 and 6 bring together four case studies of country-wide scaling-up, from Ethiopia, Vietnam, Indonesia and Bolivia. Chapters 7, 8 and 9 present three case studies of scaling-up as it is occurring in specific sectors: drainage and irrigation management in prime agricultural land in Estonia; agricultural extension and research in Zimbabwe; and slum improvement projects in India.

Part 2 focuses on organizational change. Chapters 11, 12 and 13 bring together three case studies from NGOs and community-based organizations: OUTREACH's approach to participatory watershed development in South

7

India; the Self-Help Support Programme's experience with participatory learning approaches in Sri Lanka; and approaches to community-managed programmes based on NGO experience in Somaliland. Chapters 14, 15 and 16 present three more case studies, this time of government and donor organizations: the European Union-funded Doon Valley Project in Uttar Pradesh, India; GTZ's experience of promoting and supporting participatory projects; and the introduction of participatory approaches in large public-sector organizations in Kenya, Sri Lanka and the Philippines.

Part 3, which is divided into four shorter sections, two of which are composed of individual chapters, looks to the future. Chapter 18 by Robert Leurs considers the challenges now facing PRA, based on extensive documentary research. Chapters 19 and 20 group together the reflections and recommendations made at the IDS workshop on scaling-up and organizational change. Chapter 20 presents the characteristics of the learning organization which the workshop participants considered relevant to the institutionalization of participatory approaches. In Chapter 21, John Gaventa analyses the key lessons and challenges which emerge from the preceding chapters, and suggests avenues for future research.

The book ends with a short conclusion (Chapter 22) by the main editor, James Blackburn.

PART 1

THE SCALING-UP OF PARTICIPATORY
APPROACHES: OPPORTUNITIES AND DANGERS

2
Introduction to Part 1

Scaling-up has become a catchphrase which we defined in the introduction as an expansion which has a cumulative impact. When used to describe the spread of participatory approaches, and in particular PRA, scaling-up can be situated at different levels, in specific organizations (e.g. NGOs), sectors (e.g. agricultural extension), or even entire regions or countries. The authors in this section describe how participatory approaches, in particular PRA, have spread, focusing on the country and sector levels. They show what external conditions appear to be necessary for such scaling-up to occur, and what problems and difficulties are encountered in the process. How organizations, be they NGOs, government bodies, or donor agencies, cope with the introduction and spread of participatory approaches is explored in Part 2.

Obstacles to scaling-up are many, and all the authors are (in true PRA spirit) candid about the mistakes that have been made (particularly in wanting to scale up too fast). They present practical strategies, all based on concrete experience, of how best to proceed.

Case studies of country-wide scaling-up

In Chapter 3, Dereje Wordofa, in his analysis of Save the Children's contribution to the spread of PRA in Ethiopia, examines the role of training in a scaling-up strategy. He expresses doubts about the real impact of short training cycles (the norm in PRA training) and concludes that high-quality training, as an essential feature of scaling-up, can only be sustained over the long term if participatory approaches enter more formal education arenas such as schools, universities, research institutes and so forth.

In Chapter 4, Bardolf Paul analyses how PRA has been introduced and scaled up in Vietnam, particularly in the SIDA-funded Forestry Cooperation Programme. Bardolf warns that institutional structures and personnel must be prepared for significant changes once PRA spreads. Such changes, he argues, have implications for existing funding and institutional arrangements, particularly between donors and in-country organizations, that are as yet little understood.

Nilanjana Mukherjee, in Chapter 5, describes how the Indonesian government incorporated elements of PRA to launch a nation-wide programme of participatory village planning in 60 000 villages to be completed within the 1995–6 budget year. The chapter analyses the mistakes committed in attempting to scale up too fast in the face of too many constraints, particularly the lack of sufficiently experienced trainers in-country, and the unrealistic budget and time constraints imposed by government.

Finally, James Blackburn and Costanza de Toma, in Chapter 6, analyse how NGOs in Bolivia are assisting municipal governments to work with local populations in producing the participatory municipal plans required by the country's new Law of Popular Participation, in force in the country since April 1994. The authors show that the rapid spread of PRA and related methodologies throughout Bolivia has been facilitated by the central government's decision to transfer a range of planning and resource management powers to the country's 311 municipalities, and argue that certain types of decentralization are probably integral to any long-term scaling-up strategy.

Case studies of sector-specific scaling-up

In Chapter 7, John Thompson describes how participatory social assessments led, in 1995, to the revitalizing of land and water associations in two counties of Estonia, and to the creation of a cadre of trainers in the country's Ministry of Agriculture who aim to repeat the process in other parts of the country.

Chapter 8, by Kamal Kar and Sue Phillips, analyses the experience of institutionalizing participatory approaches in the design and implementation of large-scale slum-improvement projects in India, focusing on the case of Calcutta. The authors' main conclusion is that, for scaling-up to be effective, it may be necessary to concentrate first on a handful of cases of sustained community action rather than to attempt to introduce participatory approaches across the board.

Chapter 9, by Jurgen Hagmann, E. Chuma, and K. Murwira, describes and analyses the processes involved in switching from conventional agricultural extension to participatory extension in the government agricultural extension service of Masvingo Province in Zimbabwe. The authors show how the strategy of institutionalizing participatory extension was based in this case on three factors: networking and establishing common goals with other organizations; influencing people with decision making power; and providing a thorough training and follow-up programme. The chapter warns, however, that the institutionalization of participatory approaches in hierarchically structured organizations is a highly complex intervention requiring major changes in planning, implementation, and monitoring and evaluation procedures. What these changes represent, and how they can be facilitated, is explored in greater depth in Part 2, which focuses in more detail on the specific organizational aspects of institutionalization.

3

Internalizing and Diffusing the PRA Approach: the case of Ethiopia

DEREJE WORDOFA

The author describes in this chapter his involvement since 1993 in the spread of PRA in Ethiopia, focusing on the work of the Save the Children Fund. Despite his general belief in the usefulness and effectiveness of the methodology, the author expresses some doubts about the wisdom of rapid spread: the difficulty of tackling behaviour and attitudes training when time is short; the lack of clearly defined bottom lines for good practice; and the danger that scaling-up could discredit the approach if quality issues are not tackled rigorously. The author recommends that for PRA to survive and thrive it must be introduced into mainstream education and training establishments. Influencing top decisionmakers may create the space for PRA to spread, but it is argued that high-quality training over time can only be sustained if the approach enters the formal education arenas.

This chapter attempts to show how PRA has been learned and subsequently internalized and diffused in Ethiopia by the Save the Children Fund (SCF). The views expressed are, however, my own and do not necessarily reflect the position of this organization. The first part of the chapter reflects on how PRA has been learned by exposure in Ethiopia, and on my own experience of experimenting with the approach; the second part attempts to analyse my own efforts to train others. Some suggestions as to how to ensure effectiveness in the use of PRA are also presented.

Learning and internalizing

In 1993, SCF (UK) in Ethiopia embarked on a rehabilitation programme after years of relief and emergency work. The switch challenged the organization to find new ways of working with communities. Before this, SCF (UK) in Ethiopia had no prior experience with PRA, although some community-development projects were run in the health programme. SCF has adopted PRA techniques in other countries in Africa and Asia, however. The SCF standard Project Planning Toolkit: *A Practical Guide to Assessment, Monitoring, Review and Evaluation* includes PRA as one of its key sets of tools, along with survey techniques, logical framework analysis, and cost effectiveness analysis.

My initial exposure to PRA, as a participant in the PRA workshop in Kenya sponsored by SCF (UK) in July 1994, provoked a mixture of excitement, indifference and doubt. The training workshop was organized by the Association of Land Husbandry and Organic Matter Management Network. Course participants were both junior and senior extension workers, project officers, and small-scale project coordinators from different agencies in Kenya. They represented international NGOs, grassroots indigenous NGOs and government departments. The workshop was organized primarily to introduce PRA tools and techniques into the context of organic farming approaches such as integrated pest management, environmental protection and development, and organic agriculture. The programme lasted 12 days, including both classroom training and field practices.

Generally the training was successful. The trainer and his assistants were excellent. The ice-breaking strategies, the games and interactions with communities were fun techniques, from which I learned a great deal. I witnessed how the villagers did know about themselves and their problems. I read from their faces that they were happy to be given the opportunity to talk about their situations, think problems through and take decisions. I was impressed by the amount of information we were able generate in such a short space of time and observed that the communities arrived at pragmatic solutions as a result of the exercises.

The behaviour of some of the trainees while facilitating the PRA techniques was questionable, however. In some cases they revered the opinion of the communities blindly while in others, they remained over-sceptical. I was dismayed that the core principles of PRA had not been understood by those who frequently, if not daily, interact with communities. Long-standing forms of behaviour and attitudes clearly cannot be changed in only three day of classroom training. Could the approach spread successfully if front-line development workers had problems with it?

Despite my doubts, an in-house training workshop was organized and held in August 1994 at Jijiga, in Eastern Ethiopia. It was planned and facilitated by an expatriate project manager and myself, in association with a teacher from the Agricultural University of Alemaya. About 20 project officers and field-workers, and two external participants were involved, one from a small international NGO and the other from a newly established indigenous NGO. The SCF trainees were scheduled to be deployed for project assessment and monitoring after the training.

Diffusing the methodology and influencing others

SCF produced a three-volume report from the first PRA training, bringing together the workshop proceedings, the hand-outs provided to the trainees and the trainees' own compiled reports. More than 40 copies of these reports were circulated to international and local NGOs, government departments and other SCF offices. This was the first step in diffusing and sharing our experience with others. The impact was immediate. The evidence lies in the fact that some NGOs began to ask us to organize similar workshops.

The other initiative was the organization and sponsorship of a PRA workshop by SCF (UK) to partners in government. This was held in February 1995 at Kobo in North Wollo. Middle-level managers and senior experts from different sections (planning, land use, extension) of the Ministry of Agriculture (MOA) and the Ministry of Natural Resources and Environmental Protection at zonal and regional levels were represented. Front-line extension workers and junior staff were deliberately excluded for two reasons: (i) to compare the effectiveness of the training with a different type of trainee; and (ii) as a strategy to introduce the approach in government departments. As in the previous training, two trainees were invited from international NGOs working in the area. This was in order to elicit their participation on ideas and strategies for diffusing PRA.

As in the two previous training sessions, the participants were astonished by PRA. Although they were not at ease with some of the icebreakers and games, as they were in senior positions in the hierarchy, their enthusiasm for learning was obvious. Unlike the trainees from the previous workshops, these participants were critical and serious observers. They asked questions, debated among themselves and often came up with new ideas.

PRA is now being adopted and diffused rapidly in Ethiopia. The above cases demonstrate clearly this reality. SCF (UK) Ethiopia has also introduced PRA in its programmes in the eastern and northern parts of the country. Our reports obviously triggered initiatives by other NGOs, although the impact has not yet been formally determined. The spread has, furthermore, continued into government ministries through further training and subsequent report circulation. A case in point is that of SCF (UK) in North Wollo, where PRA has been successfully introduced in agricultural pest control, livestock improvement and improved seed provision projects, together with environmental-protection and capacity-building programmes developed in partnership with government organizations. Despite the positive results, my views on the use of PRA remain mixed. I am both optimistic and cautious.

I am among those people who are trying to experiment with and learn from PRA, and I am willing to share my experience. I remain convinced that it is one of the best approaches to work with rural communities in particular. PRA is a good communication tool: villagers express themselves through it, and it is an effective way of learning for villagers and non-villagers alike. I have repeatedly seen communities use the tools of PRA to analyse their problems and forward their own solutions.

My first concern regarding PRA is that it is so open an approach with such broad scope and such a wide range of applications that it risks abuse by people who translate the empty PRA manual, in which there is only one sentence, 'use your own best judgement at all times', into a licence to 'do it the way you want: there is no formula'. The concept of the empty manual (i.e. that there are no rigid procedures to be followed) does not mean that PRA does not have its rules. There may be an unlimited number of ways of facilitating the same particular technique, yet at the core there are clear 'bottom lines' that cannot be transgressed. Indeed, whatever the tools and techniques that are used, listening to those who live in poor rural communities, recognizing and building on their knowledge, and learning from them, are fundamental principles of PRA. I suggest that they be written in the blank pages of the manual!

15

Can everybody who has attended 15 days' or a month's training understand the implicit essence of the one-sentence manual? Based on the experience presented above, I believe that it depends on who the trainees are, and how quickly they understand PRA. If looked at carefully, PRA is not easy. It may appear to be so, but at its core it requires a profound behavioural and attitudinal change. Such a change is hard indeed to achieve.

Those who work with PRA need to have a vision, an insight into 'why they do what they do'. They need to be good observers and skilful facilitators of debates, discussions and processes of negotiation. They must also refrain from becoming over-idealistic and assuming that everything the villagers say is right, hence that there is no need at all to interfere! In the Ethiopian context, where a top-down approach is deep-seated in our upbringing and culture, it is both utopian and impractical to imagine that villagers are always right. Relations between social groups in the country have largely been conditioned by civil war and authoritarian government, and it is unrealistic to expect communication between different groups to be open, trusting and relaxed.

Another reservation I have about PRA concerns the way it is spreading. Quality control is crucial, yet difficult to ensure. If PRA is to be used effectively by front-line extension workers, I believe that extended training should be given. Two weeks or even a month cannot bring about a change in behaviour. The current tendency to preach PRA in rapid bursts will only increase the rate of misuse and abuse of the approach. Perhaps the best way to tackle the quality issue head on is to incorporate the approach into the education system, but how this might be achieved remains to be seen.

Last but not least is the question of who, why and how PRA should be used. The current promotion of PRA, in which everyone is encouraged to test and experiment with the approach, also has its dangers:

- There is the danger that it will create fatigue: villagers cannot afford to be on call for outsiders wanting to do PRA, since they have to devote most of their energies to making ends meet. Villagers in many areas may already be seeing PRA as a time-consuming and tedious task that does not do much for them.
- If every training workshop, fact-finding mission and researcher continues to drag communities out for PRA-related meetings, expectations will continually be raised and frustrated, and villagers may in the end devalue the approach. This has already been presented as a problem in several places.

New ways forward?

Strategy for diffusion

Influencing senior managers, planners and policymakers to adopt PRA is the best strategy in terms of maximizing the approach's policy and institutional impact. In some cases, this strategy has limited itself to the circulation of PRA reports to decisionmakers who know nothing about the approach. Such a strategy usually has a limited impact, as PRA reports can appear bewildering, or even offensive to senior managers and decisionmakers who do not understand

16

the essence of why and how such reports were compiled in such an unconventional manner.

There is no question that the speed of PRA spread can be increased if there is material and moral support from people at a higher level within an organization, but such people need training themselves in order fully to understand what it is they are supporting and helping to propagate. In the case of SCF in Ethiopia, the spread was clearly facilitated by the fact that project managers, and myself, were properly trained in the approach.

Watch abuse while promoting

Robert Chambers advised all of us 'to start PRA, stumble, self-correct and then share it'. This is what we are now doing, but I fear that PRA might be hijacked for use as a development discourse. We may speak PRA while doing different things! The current high demand for the approach has led to a dramatic rise in PRA consultancy fees in Ethiopia. Unless this spiral is controlled, anyone versed in the PRA discourse will join the consultancy club and risk discrediting the approach.

Better training approach

I believe that PRA training will be more effective if it is included in educational institutions such as agricultural colleges, development studies institutes, colleges for extension workers, and so forth. A short training period that produces a large cadre of 'participatory development' workers and professionals will not lead to lasting change.

4

Scaling-up PRA: lessons from Vietnam

BARDOLF PAUL

Chapter 4 gives a brief overview of the use of PRA in Vietnam, focusing primarily on its use in the Vietnam–Sweden Forestry Cooperation Programme (FCP) from 1991 to 1996. The author uses a systems analysis approach to assess how PRA was introduced and scaled up in FCP. He warns that the very success of the approach threatens existing institutional structures and relationships, and project managers intent on introducing PRA elsewhere must be prepared to manage an array of organizational changes in the project(s)' administrative structures once the approach spreads. Of particular concern is staff insecurity as new roles are recognized and new positions created that can better facilitate the emergence of truly participatory projects. The author also warns that PRA is only one piece of the jigsaw. More thinking is required to determine how participation can be sustained throughout the project cycle. Such changes have implications for existing funding and institutional arrangements, particularly between donors and in-country organizations, that are as yet little understood.

Background to the Forestry Cooperation Programme

PRA as a planning tool and catalyst for participatory development has been used in Vietnam since late 1991. Prior to that time there had been some use of rapid rural appraisal (RRA) for such things as project-identification missions. Widespread use of the methodology amongst foreign-based NGOs began a few years later. The SIDA-funded Forestry Cooperation Programme (FCP) is, however, the only project that has applied PRA on a large scale over a period of several years. Even so, in the first four years of the project the scale of PRA application was limited to a total of only 70 villages in five provinces.

Some projects attempted to scale up to a greater number of villages, but did not sustain the process over time. One was an International Fund for Agricultural Development (IFAD)-funded Participatory Resource Management Project in one of the same provinces where the FCP was also operational. They used what was referred to as PRA to initiate planning in over 350 villages over a one-year period. Because personnel from the FCP were involved in the training and execution of the work, a few comments will also be made about this experience.

Much has been written about the FCP. Rather than repeat what the interested reader can find elsewhere, we will immediately examine the lessons learned from its application of the PRA approach. Some background information is provided, followed by a brief description of how the methodology was introduced and used. A short summary of the achievements and impacts will be followed by some comments on requirements and constraints.

PRA was introduced to the FCP in December 1995, and the two years that followed were spent trying out and modifying the methodology to suit the specific needs of the programme and the environment in which it was being introduced. At that time Vietnamese organizations were moving out of a period of great stability, with heavy subsidization and central control, into an era of change and much greater instability, characterized by severe downsizing and the experience of new freedoms under 'market socialism'. Because of the long years of war and the almost total use of productive resources to support the war effort, infrastructural development in all its forms lagged behind.

It was in this context that the FCP introduced the elixir of PRA. It was an opportune moment because there was no existing organization or system for extension, so nothing old had to be broken down or changed. The Vietnamese were interested, also, in trying out new things. Moreover, the PRA approach seemed to fit in well with one of Uncle Ho's dictums, that in order to create a successful revolution the People's Army had to 'live with the people, work with the people and learn from the people'.

Several other factors also created a supportive environment for PRA. The economic reforms of the early 1990s shifted the basis of production and enterprise from the cooperative to individual households. The very structure of the rural economy was profoundly affected as a result. The allocation of forest lands to individuals and groups, for example, called for the creation of new support mechanisms (such as agricultural extension services, forestry expertise) to help develop the newly opened-up lands. The role of PRA was perceived as enabling these momentous changes to take place while at the same time remaining sensitive to the particular needs of people in their own specific situations.

Other factors conducive to the adoption of PRA were the high levels of literacy and education amongst a large majority of the population, and the existence of managerial and other professional skills amongst members of many village communities. These made possible the establishment of strong community organizations capable of running project activities.

Finally the funding agency, SIDA (Swedish International Development Authority), had a very tolerant attitude towards the time required to test out new methodologies. The agency also provided large-scale funding for other programme components, which created a form of protection for experimental activities related to the introduction and spread of PRA.

How PRA was used

In the beginning PRA was used mainly as a method for extension workers to gain a greater understanding of local village conditions before initiating extension support activities. In the process, government staff and farmers together learned how to use the methodology in a focused way, and in so doing gained a much better understanding of one another.

PRA became a catalyst for initiating a development process in each village. At the end of each PRA there was a preliminary village-development plan that was later analysed and finalised by the villagers with the help of extension staff. The result was a plan based on local realities and preferences, with a genuine sense of ownership in its creation and implementation.

The PRA approach was found to be a useful method for gathering data and analysing conditions in a wide range of environmental and socio-economic conditions. Extension workers became sensitized to the knowledge and capabilities of farmers, as well as accepting the importance of involving the latter in the planning process. They also came to recognize the diversity of conditions within and between communities, and that there were no simple, broadcast solutions to farmer's problems.

Over time there was a noticeable change in the way extension staff approached and worked with problems of local-resource management and village development. They were eventually able to provide a more sophisticated and relevant set of responses to local needs. As they built up trust, they became more and more confident in delegating responsibilities to the villagers themselves.

As a catalytic influence for jump-starting the development process, PRA proved to be unrivalled. It was an effective way of involving local people in project planning and implementation. Eventually, villagers were successfully carrying out PRAs on their own in neighbouring villages, and providing follow-up services and back-up support.

A systems approach to institutionalization

One of the major objectives of the FCP was to develop methodologies that could be applied on a wider scale. After four years, it became clear that it was possible to use PRA on a large scale. However, there are constraints on, as well as certain basic requirements for, scaling-up to happen successfully.

PRA is not a stand-alone methodology. It is never an end in itself, because it is always serving some other purpose. It has to be part of a systematic approach to achieve a development objective, and is only one of many steps taken in the project cycle and development process. Understanding its place and timing in the process, and how it should be designed to fit in with everything else, is critical for it to be fully useful.

The relationships between the institutions involved have to be well understood, because most development programmes involve a variety of players and support mechanisms: policymakers, management, training, financial support (credit), material supply, technical support. The roles, responsibilities and lines of authority have to be made clear, and communicated to everyone involved.

PRA has to be carefully crafted to fit a specific development programme. There can be no fixed PRA package that will be the same from one scheme to the next. Designing variations on PRA packages takes a special talent, and a lot of experience. Standardization of PRA across a range of projects or programmes can happen all too easily. It is to be avoided at all costs.

Institutionalizing PRA requires a stable and legitimate institutional environment. Uncertainty about the future can be tremendously demoralizing. Staff must be recruited for a fixed number of years, and receive appropriate remuneration.

PRA usually requires a multi-disciplinary group of people. There may be inter-institutional barriers that prevent the bringing together of a multi-disciplinary group of people on a permanent basis.

Institutional responsibilities change over time as the system matures. Duties and tasks may start at one level in the system, and then shift elsewhere sometime later. This may be part of a gradual process of decentralization and delegation that develops out of the use of PRA (for example: a training task may start at the province level, move to the district, and then end up being carried out at village level). Somehow this process of change needs to be anticipated and planned for, because it means that changes in institutional support and relationships will happen. How to plan for this kind of process of change requires special insights and skills.

Strong local organizations are needed to support the use of PRA and the process initiated by PRA. The strength and cohesiveness of local leadership has an important impact on the success of PRA-initiated activities. Using local people and organizations to carry out PRAs in surrounding communities has proven to be a most effective strategy in spreading-out and scaling-up. The costs are lower and the outcome more rooted in local realities, resulting in more effective and efficient support.

Personnel and training

PRA is totally people-dependent. It requires a minimum critical mass of people who must have specific technical and communication skills, including the right attitude. People must also feel motivated, and not, as so often happens, sidelined from the work due to lack of appropriate salary or incentives.

It is especially important to have a few key people in the right place who really understand what PRA is all about (preferably from first-hand experience). One right-minded person can make a tremendous difference in the quality of the work that takes place. It is, however, usually a matter of good fortune to have such people in the appropriate position. Not much can be done to engineer such an outcome unless donors are particularly sensitive to the requirements of a participatory project.

Training people to be effective PRA practitioners takes a long time. Between one and two years are needed for individuals to gain sufficient understanding and self-confidence to move beyond knowing simply how to use the tools. The most important learning has to take place in the field; classroom-training on its own has limited value. Trainers themselves require special teaching. Very often the resources for training are insufficient or unavailable. Building up a body of good trainers is an essential prerequesite to staff and farmer training.

Because PRA training is so dependent on field training, this is in itself a major limitation. Using a village for training without the prospect of post-PRA activities in the village can really limit the quality of involvement from local people and compromise the quality and usefulness of the learning experience. If training always has to be linked to a commitment for project-supported village development, the numbers of villages that can be used for training are limited. There are, moreover, only a certain number of persons that can be accommodated during a PRA.

The dilemma of PRA

It is essential to distinguish between the techniques of PRA and the ideology or spirit that is behind it. PRA is driven by a philosophy that dictates how it should be done. It cannot be done properly in any other way. What is often missed is how to carry this same outlook over into every other aspect of the work that precedes and follows PRA, but without this, the good outputs from the PRA can easily get distorted or even lost.

Introducing PRA is just the tip of the iceberg. The philosophy of PRA has profound implications for how institutions function and how they are structured. This reality is by far the biggest challenge to widespread use and scaling-up of the methodology. Allowances have to be built into projects and programmes for the conversion of those who will never experience a PRA. We all know how virtually impossible it is to teach PRA without any direct involvement.

This is a serious challenge: how do we introduce the same approach in other areas? Is there some systematic way this can be done? Are major institutional changes required, or is it sufficient to be satisfied with the small, yet important gains made through farmers' involvement in processes and activities that affect them directly?

5

The Rush to Scale: lessons being learnt in Indonesia

NILANJANA MUKERJEE[1]

Chapter 5 describes how the Indonesian government sent a team to be trained in PRA in India, and subsequently incorporated elements of PRA to launch a nation-wide programme of participatory village planning, covering 60000 villages, to be completed within the 1995–6 budget year. It analyses the mistakes committed in attempting to scale up too fast in the face of too many constraints: too few sufficiently experienced in-country trainers resulting in poor-quality classroom-based training; unrealistic budget and time constraints; poor collaboration between the government team and representatives of experienced NGOs; and the strong top-down culture of development planning in Indonesia. The experience has had a number of positive spin-offs, however, in particular the nation-wide Family Welfare Movement (PKK) joining with local NGOs in the provinces to work out appropriate PRA applications for village-level assessment of women's health, and participatory analysis of the direct and underlying causes of maternal deaths. Chapter 5 shows clearly, however, that participatory approaches cannot easily be tagged on to existing national programmes, and that scaling-up will fail if it is rushed. Questions are raised that other governments keen to launch a nation-wide strategy of participatory planning should heed.

Country-wide participatory planning: how it happened

Using our own best judgement, we became involved with the incorporation of participatory approaches into the nation-wide system for village-development planning in Indonesia. What follows is a chronology of the events that took place. Readers can draw their own conclusions from a story which is probably a good example of what can happen when participatory approaches are scaled up very quickly, what it takes to make a difference, how far one can expect to go, and those things that can and cannot be controlled, and why.

The formulation of annual plans for village development has been a feature of rural life in Indonesia for more than a decade. Every January, the Department of Home Affairs sets the process in motion. Sub-district administrative staff notify village heads that they should schedule community-consultation meetings to come up with proposals for village improvement. The proposals usually include resource-sharing commitments between the villagers and different government departments. These are examined and progressively consolidated at sub-district, district, provincial and national levels. Information about approved proposals subsequently passes down the same levels in reverse order, and funds follow. What is requested is not necessarily the same as what is received. The process takes 12–14 months.

During the planning of the 1995–2000 country programe of collaboration with the Government of Indonesia, the United Nations Children's Fund (UNICEF) was requested to help improve the quality of this bottom-up planning process. Joint reviews of the existing process were carried out in six provinces in early 1995. These revealed that the process needed to focus more on human development, involve larger community groups (particularly more women) in decisionmaking, and be based on sharper analysis of the causes of local problems. A training programme for village-level facilitators of the improved planning process had already been prepared by a foreign consultant using the ZOPP (Zielorientierte Projekt Planung) methodology. Its field-testing during March–April 1995 did not, however, satisfy all the requirements.

The Department of Home Affairs has a group of national trainers and designers of training interventions. They wished to gain wider exposure to the participatory planning methods being used in other developing countries and adapt what was relevant to the conditions in Indonesia. In response, as an initial step, UNICEF arranged a one-day exposure seminar in April 1995 for national government personnel, where presentations were made by Robert Chambers, James Mascarenhas, Indonesian NGOs such as Yayasan Agro Ekonomika and Studio Driya Media, the Indonesian branch of World Education, and a GTZ consultant. One major consequence of the seminar was an urgent demand from the goverment departments and the PKK (The Family Welfare Movement, a nation-wide women's NGO which includes the wives of all top government personnel) for longer and more in-depth learning about PRA.

UNICEF agreed to support a two-week study visit to India for key government officials and trainers from the departments of Home Affairs, PKK, Adult Education, Social Affairs and Health. The 12-day study programme on applications of PRA for rural development was organized by OUTREACH at Bangalore, India, during August–September 1995.

Meanwhile, the national trainers had been instructed to re-write the training module developed and tested in April 1995. In fact they had already done so, by referring to available manuals and books documenting PRA and RRA experiences, before going on the study visit. A central-government directive had gone out to all 27 provinces of the country in early June, instructing the local-government machinery that starting with the 1995–6 cycle, bottom-up planning in villages of Indonesia would be effected following a participatory process called the 'P3MD' (*Perencanaan Partisipatif Pembangunan Masyarakat Desa*, or Participatory Village Development Planning). Training modules were scheduled to be produced centrally by October 1995 and despatched to the provinces, districts and sub-districts to train provincial trainers and, in the final instance, village-council heads in December 1995. Following this training, the village-council heads were to facilitate participatory planning in their villages during February–March 1996. Government funds had already been officially allocated for this 4-day training in over 60000 villages within the 1995–6 budget year ending in March 1996.

From the outset, the planned schedule, the groups targeted for training, the training budget and the 4-day training plan appeared to be beyond both discussion and any possibility of modification. The funds were earmarked for the year and had to be spent by March 1996. The provincial government had been given explicit instructions, along with the June directive, on how to use the money. Expenditure was to be based on the 4-day training plan, despite the fact that the contents of the training had not yet been decided. On their return from Bangalore, the national trainers' team decided to re-write their earlier training manual. They did this under the close supervision of their director, and under extreme pressure to meet the printer's deadline. The 11-volume training package was in the press by November. There had been hardly any time or opportunity for consultation with anyone outside the 4 members' writing team. We offered the assistance of NGO practitioners of PRA from Studio Driya Media and Yayasan Indonesia Sejahtera to work with the writers' team, but views proved too dissimilar to allow collaboration. We were asked to react to a semi-final draft by providing our ideas in writing to the team rather than conceptualizing it together. Field-testing was out of the question in view of the schedule.

To fit all the officially specified contents into the 4-day training module for trainers and the 3-day module for village heads, many compromises were made. Field-based methods inevitably became classroom-based and time allocations allowed only teaching rather than learning. Attitudes and behaviours received little attention in the module as it was known that existing departmental trainers at province and district levels had all received training in 'participatory andragogy' during the 1980s. The new elements in the module were the incorporation of three techniques from the PRA repertoire, i.e. resource mapping, seasonal calendars, and Venn diagramming. Information from these methods was designed to be transferred to a series of 11 tables for further processing into a Village Development Plan. Although everybody agreed that the product and the planned process left much to be desired, they felt that it would have to suffice for the current year, in order to fulfil the government's commitment already announced in June 1995. They felt that they were learning by doing and that improvements and course corrections would be made during the following year, based on the experience of applying the approach during the first year.

There was no way to stem the tide of instant replication and mass-scale training. The planned schedule was implemented relentlessly in 27 provinces and the budgets duly spent within the financial year. We were invited to observe the process and provide feedback to central decisionmakers, which we did, together with fellow-observers from the national government. The trainers observed were by and large unprepared for the role they were expected to perform. They agreed wholeheartedly with the objective of empowering the community but lacked the training necessary to foster that process. During the training of village heads they tended to rely on overhead transparencies full of text from the training manual, provided too much direction for those exercises that were to be done by community groups, asked leading questions and provided lengthy 'correct' answers themselves. The fundamental principle of learning and discovering together with their trainees seemed too unsettling and unacceptable to them and incompatible with their perception of their own role as trainers. Trainings and Trainings of Trainers (TOTs) were conducted for 60–70 people at a time, in order to complete the targets by January 1996. Reports from observers of village-level planning that followed show that little has changed in terms of process and outputs during 1997 as compared to previous years.

A summary of observations and lessons learnt was compiled at the Department of Home Affairs, using all the feedback received from departmental as well as external observers such as ourselves. There has been no review dialogue on the subject yet. Some basic premises have been revised, e.g. village teams of analysts are to be trained in the next phase rather than just the village-council heads. The team of 5 will have at least 2 women, including the village PKK leader. The small, select, core national trainers' group is working on a further revision of the training.

What we can learn from the experience

It is useful to analyse our situation with reference to Pretty and Chambers' conceptual framework for a New Learning Paradigm (1993) using the three intersecting circles.

High-level government support is an insufficient condition on its own

We began with a situation where there was, professedly, institutional support (F) and an interest in participatory approaches (E). The political climate was becoming more favourable. Terms like 'participation' and 'empowerment' of the community were becoming popular in national policies and planning documents. There was a sense of urgency among the highest levels of government to bring about visible and rapid change in the direction of more equitable development. An overall institutional thrust towards decentralising the responsibility for development was (and still is) gathering momentum as the country approaches the next general elections in 1997.

Here was a nation-wide system wishing to promote participatory approaches to improve the quality of life of the rural poor, and there appeared to be a strong motivation to learn more about how to achieve this objective. We felt that our appropriate response should be to assist this quest and thereby also to shift the focus of village development towards the situation of women and children in the village. We were aware that the 'institutional support' element had to be taken at its face value. If we wished to influence the system we had to enter when and where we were invited, and try to make a difference from that point onwards. With hindsight, perhaps it would have been more effective to emphasize the implications of adopting participatory approaches more explicitly with the top-level decisionmakers, as soon as we were in the picture. An initial laying-down of the rules of the game can help avoid unrealistic time-schedules and mismatches between processes and structures. Doing this may also alienate the top-brass who are out to score political points by appearing to bring about rapid innovations. They

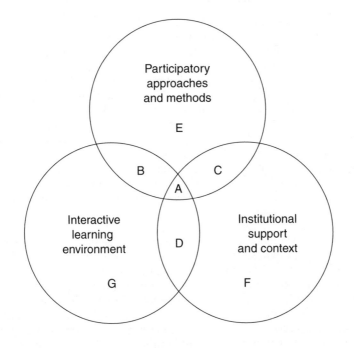

Fig. 5.1: The new learning paradigm

may prefer to approach other agencies that are happy to provide instant recipes for success, manuals, materials, training and more staff training. Could we afford to take the risk? We decided that we could not. As Robert Chambers said, we needed to 'hang in there over a matter of years', making what difference we could to the thinking of an increasing number of people who matter, in the hope of building up a critical mass of opinion. We will continue to support dialogues, promote alliances and reflection, bringing more and varied people into the picture. Already there are two other openings, with the PKK and the Department of Social Affairs, where participatory approaches are being examined and adopted under less restrictive conditions, with the help of NGOs specializing in PRA. At the PKK's national consultative meeting for 1996, a public commitment was made by the organization's leadership that all provincial PKK budgets will provide for area-specific development of PRA-based activities which aim to enhance women's participation in community decisionmaking. The PKK welcomes further collaboration with NGOs experienced in PRA. In the Department of Social Affairs, training interventions developed with NGO collaboration are being used to prepare facilitators of rural youth groups, working in the field of self-help action for poverty alleviation.

Achieving an interactive learning environment is no easy task

An interactive learning environment (G) is alien to most bureaucracies, especially large government ones. Training programmes are easy to design. Even outsiders can do it. Fostering an interactive learning environment is infinitely more difficult, particularly in top-down, hierarchial organizations where unquestioning respect for authority is often integral to social and cultural life. To achieve an interactive learning environment, the change must come from within. When working with institutions, a confrontational approach is not recommended: it is of paramount importance to respect an institutional culture. Yet at the same time, we frequently find ourselves limited by the institutional norms of our counterparts. We may try to promote reflective dialogues with certain groups in institutions, but the usual procedure is that we are asked to send our inputs in writing for consideration by the ministry. For obvious reasons, written inputs have to be less explicit and always one-way, and thus do not lead to genuine interaction.

Cultural codes of conduct may inhibit open discussion of what went wrong or did not work. Attempts at discussion may ostracize the insensitive foreigner and fail to lead to collective learning. Discussing sensitive issues with key persons prior to official meetings can help, but sometimes leads to dilution or distortion of the main point. Significant contradictions and questions involving conflicting opinions may never be opened for discussion. Under such circumstances it can become extremely problematic to define what is and what is not 'uncompromisable' according to one's personal code of ethics. It seems to help to keep the longer-term potential in mind, even if the immediate present seems too compromised.

Building a critical mass

Institutional capacity-building for the use of participatory approaches is beset with the chronic problem of staff transfers. Participatory methods need the nurturing care of not just one or two people, but of a significant group able to build up a critical mass. Just as a group is beginning to establish and develop the required work culture, however, this may be broken up and dispersed into pieces too far apart to support each other.

How does one address the problem? We have yet to find an effective solution. One idea seems to be not to put all the eggs in the same basket. Whenever field-based training is organized, it seems better to do it for people from several related ministries and disciplines together. Sensitizing people in a multi-disciplinary environment provides for more effective follow-up later. We have proposed but not yet succeeded in establishing a communication and interaction forum or network covering both government and NGO practitioners. The two still tend to remain mutually exclusive. Strengthening institutional training centres that handle mainstream staff training for government personnel is another potentially promising strategy. A start has been made in this direction with the appointment of trainers for the two national training centres of the Directorate of Community Development in Indonesia.

Progress with PKK women's groups is greatly encouraging. Within three months of the organization's national consultative meeting in February 1996, two major provinces had arranged learning workshops for PKK's district- and sub-district-level trainers. The plan was to work out ways of using the PRA methodology for improving rural women's health. Despite commendable economic progress over the past decade in Indonesia, maternal mortality remains unacceptably high. The President has called recently for urgent action to accelerate its reduction.

PKK has joined with local NGOs in the provinces to work out appropriate PRA applications for village-level assessment of women's health and participatory analysis of direct and underlying causes of maternal deaths. This is to be followed by action planning for prevention as well as proper management of obstetric emergencies at family and community level. UNICEF's support for these initiatives is limited to technical assistance for training, participatory research and alliance-building among community organizations, specialized NGOs and the providers of health services. In both provinces, local-government personnel have attended the field-based learning workshops and recognized that PRA goes far beyond 'playing with sticks and stones', as commented on by a Jakarta-based public health specialist earlier this year.

Conclusion

Experiences with the institutionalization of PRA seem to turn into an exercise in compromise. It is critical to recognize where to draw the line and prevent a slide into manipulation; on the other hand, the institutionalization of PRA can reach many more people who can make a difference than can a perfectly conducted two-village PRA exercise facilitated by good field activists. The benefits may not be immediately discernible, but over the long term the sheer volume of new thinking sparked off by institutional exposure to PRA tends to yield unexpected bonuses from many quarters.

There is a real risk associated with working on an institutionalized scale such as a government system. This is the risk of generating community initiatives and a degree of empowerment before the institution is ready or willing to respond. Those of us engaged at this level cannot disown the responsibility of continually seeking the most operationally, as well as ethically, acceptable compromise, keeping both the short- and long-term consequences clearly in mind.

6

Scaling-down as the Key to Scaling-up? The role of participatory municipal planning in Bolivia's Law of Popular Participation

JAMES BLACKBURN AND COSTANZA DE TOMA

Chapter 6 analyses the recent spread of participatory methodologies in Bolivia in the context of the profound politico-structural changes set in motion by the Law of Popular Participation enacted in May 1994. The chief characteristics of the law are first described: how central government authority and revenue is being transferred to the country's 311 municipalities; how local institutions (the basic territorial organizations and the vigilance committees) have been 'empowered' to carry out a range of planning, management and auditing activities at the municipal level; and how 'participatory planning' by local institutions and municipal governments is supposed to articulate with conventional top-down development planning by departmental and national institutions.[1]

The law offers a unique space for participatory methodologies to spread. Indeed, it endorses the use of such methodologies by requiring that participatory planning be facilitated by local institutions throughout the country. The authors are less concerned, however, with the nature of the spread as with its potential political consequences given the unique legal environment in which such a spread is occurring. The potentials and limitations of PRA and related methodologies as a tool for political empowerment in the context of the law are, therefore, considered. Particular emphasis is placed on the role of participatory methodologies in (i) strengthening the political potential of new local institutions and wider popular movements; (ii) forcing the state to reformulate its more conventional development planning procedures (and therefore policies); and (iii) allowing NGOs with expertise in participatory methodologies to exercise greater influence over government at all levels (municipal, departmental and national).

Despite evident administrative bottlenecks and cooptation, the Law of Popular Participation is seen to provide a context for users of participatory methodologies to move from micro- to macro-influencing strategies. 'Empowerment' in such a context takes on a whole new meaning.

Scaling-down, Bolivian style

As part of its widespread structural reform programme (encompassing privatization, education reform and administrative decentralization), in May 1994 Bolivia enacted a Law of Popular Participation (LPP). The law requires the country's 311 municipal governments to engage the local population in planning and managing a broad range of social, production-related and infrastructural projects, with finance transferred from central government. Not only is the LPP attempting to reverse an historical trend – the Bolivian state has always been associated with excessive centralization and little or no support for the country's municipalities, particularly those located in the more remote rural areas – it is also setting itself a colossal methodological challenge. Never before have local populations been required to 'participate' so explicitly in the planning and management of local projects. How this is to be achieved can only be seen as a highly complex and ambitious task.

Chapter 6 will explore how this challenge is being met by focusing on three fundamental aspects of the LPP: the enhanced role of local institutions, the *Organizaciones Territoriales de Base* and the *Comités de Vigilancia,* in the planning and management of projects at the municipal level; the character of 'participatory planning' sanctioned by the law and how it articulates with conventional top-down planning; finally, the NGO-state alliance without which the LPP would be difficult, if not impossible, to implement.

Transfer of government authority and revenue to the municipalities

The LPP entrusts municipal governments with political and administrative authority to draw up and manage a wider spectrum of local-development initiatives in the social, productive and infrastructural spheres than ever before. The most noticeable change is that the maintenance of school buildings, health facilities and irrigation works is now a concern of municipal authorities and no longer the responsibility of central government.

In order to finance such a devolution of authority and responsibility, the LPP calls for a 100 per cent increase in the funds allocated to municipal governments, with increases in individual municipalities varying in accordance to population size. By 1996, only two years after the law had been passed, the 100 per cent target had almost been reached, with funds allocated to the municipalities almost doubling in the 1994–6 period from $US95 million to $US160.5 million. The municipalities can also apply for funding from funding agencies (themselves largely funded by the World Bank, some bilateral donors, and with counterpart funds from the government) such as the FIS (*Fondo de Inversión Social* – Social Investment Fund) and the FDC (*Fondo de Desarrollo Campesino* – Campesino Development Fund). According to figures from the *Ministerio de Hacienda* (Booth, 1997), total municipal budgets increased from $US193 million in 1994 to $US462 million in 1995.

Despite the efficiency in the transfer of the funds, financial and administrative bottlenecks have been noted. The law stipulates that no more than 10 per cent of the extra funds are to be spent on running costs. This has proved insufficient for most municipalities, particularly small ones, which have been forced to dig into their own savings to make up the shortfall. The remaining 90 per cent are allocated to finance the implementation of projects derived from 'participatory plans' (whose methodology is described later). Even here there have been difficulties, with expended funds lagging behind the expected 90 per cent. The gap appears to result from a combination of different factors, ranging from the time-lag required for the politico-administrative structures to adjust to the LPP, to the lack of suitably trained personnel (especially in rural areas) and the failure in most cases to reach a clear consensus on the modalities for investment at the municipal-council level.

Despite these problems, what might be called the 'scaling-down' features of the law have been implemented with remarkable success, given the short time since the LPP was passed, and the significant reorientation it has entailed for the Bolivian state. The long-term success and sustainability of the law depends more, however, on the strengthening of existing and new local institutions.

New roles for local institutions: the key to making the LPP work

The LPP is more than just an exercise in administrative decentralization. Beyond transferring revenue and a range of administrative powers from central government to the country's 311 municipalities, the law also provides the legal framework for local institutions present inside municipal boundaries (which were not recognized by the state before the passage of the LPP) to participate in the following:

- *planning activities* (specifically, to draw up 'participatory plans' to determine how the new resources made available by the LPP should be spent by municipal governments);
- *management activities* (specifically, the management of development projects spawned by the participatory plans); and
- *auditing activities* (specifically, of municipal authorities to ensure that the various stipulations of the LPP are respected, and in particular that funds are properly disbursed and accounts kept transparent).

The LPP distinguishes between two types of local institutions, the *Organización Territorial de Base* (OTB) – Basic Territorial Organization – and the *Comité de Vigilancia* (CV) – Vigilance Committee, each of which will be examined in turn.

Organización Territorial de Base (OTB)

The LPP allows for the official registration of local institutions as OTBs, thus granting them a legal status they did not enjoy prior to the passage of the law. OTBs vary enormously in form, but are broadly defined as 'peasant communities, indigenous peoples and neighbourhood councils' (Rojas Ortuste, 1996). Recognized OTBs are given jurisdiction over a given territory and assigned rights and duties which cover a range of social, infrastructural, productive and environmental matters. They are also made collectively responsible for co-managing the new resources made available by the LPP, and for exercising scrutiny over the municipality's use of the assets and income assigned to it. By the end of 1995, 9772 out of a total of 11 447 OTBs had been granted legal status and officially registered (Booth *et al.*, 1996). Most of these have been indigenous councils and communities (or federations of communities: *mancomunidades*), chiefly in rural areas.

The emergence of OTBs on the Bolivian political map has presented 'complications' for the Bolivian state. In some urban areas, demonstrations 'against popular participation' were organized by unions and opposition political parties[2] which perceived the OTB formula as an instance of cooption by the ruling MNR[3] party. Another bone of contention has been that OTBs can only participate in very specific technical, as opposed to political, domains: (i) helping to draw up participatory plans to determine priorities for investment in the municipalities, and (ii) assisting in the management of projects spawned by these plans. There has been resentment that the concept of 'participation' prevalent in the LPP discourse does not extend to the political sphere, at least not explicitly.

Bolivian electoral law requires that candidates in municipal elections must be fielded in lists proposed by registered political parties. OTBs cannot present their own independent lists, thus limiting their ability to make the voices of those they represent heard directly in the municipal arena. OTBs may exercise political power only indirectly, by electing their representatives to the *comités de vigilancia* (watchdog groups responsible for auditing municipal governments – see next page), or by attempting to influence the selection of party candidates. The danger of this kind of electoral dynamic is, however, that, according to Booth (1996) 'communities wishing to influence the distribution of the significant resources now controlled by the municipal governments... can only do so by hitching themselves to the wagon of political parties'. What guarantees do they then have that the parties will maintain their promises, or that their community leaders will not become drawn in to party dynamics and forget their mandates?

Despite the potential emasculation of OTBs by the political parties, and the corruption that this could encourage, the results of the municipal elections of December 1995 returned the greatest number ever of representatives of OTBs to municipal councils. The *Secretaría Nacional para la Participación Popular* (SNPP), the central government body responsible for promoting and overseeing the implementation of the LPP, has declared that 30 per cent of the councillors elected in 1995 are of indigenous or *campesino* (small farmers who may or may not be defined as indigenous) stock, a not-insignificant result in a country in which the indigenous majority[4] has historically been largely excluded from government. Change in the composition of municipal governments has been particularly marked in the lowlands where a substantial number of Guaraní, Guarayo, Chiquitano and Yaminawe ethnic-group councillors were elected in December 1995.

Probably the most interesting case of political empowerment resulting from the LPP has been that of the *cocaleros* (coca growers) from the contentious Chapare region who have formed their own political association in response to the LPP, the *Asamblea para la Soberanía de los Pueblos* (ASP, the Assembly for the Sovereignty of the Communities). Denied the right to participate in the local elections as a political party, they put forward their lists under the name of a small local party, *Izquierda Unida* (United Left). By this astute strategy, the *cocaleros* have managed to win a majority in all the municipalities of the Chapare, thus building a power base to advance their struggle.

They are now vociferous actors on the Bolivian political scene, putting up stiff resistance to the government's US-imposed coca-eradication programme.

Comité de Vigilancia (CV)

Vigilance committees (CVs) act as a 'nexus' between the municipal government and local OTBs in monitoring how resources are managed, both in the process of participatory planning sanctioned by the LPP and in the implementation of projects. Individual CV members are elected by district (the loosely defined administrative unit which lies between the municipality and the community) and have a watchdog role over the activities of the municipal government. In case of any irregularities, or complaints against the municipal administration, the CV is required to report to the Finance Ministry (*Ministerio de Hacienda*) which is in turn required to investigate and pass a report to Congress within 30 days. If the complaint is accepted and proven, the municipality's funding can be frozen indefinitely by Congress.

By the end of 1995, CVs had been constituted in less than 50 per cent of the 311 municipalities. Growth has been hampered by bureaucracy. It has been difficult to recruit sufficient numbers of CV personnel with the required technical qualifications. The committees have also been perceived in some municipalities as an ingenious mechanism by the state to divert popular protest into safe channels, stifling potentially disruptive social action with bureaucracy. Finally, there have been instances of corruption of CV members by municipal authorities. The development of clientelistic relationships between OTBs and CVs has been observed in some municipalities.

The state's recognition and promotion of OTBs and CVs as the linchpin of the LPP is unprecedented in Bolivian history. A state characterized historically by excessive centralization appears to be doing an about-face, not only transferring resources and authority to municipal governments but going one step further: recognizing and strengthening local institutions as significant actors in planning, management and auditing activities. The evidence so far suggests that the political consequences of this transformation are likely to be significant. The extent to which the state is likely to gain, or lose, from the new scenario is as yet unclear. What is certain is that a space has opened for the Bolivian people to have their voices heard in a new way.

State-sanctioned participatory planning: a contradiction in terms?

A central feature of the LPP calls for OTBs, municipal governments and NGOs to collaborate in the facilitation and elaboration of participatory plans. When a law passed by a government which has been democratic (formally) only since 1982 expounds on the virtues of participatory planning, questions relating to methodology are in order. How are these plans to be elaborated (i.e. using which methodologies)? To what extent do local people really conduct the necessary research and determine priorities for action? More importantly, how do participatory plans at the municipal level fit in with the state's own planning authorities and mechanisms? Put another way, how does scaling-down (by government) meet scaling-up (by local people through local institutions)?

34

Since the passage of the LPP in April 1994, the Bolivian state's annual Social and Economic Development Plan now hinges upon the articulation of central development programmes devised by the Ministry of the Environment and Sustainable Development with participatory plans coming from the OTBs at municipal level. It is at the departmental level that the two are combined for the elaboration of micro-regional or departmental programmes which are arrived at as a result of a process of negotiation and consensus-building between municipal councils, the *Corporaciones Regionales de Desarrollo* (CORDES)[5] and the National Planning Secretariat based in the capital.

Development planning in Bolivia is thus articulated at three different levels: national, departmental and municipal. At the national level, it is Congress which has the final say on the programmes, while the National Development Council and the National Planning Secretariat have a coordinating and supervisory role in recommending development policies and offering technical support to the lower levels in a consultative role (so-called indicative planning).

Participatory planning, as opposed to indicative planning, is supposed to take place at the municipal level, with OTBs and CVs as its main protagonists. The main outcomes of the process are the *Plan Anual Operativo* (PAO)[6] – Annual Operative Plan – and the *Plan de Desarrollo Municipal* (PDM) – Municipal Development Plan – both prerequisites for gaining access to the new funds made available by the LPP. Drawing up the plans involves the use of participatory appraisal methodologies in the investigative phase at grassroots level, followed by politico-administrative negotiations between the different interest groups once a plan is consolidated. The central question is, however, the extent to which the original priorities set out in the appraisal phase can be retained as the plan moves up the administrative ladder. Indeed, as the participatory plans scale up from OTBs to municipal governments, and finally to the departments, there is a real danger that diversity will be lost and that the more powerful interest groups succeed in pushing through the particular changes they want to the detriment of the poor and vulnerable.[7]

Dangers of bureaucratizing participatory methodologies

The great majority of municipalities have complied with the LPP in drawing up PAOs and PDMs. Although the the law was promulgated in April 1994, 281 out of 311 municipalities managed to present a PAO the same year and the number grew to 293 the following year (Arrieta, 1995). However, despite the impressive spread of participatory planning as a result of the implementation of the LPP, doubts have been raised as to the participatory nature of the planning process (Arrieta, 1995; Booth, *et al.*, 1996; Galindo, 1995; Peres Arenas, 1996a). It has been argued that, especially during 1994, the formulation of PAOs and PDMs was heavily influenced by external consultants belonging to the *Unidades de Fortalecimiento Municipal* (Municipal Strengthening Units) from the CORDES (the regional development corporations). These consultants provided facilitation and training in participatory methodologies to help articulate local needs, perceptions and priorities. However, these same consultants were also required to fit local priorities into a standard format to be presented to departmental authorities.

The use of a standard format has clearly reduced much of the specificity and diversity of the needs and priorities which had been expressed in the different communities. The powerful influence which some of these consultants appear to have exercised over the process has even come to the notice of the *Secretría Nacional de Participación Popular* (SNPP) – National Secretariat for Popular Participation – which is part of the Ministry of Human Development. Indeed, the secretariat has reported a bias towards investment in infrastructural rather than production-related projects in the participatory plans of municipalities where external consultants are known to have played a prominent role in the process of drawing up PDMs and PAOs (Peres Arenas, 1996a).

The use of PRA

There has been much methodological 'blending' in the way PAOs and PDMs have been drawn up. In a growing number of cases, PRA is clearly recognizable, most commonly in the methods used and, increasingly, in the attention paid to behaviour and attitudes. The use of PRA-type approaches, often mixed with elements of stakeholder analysis, and Latin American home-grown popular education techniques, has become more popular, especially in the appraisal phase at the OTB level. The use of PRA has also been supported by the World Bank (keen to be seen to be doing something participatory) and FAO, as well as bilateral agencies such as GTZ (Germany) and DANIDA (Denmark), and large international NGOs, notably CARE. The usual scenario is for one or more of these organizations to work through local NGOs and government organizations. In projects independent of the LPP which are financed directly by northern support organizations, PRA is fast becoming a prerequisite for funding, not only for appraisal but also, and more significantly, for the monitoring and evaluation of projects. The general spread of PRA in the country has without doubt had an impact on the methodologies used in the LPP. Booth *et al.* (1996) notes that PRA, promoted by the World Bank[8] and bilateral support agencies, had been used in the context of the LPP in 96 municipalities as of the end of 1995.

The use of PRA has been particularly successful amongst lowland indigenous people in the *Territorio Indígena Multietnico* (TIM, Indigenous Multiethnic Territory, a territory bordering Brazil and covering almost 2 million hectares, inhabited by Amazonian ethnic groups). The training was requested by CIDOB (Confederation of Eastern Bolivian Indigenous Peoples) in 1995, and was carried out by consultants from Núr University (Santa Cruz) and CERES (Centre for Studies on Economic and Social Reality in Cochabamba) mainly with community leaders and *promotores* (community-development workers). The collaboration between Núr University and local organizations resulted in the formulation of a plan for sustainable forestry which has been endorsed by the TIM government. The plan was later ratified by the departmental government and is currently being implemented. It has also strengthened the TIM government's lobbying activities against commercial logging in the area.

NGO–state relations and the LPP

A tenuous relationship

The relationship of NGOs with the state in Bolivia has traditionally been confrontational (Bebbington and Thiele *et al.*, 1993; ILDIS, 1992). During General Banzer's and General Garcia Meza's repressive presidencies over most of the period 1971–82, NGOs saw their role in essentially political terms: abuses of power, human-rights violations and social inequities had to be denounced, and a new, more open and democratic society needed to be built. The relative success of the Cuban Revolution, together with the continued irritant of US interference in Latin American affairs, made NGOs particularly sensitive to a range of Marxist thinking, much of it home-grown.

Especially popular were the ideas of Paulo Freire, Liberation Theology and, a little later, participatory action research, all of which developed a range of approaches which aimed to facilitate the conscientization and eventual emancipation of what were then called the 'oppressed' and are now called less flamboyantly 'the poor'. The concept of participation up-held by a significant number of Bolivian NGOs has therefore always had revolutionary connotations. It is associated more with the mobilization of the poor to achieve political change in favour of greater social justice rather than the more technical meaning it is given today, i.e. the involvement of the poor in doing their own research, establishing priorities for investment and 'participating' in the management, monitoring and evaluation of specific projects.

Now, with the end of the Cold War, most Bolivian NGOs feel they have lost their political and ideological *raison d'être*. Leftist rhetoric has lost much of its resonance as the state can no longer be so clearly defined as an ogre to be opposed. Indeed, with the LPP, the state has stolen much of the NGOs' rhetoric and methods, and is pressing to make allies of its former critics. Three years before the LPP was passed, in 1991, it called for all NGOs to register and agree on state–NGO collaborative arrangements. Although the proposal was turned down by most NGOs, some did opt for closer collaboration with government on programmes of poverty alleviation. These have renamed themselves *Instituciones Privadas de Desarrollo Social* (IPDS, Private Institutions for Social Development).

With the passage of the LPP, state–NGO collaboration has entered a new phase. In fact, it is now government policy that NGOs be integrated in the process of participatory municipal planning sanctioned by the LPP. It is significant, however, that very few NGOs took part in drawing up the LPP; there was resentment (but little opposition) at the government's appropriation and re-interpretation of concepts which were widely perceived to have originated in civil society. Since the promulgation of the law, they have, nevertheless joined in the capacity-building process, drawing on their long experience of strengthening local institutions, through such means as literacy training, popular education, credit support and indigenous-technology generation.

NGOs have been key actors in providing training in participatory methodologies (especially PRA) to involve local people, through the OTBs, in the elaboration of the participatory plans required by the LPP. The enthusiasm PRA has generated in some NGOs resulted in the creation in 1995 of a national PRA network spearheaded by Núr University in Santa Cruz. The network, composed of some ten NGO and government organizations, has facilitated a series of workshops to share experiences in the use of PRA and related methodologies, in the specific context of implementing the LPP, or in general. Seminal articles on PRA have also been translated from English into Spanish and disseminated to interested organizations, both in Bolivia and more widely throughout Latin America.[9]

The government's capacity-building programme

The government's capacity-building programme has been aimed primarily at strengthening the administrative capacity of municipal governments, rather than working with the OTBs (the preferred domain of NGOs). The *Programa Nacional de Fortalecimiento Municipal* (National Programme for Municipal Strengthening) launched a massive training campaign in April 1994, days before the official promulgation of the LPP, covering more than 90 per cent of the municipalities. The campaign was coordinated by the National Secretariat for Popular Participation and managed by the Regional Development Corporations (CORDES) and the *Unidades de Fortalecimiento Municipal* (Municipal Strengthening Units). The programme began with the training of 117 trainers in the basic contents of the LPP, and in the administrative skills required to formulate PAOs. The first phase of the training focused primarily on the administrative and financial aspects of municipal management, with specific courses in accountancy and budgeting skills. At a later stage, participatory planning was covered, although this was limited to the bureaucratic aspects involved in formulating the plans and did not, as such, address the question of how to facilitate participatory methods in the field.

Ardaya Salinas (1996) claims that the outcome of the national training campaign has been 'miraculous'. Between 1993 and 1995, the number of municipal governments which received training and acquired planning responsibilities increased from 26 to 305. The SNPP (quoted in Ardaya Salinas, 1996) reports that the number of investment projects in the municipalities increased from 400 in 1993 to over 2000 in 1994, reaching a total of over 9000 programmed for 1995. As Table 6.1 shows, over 80 per cent of the projects were initially in the social sector (mostly in education and urban development), though a slow shift towards production-related projects is now discernible.

Overall, despite historically loaded ideological discrepancies, the state and the NGOs are playing a complementary role in capacity-building for the implementation of the LPP. Clearly, the outcome has been heterogeneous and different OTBs have benefited to a lesser or greater extent, depending upon the timing and quality of the training they have received.

Table 6.1: Sectoral Distribution of Municipal Investment in Bolivia, 1994–5

Sector	Projects 1994		Programmed 1995	
	No	%	No	%
Production	86	3.7	562	6.0
Infrastructure	216	9.4	1144	12.2
Social	1930	84.1	7552	80.4
Multisectorial	63	2.7	132	1.4
Total	2295	100.00	9390	100.00

Source: Ardaya Salinas (1996).

A realignment of political forces?

What appears to be happening in Bolivia is more than 'decentralization with a bit of PRA etc. thrown in for good measure'. The LPP is not only a technical transfer of revenue and authority from central government to local authorities, as is characteristic of most models of decentralization. As its name suggests, the law aims to encourage participation; indeed, many of its stipulations provide concrete mechanisms for participation to happen: local institutions have been formally recognized by the state and are expected to play an active role in helping to implement the law; conventional planning methodologies are being reconsidered through the law's endorsement of participatory planning; and NGOs, former ideological opponents of the state, are now finding that participation with rather than against the state, as the law calls for, may be a more intelligent political strategy.

New and old actors are participating, then, in a venture spawned by the state. Local people and popular movements, with or without NGOs, now have the space to articulate their demands in ways that were impossible before the law came into effect: through newly recognized local institutions; through participatory planning (although the participatory nature of such planning still leaves much to be desired); and through increased control over the management of municipal-development projects, and the auditing of municipal government. New forms of collaboration with northern NGOs and international organizations have also been made possible.

To what extent all these changes will result in a profound realignment of political forces in the country remains, however, to be seen. Bolivia remains the poorest country on the Latin American mainland. It has also one of the highest proportions of indigenous peoples (c. 60 per cent). Contradictions are bound to surface with growing regularity. An almost exclusively white and *mestizo* government which is scaling down and using participation and 'empowerment' as central features of its new rhetoric may not be prepared to disempower itself in favour of groups, particularly the indigenous and the marginalized, calling for empowerment from the grassroots. How these contradictions are played out in the years to come, and who will gain and lose from the LPP and the processes that have been sparked off by it, should provide some important lessons for other countries interested in combining decentralization with participation.

7

Participatory Social Assessment in an Economy in Transition: strengthening capacity and influencing policy in Estonia

JOHN THOMPSON

Chapter 7 describes how participatory social assessments (PSAs) were facilitated by local technical agents and researchers to initiate a process of revitalizing farmers' associations in two counties of Estonia. The author discusses only the results of the first phase of what is to be a three-phase programme. Completed in October 1995, Phase One has enabled the Estonian Ministry of Agriculture to ascertain farmers' knowledge and perceptions of existing field-drainage systems. It has led to the creation of local land and water associations (LWAs) which will assume responsibilities for operation and maintenance of the drainage systems, as well as share costs. It has also led to the establishment of a cadre of trainers in the Estonian Ministry of Agriculture which will facilitate ongoing collaboration between the newly formed associations and the ministry.

The chapter describes how training in a participatory approach can have a strategic effect – revitalizing weakened structures, building new links between organizations working at different levels and, ultimately, influencing policy. The scaling-up that is occurring in parts of rural Estonia as a result of the spread and popularity of PSAs can be described as a multi-institutional process. Its long-term effects remain to be seen.

The context

As the institutions of Soviet agriculture were dismantled in Estonia in 1991, routine maintenance of the drainage infrastructure, engineered to the scale requirements of collective farms, was neglected, to the point where permanent damage to the systems will occur unless repairs are made and effective operation and maintenance is restored.

Countries in transition from centrally planned to market economies, such as Estonia, face several policy challenges when planning investments and designing agricultural-development programmes. These include lack of information concerning the capacities and priorities of local groups, and the collapse of institutions maintained by the state prior to transition. During preparation of the World Bank-supported Estonia Agriculture Project, the Sustainable Agriculture Programme of the International Institute for Environment and Development (IIED) in London was invited to support local technical agents and researchers to undertake participatory social assessments (PSAs), essentially a combination of participatory rural appraisal (PRA), rapid rural appraisal (RRA) and stakeholder analysis, to fill in information gaps and initiate a process of creating new and revitalizing the vestiges of existing, farmers' associations.[1]

The programme was divided into three phases, with the overall objectives of: (i) building institutional capacity at both the local and national levels; and (ii) informing the government's policy of land rehabilitation. Phase I was completed in October 1995, and has enabled the Ministry of Agriculture (MoA) to ascertain farmers' understanding of and commitment to the rehabilitation of field-drainage systems, and their willingness to form land and water associations (LWAs) which will share costs and assume responsibilities for operation and maintenance. It also led to the establishment of a new participatory training team in the MoA, which will support the collaboration between the LWAs and the ministry.

The challenge

Since regaining independence in 1991, Estonia has stabilized its macroeconomic situation and moved rapidly towards a market economy. Living standards, which declined dramatically in 1992–3, have begun to rise in urban areas where enterprises have been privatized and industrial production has been revived. Despite the country's potential to be competitive in agriculture, similar results have not materialized in the rural areas due to a number of technical and institutional constraints. The Estonia Agriculture Project, a World Bank-financed initiative, is expected to address some of these obstacles, principally the rehabilitation of field-drainage systems in the most fertile parts of the country.

The artificial drainage systems that were constructed over the past 40 years enabled Estonian farmers to raise the productivity of 740 000 ha (66 per cent) of the country's arable land. As was characteristic of Soviet agriculture, drainage systems were engineered to the scale requirements of collective farms and were centrally managed with little or no input from farmers. When collective farms were dismantled after 1991, routine maintenance of the drainage infrastructure was neglected and many systems fell into disrepair.

Rehabilitation of the entire drainage system would be technically complex and economically unjustifiable in a cash-strapped economy. The Government of Estonia has therefore requested funds from the World Bank to rehabilitate systems in five counties on 60 000 ha of the most productive lands. In order for these investments to be sustainable, farmers are required to form LWAs. The LWAs will negotiate with the government on the design of improvements, collect farmers' contributions of 20 per cent of the rehabilitation costs (in cash or kind), and assume the new, and sole, responsibility for managing and financing drainage-system operation and maintenance.

When selecting the rehabilitation areas, the MoA applied a rigorous screening process on technical and environmental criteria, but lacked knowledge of farmers' attitudes towards the proposed project. It was unclear also whether all the farmers in the identified catchment areas would continue farming, as some were moving out of agriculture, which is perceived as being unproductive, or whether the uncertainty over land ownership would be a major disincentive to investment in drainage improvements. The MoA reasoned that if farmers did not consider drainage rehabilitation a priority, were unable and/or unwilling to pay construction and operation and maintenance (O&M) costs, or were uninterested in acting collectively through LWAs, then the proposed investment would not be feasible or sustainable.

The participatory social assessment (PSA)

To fill in the information gaps and to develop a participatory process for involving farmers, the MoA, through the World Bank, requested IIED's assistance to carry out PSAs in five counties. The broad objectives of the PSAs were to:

- identify key stakeholders and obtain their views;
- collect information on social factors for selecting and screening appropriate sites;
- strengthen the MoA's ability to communicate with farmers and understand local priorities and capacities;
- develop a process to enable farmers to identify drainage problems, analyse constraints and propose viable solutions;
- identify procedures for decisionmaking and planning of LWA functions;
- anticipate the types of support (such as training and technical assistance) required by LWAs; and
- generate a commitment and ownership for farmers' participation in drainage rehabilitation and management.

The PSA was divided into three phases: during Phase I, training was provided to key stakeholders in PSA and participatory planning, and a PSA process was launched in two of the five counties selected for drainage rehabilitation; Phase II, planned for late 1996, was to be conducted in three other counties; and Phase III, scheduled for early 1997, was to focus on consolidation of stakeholder knowledge, and participation through workshops and farmer-to-farmer exchange events.

As part of Phase I, an intensive, national-level, introductory workshop on participatory social assessment was organized by the Amelioration Unit of the Estonian Ministry of Agriculture, with financial support from the European Community. The training, fieldwork preparations and review took place at the Vigala Agricultural Polytechnic in Rapla Maakond, Vana-Vigala, in October 1995. Twenty-four persons took part in the introductory training and fieldwork in three subsequent participatory social assessments in Pärnu and Tartu counties, among them: representatives of the county amelioration bureaus (the agencies responsible for implementing the drainage-rehabilitation programme); the county-land boards, local municipalities, the Agricultural Producers' Union, the Central Farmers' Union, the Institute of Philosophy and Rural Sociology of the Estonian Agricultural University, and Tartu University.

Participants represented a range of professional and academic disciplines, including agronomy, anthropology, amelioration planning, drainage engineering, land management and rural sociology.

There primary objectives of these activities were to:

(1) introduce an interdisciplinary and interinstitutional group of government planners, farmer representatives and university researchers to the key concepts, core principles and main methods of PRA, RRA and stakeholder analysis for participatory social assessment;

(2) strengthen the capacity of the collaborating organizations to design and undertake effective participatory social assessments for assessing farmer priorities, capacities and willingness to create LWAs for rehabilitating, operating and maintaining their drainage systems; and

(3) conduct participatory social assessments with farmers in several sites in Pärnu and Tartu counties in order to analyse local conditions, identify priority problems and develop an effective strategy for implementing the development of sustainable LWAs.

During the training and fieldwork, the participants were introduced to a wide variety of methods (Table 7.1) and worked with farmers to prepare catchment drainage maps (where drainage problems were identified and tenure issues were discussed), farm profiles, seasonal diagrams of agricultural production, labour demand and income and expenditure, pairwise rankings of priority projects, network and Venn diagrams of institutional linkages and information flows, and so on.

Findings of Phase I

The Phase I PSAs produced several unanticipated findings and clarified a number of issues. For example:

- farmers' perceptions of land-tenure issues appeared to be less of a bottleneck to LWA formation than anticipated by the MoA and the World Bank;
- prior to the PSAs, the MoA and the World Bank expected that the formation of the LWAs and their operation would be standardized across the counties. The social diversity apparent during Phase I illustrated the need for a more flexible and contextualized approach if farmers were to develop a sense of trust and be committed to their LWA;

Box 7.1: Responding to farmers' concerns

One important lesson to emerge from the fieldwork was the difficulty farmers had in understanding the financial arrangements for the drainage-rehabilitation work. Many of the questions raised at the large feedback meetings demonstrated this confusion and concern about financial disbursement and control. The PSA teams eventually decided that a summary of the project should be prepared, with a sample catchment map and schematic diagram, to serve as a briefing paper on the financial procedures, the flow of financial resources, institutional roles and responsibilities, and potential obligations of farmers. This briefing paper will be used early in the public consultation process.

Table 7.1: Methods for participatory social assessment

METHODS	APPLICATIONS
Semi-structured interviews and focus-group discussions	• identification and analysis of local criteria, perceptions, priorities, problems and opportunities regarding drainage amelioration, the formation and functioning of LWAs, land tenure and other land-management issues • identification and consultation with various social groups, focus groups and key informants
Farm profiles	• analysis of drainage and other resource problems at individual farm level • changes in productivity of fields, intensity of resource use, resource degradation, etc.
Resource maps at catchment or community level	• analysis of drainage and other resource problems at catchment level, enabling farmers to see interconnections between their individual land- and water-management problems and practices • identification of present land-use patterns and practices • inventory of resources in catchment level
Social maps at catchment or community level	• exploration of land-tenure and land-management issues • identification of different social groups using locally defined criteria • assessment of the distribution of assets (e.g., land, livestock, farm machinery, etc.) across social groups • identification of potential focus groups and key informants • identification of local innovators and experimenters
Trends analysis (using maps and other diagrams)	• analysis of trends and changes in: • land-use patterns and practices (past, present and future), including drainage-system development and management • agricultural productivity • income and expenditure, and diversification of livelihoods • institutional activities and interactions
Seasonal calendars	• planning of timing of drainage-rehabilitation activities • identification of trends in seasonal labour demand and availability • analysis of the annual agricultural calendar, including seasonal patterns of precipitation, cropping, marketing, income and expenditure
Venn diagrams	• identification of key local and external organizations • examination of past and present experiences with farmers' associations and local users' groups • exploration of local views of the core characteristics of effective farmer associations • understanding local perceptions of the relative importance, and frequency, strength and quality of interactions between local and external groups and agencies • identification and analysis of sources of conflict and cooperation between local and external interest groups
Matrix scoring	• conducting systematic comparisons of drainage technologies, amelioration strategies, land-management practices, marketing options, according to locally generated criteria • analysis of local priority problems and/or opportunities according to different interest groups • quantification of potential costs and benefits
Village meetings and exhibitions	• sharing, analysis and cross-checking of preliminary findings and information • supporting farmer-to-farmer exchanges • facilitating role reversals • preparing participatory action plans • conducting periodic monitoring of activities

- farmers were most concerned with local contractors' expertise and the possible impact of poor rehabilitation work on their future maintenance obligations and costs (Box 7.1).

Outcomes of Phase I

The PSAs conducted during Phase I led to a number of important outcomes:

(1) Farmers' interests and needs were more clearly identified and understood. The farm profiles provided the basis for identifying household assets and the conditions which affect potential LWA members' ability to utilize improved drainage and apply new farming practices. This information will be available to LWAs, MoA facilitators and design engineers when planning and budgeting for the rehabilitation works.

(2) A participatory planning process was set in motion. The participatory analyses became a means for giving voice to farmers. The catchment mapping enabled farmers to articulate their priorities and assess how they could cooperate and agree on the modalities for LWAs. During Phase II of the PSA work, the MoA and IIED team will test the participatory planning process to design improved schemes and management plans (see Box 7.2).

(3) Strategies for capacity building were developed. The MoA will continue to support technical assistance to LWAs during implementation in order to strengthen farmers' planning and management abilities. As part of this capacity-strengthening, during Phase III, a participatory monitoring and evaluation process will be tested to develop appropriate performance indicators with the LWAs, so that they may assess their progress and that of the MoA.

Box 7.2: Creating a National Training Team (NTT) in the Ministry of Agriculture

During the preparation phase of the Estonia Agriculture Project, the World Bank had assumed that social scientists from Estonia Agricultural University would be the appropriate actors to be conducting the PSAs and supporting the establishment of LWAs. This proved problematic, however, as the scientists were resistant to handing over control of these participatory analyses to the farmers. Instead, the MoA engineers were more adept at learning from farmers and setting the participatory tone for the fieldwork. In fact, they were so determined to build on the techniques they were learning, they recommended that the MoA establish a national training team (NTT) for participatory social assessment which would be in place for Phase II and become the resource unit for the project. This recommendation was endorsed by the MoA and the World Bank. Recently, the three-person NTT facilitated four county-level trainings of government staff and appears on its way to developing a flexible training programme which will be implemented across the five counties where drainage rehabilitation will occur. In the meantime, the university is reviewing its social science teaching and research methods to incorporate the new techniques gained from the PSA.

Learning from the past, building for the future

Since October 1995, 15 LWAs have been formed with the help of the national training team (NTT) and the county amelioration units. The use of the participatory social assessment has enabled MoA staff to screen the selected sites according to social criteria, primarily indicators of readiness to form and manage an LWA, and to develop a continuum of sites primed for collaboration in the programme. The Land Board of Estonia has endorsed and supported the screening process by accelerating its assistance for land titling in those areas selected for rehabilitation.

The social-assessment process also established an enabling environment for the MoA facilitators, by systematically including local-level stakeholders in the training events and social assessments undertaken so far, so that all interest groups are aware of the planning and conditions for LWA formation.

In early 1996, the NTT registered itself as a non-governmental organization, the Voluntary Society for Amelioration, with the intention of educating a wider public about Estonia's history and future in land and water management. It has been compiling numerous maps and documents relating to the distribution, membership and activities of LWAs across Estonia in the pre-Soviet era. These historical records and plans of local amelioration works, many of which have been held in town halls and private homes for over 50 years, indicate that farmer participation in voluntary associations to manage common land and water resources was widespread throughout the 1920s to the end of the 1930s. This ethnography of land and water management is a steadily growing collection and will be maintained by the Voluntary Society for Amelioration. This material will be used during discussions with new LWAs to draw connections between the past and the present, and trace family involvement in land- and water-management activities across the generations. In this way, participatory social assessment is being used to revitalize a nearly moribund cultural tradition and rekindle farmers' interest in the joint management of their drainage systems.

8

Scaling-up of Participatory Approaches through Institutionalization in Government Services: the case of agricultural extension in Masvingo Province, Zimbabwe

JURGEN HAGMANN,[1] EDWARD CHUMA,[2] and KUDAKWASHE MURWIRA[3]

Chapter 8 begins by describing how two agricultural extension projects in Zimbabwe switched from a conventional to a participatory approach in which elements of training for transformation (TFT) and PRA were tested. It then analyses how the approach was subsequently institutionalized in the agricultural extension service in Masvingo Province. The strategy adopted to institutionalize the participatory extension approach involved networking with other organizations, establishing common goals and launching a campaign to familiarize staff with the new procedure. The provision of ongoing training and follow-up over the medium-to-long-term was also considered crucial to facilitate the required attitudinal change.

The chapter concludes that the institutionalization of participatory approaches into hierarchically structured organizations is a highly complex intervention. In order to succeed, major changes are required in planning, implementation, and monitoring and evaluation procedures. Such profound changes require a process of at least five to ten years' duration as well as strong commitment by institutional staff at all levels, including donors.

Concept and approach for participatory innovation development and extension

In the Conservation Tillage for Sustainable Crop Production System project (CONTILL), adaptive on-farm trials in a farming-systems perspective were in use from 1991. Early experiences of technology development between small-holder farmers and extension staff soon revealed that the approach needed to be refined further into what would become a comprehensive methodology for participatory extension.

It proved to be unlikely that flexible, often site-specific innovations developed in the framework of the project would spread effectively if promoted through the existing approach of the agricultural extension service (AGRI-TEX). Two main limitations were identified (for more detail, see Madondo, 1992, 1993): (i) the outreach of the extension service concentrated on a 'master-farmer programme' which involved only about 10 per cent of the farming households; (ii) these farmers were being taught normative, blanket recommendations delivered in a top-down manner, a far cry from the dialogical, interactive-learning approach we wanted to introduce. Besides the question of technical innovations, it was also recognized that developments and innovation in the socio-organizational sphere had to be considered and addressed.

A participatory extension approach was developed, therefore, not as a desk-based blueprint, but as the result of a process driven by practical experience gained while working with individuals and communities (Hagmann et al., 1997).

The goal of the new participatory approach is to achieve the sustainable management of natural resources and higher levels of food security in small-holder farming areas in Zimbabwe. It aims to do this by developing and spreading sustainable farming practices and enabling rural communities better to handle their problems without depending on incentives from outside. It addresses communities as a whole, as well as individual families.

Participatory innovation development and extension is based on three inter-linked concepts: dialogical communication, farmer experimentation, and the strengthening of the self-organizational capacities of rural communities. The encouragement of active participation and dialogue by all actors at the local level as partners, e.g. farmers and their institutions, extensionists and researchers, is the mainstay of the approach.

Farmer experimentation

Dialogue and farmer experimentation is being encouraged in an environment where a powerful top-down extension service has considered farmers' knowledge to be backward and of no importance for nearly three generations, and where farmers have been conditioned to accept externally developed standardized technologies (Madondo, 1995). The stimulation of local experimentation has proved to be useful in recognizing the value of traditional and indigenous forms of knowledge, and has strengthened the farmers' confidence in finding their own solutions, and choosing options appropriate to their specific ecological, economic and socio-cultural conditions and circumstances. This process aims to transform the present standard-oriented extension methodology into an output-oriented approach in which general impacts, such as the efficient conservation of soil and water rather than the adoption of one specific technique are, for example, considered indicators of success.

Strengthening capacities for self-organization at the grassroots level

Strengthening the capacities of rural communities to organize often requires improvements in communication flows at the level of village institutions, which farmers themselves have assessed as too hierarchical, weak and closed to allow for the active participation of villagers in community activities (Hagmann, 1993). In addition, the conflict between traditional leadership structures and modern, government-introduced systems of representation has weakened local institutions and precipitated authority conflicts. Leadership training and the facilitation of dialogical communication in village workshops are elements which have shown high potential for improving cooperation, sharing knowledge and improving the participation of all gender and age groups in extension and rural development (Hagmann and Murwira, 1996).

The strengthening of local institutions, together with the increase in confidence that comes from the gain in knowledge and recognition during the experimentation process, creates an atmosphere conducive to the sharing of experiences, innovations and knowledge, and leads to effective farmer to farmer extension.

Philosophy and tools

Our experience has shown that the concept of strengthening local organizations, in particular its component of stimulating leadership and cooperation, requires more than a number of practical PRA tools to set it in motion (see, for example, Theis and Grady, 1991). A broader philosophical framework for the participatory development process was required and introduced in the form of training for transformation (TFT). This training programme was developed in Kenya in 1974 and adapted to Zimbabwean conditions by Hope and Timmel (1984). It originates in the pedagogy of Freire (1982) and is built on the notion of conscientization through participatory education, where learning is based on the experience of confronting and reflecting together on problems and issues as they occur. Teaching consists of facilitating dialogues centred on the technique of problem posing. Identifying, 'naming', to use the Freirean terminology, and reflecting on problems requires the facilitation of communication flows which allow groups to ask relevant questions and find causes and solutions for themselves, rather than receive teaching based on 'foreign' knowledge and realities.

TFT provides concrete methods and tools (e.g. codes, role plays, poems) to implement Freire's approach practically. It empowers local people to gain greater control over their circumstances by participating actively in their own development through the sharing and joint construction of ideas and knowledge. It stresses the importance of participation and cooperation as key elements in the building and strengthening of institutions which enable people to become self-reliant. It also aims to strengthen people's confidence, and includes tools to facilitate social analysis to help groups find the causes of problems (Hope and Timmel, 1984). The philosophical depth of Freire's concepts of dialogue and concientization has made his broad approach relevant and powerful for people of different disciplines, backgrounds, status and personality. It manages to integrate and unite divergent interests under one umbrella.

The approach is of great importance in societies where rapid and disruptive socio-cultural change has weakened social structures based on traditional rules and regulations (Hagmann, 1993; Nyagumbo, 1995). In our experience, a new 'umbrella' which can replace or at least partly substitute for a greater social cohesion that existed in the past is particularly important. The human

49

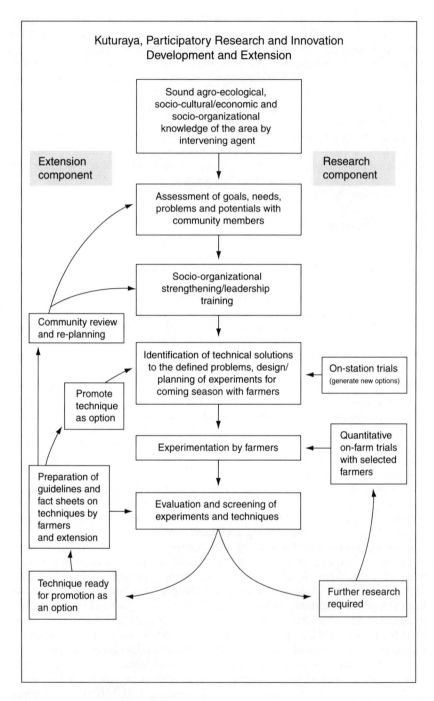

Fig. 8.1: Conceptual model for participatory research/innovation development and extension

desire for social harmony is very strong, in particular in the socio-cultural set-up within Zimbabwe, and largely determines most of the decisions taken by individuals and groups. Without providing a platform to develop a new umbrella, cooperation and leadership structures in rural communities will generally remain weak and a prey to unresolved social conflicts, which in turn adversely affect innovation development and extension.

Farmers are introduced to TFT at the beginning of the process in aware-ness-raising community workshops. Elements of TFT are utilized selectively and complemented by tools originating in PRA, diagnostic survey (Raintree, 1987) and goal-oriented planning (ZOPP) (GTZ, 1987), as well as by materi-als and aids for dialogical teaching to initiate and follow up on participatory innovation development and extension.

Figure 8.1 illustrates the concepts of participatory research, and innova-tion development and extension that form the core of the approach. It con-sists of three main components: (i) the 'process of learning and development through experimentation'; (ii) the research component and (iii) the extension component.

- *The 'learning and development through experimentation' process* The main process (centre column, Fig. 8.1) can be conceived as 'learning and development through experimentation', initiated and facilitated by exten-sion workers. It is people-centred in that villagers analyse and define their problems, needs and potentials, and the activities they want to carry out. Outside intervention contributes methodologies to facilitate the process, raise awareness and provide inspiration through the presentation of poten-tial technical options but people are not pushed by outsiders to carry out certain preconceived activities. It is an open-ended development process in which research and extension agencies do their best to participate in peo-ples' programmes and not vice versa.
- *Development of innovative techniques (research component in Fig. 8.1)* Innovation development is based on the trial-and-error principle. Farmers are encouraged to experiment with ideas and techniques emanating from their own knowledge base, on their own or in combination with outside sources. The problems identified during the needs and problems assessment form the basis for a research agenda and the experimentation process. If the specific technical processes are not fully understood, the farmers' ideas are taken to the research station for further research under controlled conditions.
- *Spreading innovative techniques (extension component in Fig. 8.1)* Spread is facilitated through the strengthening of the self-organizational capacities of rural communities and institutions. Improvements in commu-nication structures and skills are facilitated with the help of the TFT phil-osophy and tools, whereby an environment is created in which people feel free to communicate and share their skills and experiences with all the members of the community. Once this level of communication flow is reached in the communities, higher levels of farmer-to-farmer sharing and extension should result. In technical terms, it is not new technologies as such that are promoted but rather that experimentation based largely on indigenous technical knowledge (ITK) is encouraged. The experiences and results of the experiments are shared between farmers and extension staff,

51

Fig. 8.2: The main elements of the facilitator role

and contribute to the preparation of guidelines and training materials which focus on understanding the factors which make certain techniques succeed or fail. Important tools are mid-season evaluation tours and annual community reviews where technical and socio-organizational progress is reviewed and evaluated, and adaptations to planning forecasts made.

The new role of the agricultural extension worker

At present agricultural extension workers (AEWs) in the projects see themselves as teachers. A participatory approach requires a major role shift from teacher to facilitator. This implies that the AEW is no longer the main carrier of a message or knowledge, but the one who coordinates and organizes the acquisition of knowledge from several sources. Using the TFT philosophy and tools, the AEW initiates a participatory process in communities in which the focus is on local institutional strengthening, needs' identification and prioritization. S/he assists farmers in facilitating discussions around different options, for example by organizing 'look-and-learn' visits to innovative farmers and research stations, and encourages farmers to experiment with options and ideas as they come up. The AEW also encourages farmers to hold feedback sessions for those who could not participate directly. With time, the facilitator's role will be taken over by community leaders who are in the process of being trained in facilitation skills. Figure 8.2 summarises the main elements of the facilitator's role.

Strategy for institutionalizing the participatory approach

Pilot activities were carried out by the CONTILL Project, the ITDG Food Security Project and the Community-level Planning and Development operations of the Integrated Rural Development Programme (IRDEP) which is supported by GTZ. These activities served as case studies which monitored the processes, impacts and reactions of both farmers and extension staff to the introduction of the new approach. The success of the three projects in terms of the development and extension of innovations (Hagmann *et al.*, 1996), improvements in the organizational capacity of the communities (Hagmann and Murwira, 1994) and the growth in the number of community-planned and -implemented projects (Göricke, 1993) provided, we felt, sufficient justification to scale up the approach. A strategy for institutionalizing the participatory approach was therefore developed for Masvingo Province. Its key elements are described below.

- *Networking* Several organizations and projects in Masvingo Province use participatory approaches in one way or another. The focuses differ, but all of them work in close collaboration with AGRITEX, the extension service, as this is the institution which is most strongly represented at field level. The sharing of experiences between projects has been extremely valuable, and we were able to cooperate closely with ITDG and IRDEP and coordinate activities designed to facilitate the institutionalization of participatory approaches in AGRITEX. The informal networking and joint lobbying has allowed us to learn from each other's experiences. We also worked on joint papers and workshops. It was crucial to build up a critical mass of people in the different organizations that could draw attention to the participatory approaches and corresponding pilot activities. At the end of 1994, after several presentations in various provincial, national and international workshops, the network was expanding as various organizations from other provinces also showed a vivid interest in adopting a more participatory style in their work.

- *Familiarization of staff of all levels*
  Once the participatory approaches had gained a foothold in AGRITEX's operations, familiarization of extension staff of all levels became a priority. Besides providing reports and other relevant literature, several workshops were organized and supported by the three projects. These workshops were combined with field visits to the case-study areas in which participatory approaches were presented and experiences discussed. The field visits enabled higher-level staff to get fully involved in the process and decide to adopt the new ideas. Conversations with farmers who analysed the difference between the conventional and the participatory approach were particularly convincing. In addition to these formal activities, informal discussions based on good personal relationships, together with informal field visits, proved to be key elements in familiarizing AGRITEX officers with the participatory process and convincing them of its worth. Once high-level officers were convinced of the potential of the new approach, AGRITEX Masvingo organized a familiarization workshop for all its staff in the province in 1995.

- *Elaboration of a training and follow-up programme for extension workers*
  After the familiarization of the key players, a systematic training of 30 extension workers in TFT, and participatory tools and methods drawn from PRA began. An initial two-week course attended by extension workers and farmers together was followed by a report-back workshop to the communities which had chosen the farmers as their representatives, and to AGRITEX district staff. Extension workers then chose communities in which they wanted to apply and practise their new skills. A follow-up facilitation training was also provided over one year at 3–6 monthly intervals. These follow-up workshops gave extension workers a chance to assist each other, share experiences and improve their facilitation skills continuously in day-

to-day practice. The experiences of this training process were still being documented at the time of writing. A final evaluation will reveal its effectiveness.

- *Framework for organizational development*
  Based on the increased awareness for a required change within the organization, AGRITEX Masvingo recently launched an organizational-development programme, supported by GTZ/IRDEP and initiated by the Chief Agricultural Extension Officer, whose purpose was to improve 'relevant aggregate output at all levels of AGRITEX staff in Masvingo Province' (AGRITEX, 1995). As participatory extension had shown to be the most promising approach for improving the extension-delivery system, it became an integral part of the organizational-development strategy.

Lessons learnt from experience

Our experiences with institutionalization in Masvingo were based on an effort over a period of two years to integrate participatory approaches, not only in the operations of the projects in question but also in the very structures of the project's systems of organization. The full cycle, including training and follow-up programmes for extension workers, was initiated only in 1994, however, and has not yet been completed. Some of the constraints we faced in attempting to institutionalize a more participatory approach are discussed below. More details are described in Hagmann, Chuma, Murwira and Moyo (1995).

Participatory approaches showed high potential for increasing the efficiency of extension and rural development activities

The impact of the use of participatory approaches in the three projects was positive in three ways: (i) greater farmer participation was stimulated in innovation development; (ii) increased rates of adoption of technologies and innovations were recorded; and (iii) improvements were made in the capacity of communities to organize and set their own targets. In some areas, up to 80 per cent of the households were involved in developing and testing soil- and water-conservation techniques identified and promoted largely as a result of participatory research.

Implementing participatory approaches requires a change in attitudes

The case studies showed that a change in the attitudes of extension staff towards smallholder farmers is the key determinant for the success of the approach. In a hierarchically structured society, where hierarchy is based mostly on the level of formal education, it is difficult for formally educated staff to accept farmers' traditional- and experience-based knowledge systems as equal, and to learn from them. Attitudes cannot be changed only by applying certain participatory methods. That requires a philosophical framework sufficient to create conditions conducive to such a process. TFT (Hope and Timmel, 1984) is an approach that has the philosophical depth needed to frame a 'change in attitudes' in a broader context.

Ability to develop participatory skills depends on personalities

As attitudes are dependent largely on personality types, it is doubtful whether staff who have been professionally socialized and to a certain extent conditioned under colonial rule can truly reverse top-down approaches as this would force them to question most of their working life. The same applies to older farmers who have accepted a subordinate role and now identify with it. The impact chiefly depends, therefore, on the personality of each individual AEW. One cannot expect this to be uniform.

Training in participatory approaches as a continuous, medium-term process

Training courses in TFT and participatory tools were initially successful, but it was revealed that without a consistent follow-up of the process of change over a medium-term time span, the impact is low. Intensive training, support and follow-up are extremely important in order to avoid these kinds of initiatives being labelled participatory simply because participation is the talk of the day (something which has occurred with other approaches in the past). During the transition phase in particular, extension workers need strong support to overcome the insecurity and fear of losing power that often comes from giving up the teacher role.

Developing more effective staff-appraisal systems

Various levels of staff have frequently misinterpreted participatory approaches as 'AEWs pulling out', 'letting farmers do what they want', and as no longer being accountable for failures. To avoid this danger, besides proper training and follow-up, a more effective and appropriate staff-appraisal and -counselling system (including new types of performance criteria) has to be developed and made effective from the moment the participatory approach begins to be implemented. This requires a strong commitment on the part of higher-level staff to provide direction and create incentives for extension workers to sustain the participatory process. A key move has been to encourage appraisals of extension workers by farmers themselves, so increasing the accountability of extension workers towards their clients (i.e: the farmers). Farmer appraisals have since been integrated into the monitoring and evaluation system of the projects. Another important job-evaluation criterion is the AEW's performance in documenting farmer knowledge. This provides an incentive for the AEW to learn from farmers and recognize the value and importance of indigenous knowledge systems.

Developing criteria and indicators for monitoring and evaluating the impacts of participatory extension

The present M&E system is still based on quantitative indicators which measure the adoption of certain practices designed to increase and sustain production. Such indicators cannot measure the success or otherwise of participatory processes. More thinking is needed to develop qualitative indicators which better reflect the medium- to long-term impacts of working with participatory approaches. But aspects such as increases in self-reliance and self-organization are notoriously difficult to measure, even subjectively. Experience from other comparable projects would be most welcome.

Conclusions and recommendations

(1) The institutionalization of participatory approaches into a hierarchically structured organization is a highly complex intervention that must be considered a medium- to long-term objective. It requires a major reorientation of planning, implementation and monitoring and evaluation systems for which high commitment from all staff is imperative.

(2) Case studies or pilot activities in which participatory approaches are developed, tested and adapted are important. They serve as practical examples to familiarize and convince institutional staff and thereby influence policies from the bottom-up. Detailed monitoring of those operations should be continued in parallel with other aspects of institutionalization. Gradual rather than rapid scaling-up is recommended in order to detect pitfalls and mistakes as the process unfolds.

(3) It is crucial to make intensive efforts to familiarize and train staff of all levels. Networking and coordination of activities with other projects also appear to be important elements in building up the critical mass needed to sustain the process.

(4) Once there is a commitment from higher-level staff, intensive training, support and follow-up of field extension staff must have priority in the process of institutionalizing participatory approaches. Extension workers who are at the interface between farmers and the extension agency require new skills and competences if they are to switch from a teaching to a facilitating role. As staff turnover at the field level is low, intensive training at this level has a better chance of a lasting impact.

(5) Despite the favourable conditions that exist in Masvingo Province, the effective institutionalization of participatory innovation development and extension in the agricultural extension service will require a process of at least 5 to 10 years. Continuous commitment by the institution as well as by donors during this period is considered critical to its success.

(6) The process of organizational development is open-ended and unpredictable. The results of the process in Masvingo cannot be transferred to any other province, but the methodology and lessons·learnt during the process can act as cornerstones for a process elsewhere. This will be documented in the future.

9

Scaling-up or Scaling-down? The experience of institutionalizing PRA in the slum improvement projects in India

KAMAL KAR[1] AND SUE PHILLIPS[2]

Chapter 9 analyses the experience of institutionalizing participatory approaches in the design and implementation of ODA-supported slum-improvement projects in India, focusing on the case of Calcutta. The authors highlight the excessively compartmentalized structure of the project institutions (strictly divided between Engineering, Health, and Community Development) as the most significant obstacle to the effective adoption and spread of participatory approaches. Despite staff enthusiasm for PRA techniques, these were considered useful primarily to extract information rather than for planning. Another limitation was the insufficient attention paid to behaviour and attitudes training. The main conclusion was that for scaling-up to be effective, scaling-down may first be necessary by concentrating on a handful of cases of sustained community action in which participatory approaches play an important part, and using such cases as learning laboratories.

Background

The slum-improvement projects (SIPs) are being implemented with the broad objective of improving the standards of living of city slum dwellers in India. SIPs include infrastructural improvements such as drinking-water provision, sanitation, roads, drainage, garbage collection and electricity, together with the development of primary health care and community-development programmes such as pre-school, non-formal education, adult literacy and economic development. Since the early 1990s, the Overseas Development Administration (ODA) has funded SIPs in five major cities, and funding has just been extended to two more. They are Hyderabad, Vishakapatnam and Vijaywada in Andhira Pradesh, Calcutta in West Bengal, Indore in Madhya Pradesh, Cuttack in Orissa and Cochin in Kerala.

In this chapter we attempt to share some of our experiences of institutionalizing participatory approaches, especially participatory analysis and learning methods (PALM), a variant of PRA, in the slum-improvement projects, with a special focus on the Calcutta Slum-improvement Project (CSIP), which is being implemented by the Calcutta Metropolitan Development Authority (CMDA). This ODA-supported programme covers some 280 000 slum dwellers living in 15 wards, comprising roughly 250 slums, in and around the city of Calcutta. Although the project began in 1991 with the central idea of promoting community participation, in practice its mode of implementation was traditional.

In 1993, it was decided that a more participatory approach be adopted to ensure people's participation at every stage in the planning and implementation of the scheme. The local CMDA actors had been implementing the programme in the conventional government style. Keeping up with area coverage, achieving pre-set targets, using funds by certain dates, preparing timely reports etc. were considered priority concerns. Now for the first time, PRA approaches were introduced to CMDA staff. The idea of ensuring people's participation was not need-driven from the side of CMDA, however, but rather introduced by the donor agency. Terms such as participation, empowerment of community and local people, participatory planning and implementation, participatory monitoring and evaluation, community decisionmaking and so forth were coming up occasionally in seminars and workshops, but there were few signs that such rhetoric would be transformed into action.

The structure of the Community Slum-improvement Project (CSIP)

The CSIP is composed of three sections: engineering, health and community development. Each section has its programme manager: the director of engineering, the chief co-ordinator for community development, and the advisor for health. There are also assistant directors in Health and Community Development (CD) and executive, divisional and assistant engineers in the Engineering Department.

Before participatory approaches were introduced, part-time workers from the local area were recruited on a temporary basis to work in the *bustees* (slums). They were non-formal and pre-primary school teachers, community-development workers and health supervisors. While most of these part-time workers were women, there were hardly any women amongst the officials and staff in the levels above: none in community development and engineering, and only a few medical professionals in the health section. In engineering, the staff came from regular government departments, whereas most of the officials in CD and health were professionals and doctors from various government organizations recruited on short-term contracts. Most had worked for many years in the government bureaucracy. Only one or two young officials had had some earlier experience of working with the private sector or NGOs.

In every respect each section had its own agenda, targets and *modus operandi*. This was further reflected in the timing of the fieldwork, in which there was absolutely no coordination between the staff of each section at the level of the slum. Moreover, the heads of each section came together only in occasional meetings, such as the visits of outside delegates. Down the line there was no common platform, neither did there exist any regular event where the staff of all three sections could meet and exchange their views, experiences and ideas, and plan common actions. The CSIP was so compartmentalized that to an outsider it looked like three different institutes.

Training of CSIP staff in participatory approaches

The task of orienting the rank and file of CSIP (and other SIPs) in participatory approaches and methodology was time-consuming, and required much patience and persuasion. A number of training workshops for both officials and field staff was organized over a period of one year in four different stages:

(1) short exposure to PALM for the most senior staff of the five SIPs in India;
(2) training of middle-level officials and heads of departments of all the sections on PALM/PRA, with a slant on the training of trainers;
(3) training of trainers in PALM/PRA; and
(4) training of field-level staff in different SIPs by the newly trained trainers under the guidance of experienced trainers.

Interestingly, staff of all levels enjoyed the idea of a participatory approach and absorbed the techniques with great interest. There were, however, many difficulties, the most important of which are listed below.

It was initially very difficult to bring the staff of all the three sections of CSIP into one common training programme. Each wanted to have separate training workshops on PRA. Compartmentalization was so deep-set in the institutional culture of CSIP that it was difficult for the staff to imagine a common workshop setting.

The initial difficulty and stiffness of the higher-level staff when engaging in spontaneous and frank exchange with field staff and community groups was gradually overcome. Introduction games like hat selection, seed mixer, group drawings of personal images were useful as ice-breakers and rapport-builders during the workshops.

The specific interventions of each section were different. While the CD and health sections were providing inputs chiefly for long-term improvement in health, education and income generation, the engineering section was engaged in building infrastructure for immediate benefit. When PALM was introduced, most of the engineering plans for the slums had already been completed. The engineers consequently saw little relevance in an approach centred on participatory planning. The CD and health sections, meanwhile, found it difficult to move beyond appraisal. They felt their plans did not need to be modified.

Problems of scaling-up

A number of workshops, dialogues and discussions, which the staff from all three sections greatly enjoyed, were organized. For the first time they experienced the feeling of belonging to one integrated project. Ironically it was at this juncture that inter-sectional struggle in facilitating slum-improvement plans really began. One way the struggle was played out was for each section to apply the techniques of PRA/PALM quickly and haphazardly, here and there, in the slums.

59

The CD section, which was supposed to have the overall responsibility for the social dimensions of the project interventions, used the approach most. The staff had the feeling that they were doing their PRAs well. Hundreds of social maps, seasonal calendars of various kinds and matrices began to appear. Many of the so-called PRAs were facilitated in the slums during office hours (10:00 am–5:00 pm), and most of the drawings were made by women and children who were present in the slum community at that time. Since young and middle-aged men in slums are not generally available until after 5:00 or 6:00 in the evening, their contribution was minimal. In most cases the products of these so-called PRAs were not used in any comprehensive planning or sustained action by the community.

As for the engineers, although they thought the PALM techniques good, they were adamant that their planning phase was over, and that they were in the later stage of implementing all the plans already developed by the planners and engineers. At best, PRA/PALM could confirm what they knew.

Finally, the health section did have some success in using seasonal calendars to facilitate health discussions with mothers about the link between sickness and seasonally occurring events.

It was clear that the compartmentalization of SIPs into engineering, health and community development reduced the effectiveness of the use of PRA. All three sections tried to use PRA in isolation. The problems and solutions that were raised demanded a more comprehensive intervention and a consolidated approach. Each section expected the participation of the slum community, but there was no participation in-house. Compartmentalization tended to perpetuate a service-provision approach rather than to encourage a demand-driven response.

In Vijaywada (a city in South India) a senior officer of the SIP even made it compulsory for project staff to do PRA from 10:00 to 11:00 in the morning every day. Scores of social maps, calendars and diagrams were produced in slums, and it was not for some time that the officer was transferred. The project staff, who were by then tired of PRA, became critical of the approach. The lessons learnt from the Vijawada SIP were

- that without initiating a change in the behaviour and attitude of the project staff, it might be dangerous and risky to make large-scale use of PRA/PALM techniques;
- sufficient time and training input is needed to sensitize senior staff in the project bureaucracy about the implications of a participatory process of development for their organization; and
- a more integrated approach, not merely issuing government orders, is required to implement a people-centred development programme.

Efforts to scale down and create small examples of sustained community action

Situations whereby techniques were being used at random, with little concrete planning, and still less action, led us to scale down the introduction of the participatory approach by focusing on a few small examples of real-life community participation. It was thought that these showcases, or examples of community participation, would become process-learning centres for staff and other slum communities in which insiders (slum dwellers in this case) would tell their own story to others. This approach worked fairly well in Calcutta.[3]

The question was then raised whether the slum dwellers' participation could go beyond appraisal and planning and include the maintenance of the community infrastructure created by the project, through the formation of slum groups.

Our experience of facilitating attitudinal change in government staff has also been quite exciting. A different kind of training module was adopted whereby the poor from the *bustees* were brought in as consultants. In workshop settings, the slum dwellers took the lead in discussions regarding their conditions of life and experiences, and the government official's role was primarily to listen and learn. Slum dwellers were also brought from the city of Bombay (in the west) to Cuttuck (in the east) and vice versa, to share experiences and engage in mutual learning.

In the Calcutta SIP, a number of different activities were tried out over a period of 18 months to institutionalize the participatory approach, moving beyond the adoption of techniques to sustained community action in the slums. Some of the important novel actions that were tried out are listed below.

A series of joint workshops and meetings was conducted with the senior and middle-level officials from the three sections of CMDA on the pressing need to integrate their actions to make community participation more meaningful and effective. All the meetings were conducted in a fully participatory mode, with changed seating arrangements, group games, group sharing, joint presentations and the drawing-up of joint follow-up plans. Given the busy schedule of the officials, workshops and meetings generally had to be of a shorter duration (one day or half a day) than is normally the case. In all of these workshops, maximum emphasis was placed on the question of behaviour and attitudes as central to the success of participatory initiatives.

Officials from each section appreciated the need for a more integrated approach and suggested forming a core interdisciplinary team. It was felt by many that before advocating community participation, lack of in-house coordination and understanding of the implications of adopting a participatory approach had to be addressed. At the community level, six action groups were formed, drawing staff from each section responsible for a certain area. The whole idea was to integrate the interventions of all three sections to support and strengthen the implementation of community participatory plans. It was very difficult to reach this stage as the working hours for the field staff of CD and health were different, as were the location of their work stations, and even their salary and conditions of employment.

Special short workshops were organized for the joint orientation of the six community-action groups in facilitation skills for community participatory planning at the level of the slum.

Short one-day orientation workshops on participatory approaches for CSIPs were organized for the ward councillors of the municipal corporation. This initiative was essential because the councillors, who represent different political parties, are the most powerful elected representatives at the local level. CSIP staff on many earlier occasions had experienced difficulty in handling local ward councillors, who often tried to use project interventions to strengthen their own political positions. The results of the workshops were generally good, as most ward councillors gave the new participatory approach their blessing. It was realized that facilitating community participation at the slum level was more than a project. It was also about power.

Such workshops had to be facilitated very carefully, therefore, since they were attended by councillors of different political parties with different political agendas. Although the councillors had different views and opinions about CSIP, they all appreciated the participatory approach and promised their help and support.

Efforts were made to encourage staff to develop showcases of community participation in selected slums through concerted and prolonged action. One such slum, in Calcutta, became a model, and has since been visited by many officials of different SIPs, as well as outsiders. Slum members themselves have explained to these visitors the process of change that has taken place and how they have built up their own organizations to carry through the activities they planned.

The activities that were most effective in gradually institutionalizing the participatory approach in the CSIP, and more especially in building up strong and sustainable community organizations, were as follows:

- creating new slum-based community organizations and strengthening existing ones;
- integrating all SIP interventions at the level of slum-based community organizations and supporting only those activities set out in the participatory plan;
- facilitating exchanges between community members of a successful slum, and slum dwellers from elsewhere, in large meetings attended by slum dwellers and CMDA officials;
- organizing slum community meetings in the evenings (after normal office hours) when all the members of the community were generally present. In such *Sahajog* (co-operation) meetings attendance was high, as was the level of enthusiasm. Senior officials such as the chief engineer, the chief health advisor, the chief of CD, and others, shared the same floor with the slum community, and it was the local field workers and slum leaders who facilitated the group activities. Slum dwellers evaluated the progress of the work of the infrastructure done by the CSIP, suggested improvements, and promised to make contributions and participate.

Lessons learnt and conclusions

(1) It is absolutely essential in a participatory process that local people be involved right from the beginning, even before project formulation. The slum communities for whom the SIPs were designed were not consulted during the planning and implementation of the first SIP activities. Only halfway through the project was the decision to bring in a more participatory approach taken, and the staff trained in PRA/PALM.

(2) The pressure of achieving set targets within a given time frame interfered with the staff's ability to internalize the new participatory approach and reorganize themselves accordingly, in particular to adopt a more concerted and integrated inter-sectoral approach. Even after the participatory

62

approach had been up and running for 12 months, the staff remained concerned about sectional targets and time limits. It is necessary to allow some time to build up the participatory process at the early stage of the project so as to overcome apprehension of this kind among staff. This should be built into the project document.

(3) More thinking is needed to determine how best to develop non-conventional indicators that are suitable for participatory monitoring and evaluation. The conventional indicators used in traditional evaluations were clearly incompatible with a participatory mode of working with community groups and project staff. There appears to be a growing consensus among those with considerable experience with participatory approaches that the best way forward is for local people to define their own indicators. In this way, participatory monitoring and evaluation also becomes part of an institution- and capacity-building process.

(4) In the project document, the newly created infrastructures and other delivery systems were supposed to be handed over to the local authorities, community-based organizations, NGOs and slum community groups for future maintenance. The staff became concerned that community groups should be adequately prepared. These and other groups were not, however, expected to join as partners in the planning stage. Clearly, the community groups should have been involved right from the planning stage of the project. This oversight begs the question: Who participates in whose programme?

(5) Considerable time, effort and tact is needed to bring about the desired change in the attitude and behaviours of the staff in a project of this nature. Such a change is unlikely to be achieved in one or two occasional training sessions. A much longer-term input and a host of training-related activities needs to be considered.

(6) The commitment of only one or two people at critical moments can make a significant difference. Staff and officials who emerge as natural leaders in participatory development and show the right kind of attitude are not many. Sometimes they face obstructions from others in the system and may not get support and cooperation from those in authority. Such persons need to be identified, supported and encouraged. Innovative ways to sustain the spirit and motivation of such people need to be developed.

(7) The impact of ongoing and new programmes could be greatly influenced if the appropriate actions, based on the lessons learnt, are taken. The selection of the right person and the right venue for training is of utmost importance. Although the project life of some SIPs in India has almost come to an end, many are still in the middle of their implementation process and some new ones are coming up.

PART 2

ORGANIZATIONAL CHANGE: THE KEY TO INSTITUTIONALIZING PARTICIPATION?

10
Introduction to Part 2

In Part 1, we saw how participatory approaches, in particular PRA, have spread in markedly different settings, in countries as diverse as Ethiopia, Vietnam and Bolivia, and in sectors as different as agricultural extension in Zimbabwe and slum improvement in India. In most of these cases, the authors pointed out that the main constraints facing the scaling-up of PRA and related approaches are organizational. Be they NGOs, government organizations or donors (or a combination of these), development agencies are ill-equipped to cope with the changes implied by the introduction and spread of an approach such as PRA.

Adopting PRA and/or related methodologies involves much more than training field staff in the approach and leaving everything else untouched. Significant internal organizational changes are required across the board, in structures as well as procedures. How funds are disbursed, to whom and how, and who decides what is important are some of the fundamental questions which the use of participatory methodologies oblige us to consider. The cases explored below, of non-governmental and community-based organizations in India, Sri Lanka, and Somaliland, and of government and donor organizations (EU-Government of India, GTZ (Germany) and large public institutions more generally), show that the organizational changes required by the adoption of participatory approaches are multi-level and cross-sectoral. Moreover, since organizations are increasingly interlinked, whether through funding arrangements or joint agendas, changes in one are bound to affect others. Organizational change is as much inter-institutional as intra-institutional.

Chapters 11–13 present three case studies of how NGOs and community-based organizations are responding to the organizational challenges of introducing and sustaining participatory approaches in their work.

In Chapter 11, James Mascarenhas reviews the experience of OUTREACH, an Indian NGO, in facilitating participatory watershed development in semi-arid and drought-prone areas of South India. The chapter describes five stages that the author considers essential to the introduction and spread of a participatory approach. Emphasis is placed on the importance of pre-project preparatory processes, as well as planning, before any intervention is considered. Inter-institutional consultation and coordination are also seen as crucial elements of the kind of organizational change strategy that is required for participatory approaches to take root.

Chapter 12, by Mallika Samaranayake, analyses in some detail the various organizational challenges faced by a Sri Lankan NGO, the Self-help Support Programme, as it gradually introduced PRA in every phase of all its projects over a period of five years. The chapter gives useful practical tips to those hoping to embark on a similar venture. It shows in candid terms that turning an NGO, or indeed any organization, into a truly participatory institution is no easy task, but that careful attention paid to the way funds are disbursed, both by donors and within an organization, can forestall many of the difficulties that seem to occur once a participatory approach is adopted across the board.

Chapter 13, by Sam Joseph, reflects on how certain NGOs are responding to the organizational challenges of participation in Somaliland. Joseph argues that for development workers to support participatory programmes implies long-term commitment and the adoption of management styles that coach and facilitate rather than supervise and dictate. For local leadership to flower, a ten-year period of support is recommended, in the form of advice or patronage, for each community-managed programme, to ensure continuity and consistency regardless of changes of staff or structure.

Chapters 14–16 group together three case studies of how different government and donor agencies are taking on the organizational challenges of going 'participatory.'

Chapter 14, by Andrew Shepherd, analyses the experience of the Government of Uttar Pradesh's (India) European Union-funded Watershed Management Doon Valley Project, in which participatory planning at the village level has been initiated. It addresses issues to do with organizational structure and procedures, training and the dynamics of social change more generally, and compares the experience of the Doon Valley Project with other similar initiatives, in particular the experience of participatory irrigation management in the Philippines. The chapter's key lesson is that participation cannot simply be bolted on to an existing project concept as an add-on because it has implications for the project's entire gamut of working practices.

Chapter 15, by Heinrich Eylers and Reiner Forster, reviews GTZ's experience with participatory approaches since 1991. It outlines some concrete recommendations to re-orient GTZ's approach to management, and argues that more research is needed to understand the impacts that these approaches have, both on the beneficiaries and on the wider social and political systems that exist in partner countries. The authors recommend a regular exchange in learning groups at a regional or national level to reflect on common experience with participation and suggest new ways forward.

In Chapter 16, John Thompson shows how the challenge for large public institutions attempting to employ participatory approaches is to facilitate the emergence of new ways of knowing and behaving so as to manage change creatively. The author argues that this will offset growing concerns over the co-opting of the term 'participatory' by those with short time horizons and narrow agendas who may be promoting stasis and the status quo rather than change, innovation and, eventually, transformation.

11

The Participatory Watershed-development Implementation Process: some practical tips drawn from OUTREACH in South India

JAMES MASCARENHAS

Chapter 11 reviews the experience of OUTREACH, an Indian NGO, in facilitating participatory watershed development in semi-arid and drought-prone areas of South India. It describes five stages, over a period of four to six years, that the author considers essential to the successful introduction and institutionalization of a participatory approach to natural resource management. Emphasis is placed on pre-project preparatory processes, such as the creation of self-help groups, as well as participatory planning based on PRAs, before any intervention is considered. Consultation and coordination between newly formed watershed associations, other NGOs, and local government institutions are also considered crucial at every stage of the process.

The author makes a strong case for a gradual, progressive institutionalization of participatory approaches whose central aim is the strengthening of emerging community-based organizations (CBOs). 'Success' is defined as the moment that CBOs in the watersheds no longer need a supporting agency, and are able to manage their own projects and apply for outside assistance as and when necessary.

This chapter brings together the experience of OUTREACH, an NGO specializing in facilitating participatory approaches to natural resource management (NRM) in South India. The context that is described is that of watershed development in semi-arid and drought-prone areas in the states of Karnataka, Andhra Pradesh and Tamil Nadu in South India. These are areas in which the staff of OUTREACH has been involved for more than ten years in developing approaches to NRM that are relevant, participatory and sustainable. More importantly, this chapter attempts to offer some guidelines for practitioners who are engaged in this enormous and complex task.

The process of implementing participatory watershed-development activities involves several stages and activities. These stages, described below, are not rigid and indeed they often overlap. Each stage is fundamental, however, to the fostering of community participation over the long term.

Stage 1: preparation time and the creation of self-help groups

In areas where NGOs have had a substantial presence, it is often the case that communities will already have formed their self-help groups and are able to place demands on the 'delivery system'. The delivery system in this case exists in the form of an NGO which provides inputs, and assists individuals and groups to draw benefits from government programmes in the form of minikits, IRDP loans, forestry plants, susbsidized horticultural plants, drinking water, old-age pensions and so on.

When watershed development is introduced as a new concept in the communities, a preparatory period of five to six months is needed. This time is spent in a combination of discussion forums, exposure trips and field interactions with other well-established watershed communities.

Areas where no NGOs are present need a longer start-up period, in terms of community preparation (about 12–18 months). The process begins with activities aimed at generating community participation, initiating self-help groups, setting up savings and credit schemes, and raising environmental and wastershed awareness. 'Preliminary' PRAs are conducted to understand more about the watershed community, its history and livelihood systems, and its various interest groups. These preliminary PRAs lead to the identification of entry-point activities for the project. They also throw up key issues around which local communities can mobilize by forming self-help groups. Particularly important at this stage in the formation of self-help groups is the establishment of micro-credit schemes to help generate local funds and shape group solidarity. Training is provided in savings and credit management.

Stage 2: participatory planning processes and procedures

Once the watershed has been delineated (based on the preliminary PRAs facilitated in the preparatory period), the stakeholders identified and an initial study conducted, a planning process is set in motion. In the first phase, PRA is used again, this time to generate information which will be fed into the watershed-management plan. In the second phase, the plan itself is drawn up in its various components.

Generating the information

A range of PRA methods is facilitated over a period of three to four days to build up a complex picture of the watershed, especially of its agroclimatic and socio-economic conditions and the manner in which they interact. It is important to note that the Gramsabha and the Panchayat (local councils) are invited to take part at this stage. Their presence is essential to the success of the various plans that will evolve subsequently.

Historical transects generate trends in resource use, land-based and non land-based livelihood systems and the traditional ways in which watershed resources have been managed and used. The problems, constraints and opportunities facing the watershed are addressed in some detail, covering relations between the main village and neighbouring villages, the role of informal institutions and their relevance, and seasonal patterns in agricultural work, migration, diseases, fodder availability and credit needs. Of particular importance are the social and natural-resource mapping exercises to study the management and use of resources, and the wealth-ranking exercises which help identify who the poorest members of the community are. Sweeping transects of the watersheds are also carried out by members of the communities, as well as representatives of outside agencies and local councils, to identify problems and opportunities specifically connected with the land.

Likely to arise during this process are discussions on the use and management of fallow lands, and of the upper reaches of the watersheds, whether commonly or privately used and whether owned by the revenue or forestry departments or members of the community. This also touches upon grazing land and its management. It is usually the case that members of the micro-watershed community are willing to make plans that apply to their own land where the title and benefits are clear. Common lands, on the other hand, do not offer such clarity. Individual responsibilities and obligations, in terms of investments, usufruct rights, process and procedure for joint management, and so on, have to be negotiated. These questions are addressed more thoroughly at the end of Stage 3 in the process.

The problems and opportunities detected as a result of the transects lead to the identification of treatment activities in the micro-watershed. These are represented visually on a map of the micro-watershed prepared by the community. This map indicates and illustrates the treatment plan as proposed by the micro-watershed community in physical terms such as contour bunds, plots for horticulture, check dams and diversion drains. Different 'official' maps, such as the revenue and topographical maps (if available), are at this point cross-checked with the villagers' treatment maps. Initial discussions are held between the various parties involved to determine who will undertake which treatments, whether on individual or common lands. This exercise leads to the elaboration of a micro-watershed development plan consisting of five parts.

Elaborating the plan in its various components

Treatment plans

How these are drawn up has been discussed in some detail above. The finalization of the treatment plan – reaching agreement on the sites of major works and who will do what where – requires the formal approval of the whole micro-watershed community or group.

Financial (budget) plan

Here the costing for the different activities is worked out, as well as the contribution from the community, NGOs, government and others. It is during this stage that agreements are negotiated with the community regarding cost-sharing, common-property resource management, the sharing of work between men and women, and how landless labourers are to be involved. Who contributes, how much and what for is carefully established. It is important to note that the exercise distinguishes between activities that have zero or very low cost, and those that have medium or high cost, in order to emphasize that resource mobilization can come from different sources including the community itself.

71

Time plan

The time plan is drawn up by means of a seasonality exercise indicating the peak periods and slack periods in the watershed communities' annual calendar. The plan determines the timings for execution of the various watershed-development activities, according to the preferences set by the communities themselves.

Implementation plan

The implementation plan deals with questions that are purely operational, i.e. which group or individual is responsible for each activity or sub-activity. For example, if the activity is tree planting, then who will select the species to be planted? Who will raise the nursery? Who will transport the plants to the field? Who will dig the pits and trenches? What layout and type of pit or trench? Who will do the planting, etc.?

Management plan

Similar to the implementation plan, the management plan determines who will manage various aspects of the work once completed. To continue with the above illustration, who will protect the plants? Who will water, manure and maintain them?

It is also at this time that decisions are taken regarding the composition of the watershed management committee (WMC), its precise functions and the frequency of its meetings. All the above agreements are entered into and signed by all parties on an agreement form.

Stage 3: the implementation plan

After the planning is complete, the actual process of implementing watershed-development activities begins. Assuming that the lead-up to the beginning of this phase (at the end of the participatory planning exercise) takes 6 to 18 months (depending on whether there is an existing NGO presence or none at all, as discussed earlier), this period will take between two and two and a half years, and involves the following sub-stages:

(1) *Strengthening of community organizations within the watershed*
It is not to be assumed that community organization and the establishment of the WMC, as well as other micro-watershed groups, is a one-off activity. It continues throughout this period through group-strengthening activities such as training, discussions and exposure trips. The groups have to be supported in their attempts to evolve, and, at least initially, assisted in various activities, particularly in the field of credit management and common-property resource management. It is interesting to observe how the various groups deal with their respective situations, take decisions and act on them.
This is a period of growth which is critical to the process of development. Groups must be given opportunities to learn and grow, even if some of these have to be created deliberately. For example, in most cases the entire experience of bookkeeping is new, as is the opening of a joint bank account, the concept of monitoring quality or the negotiating of rebates

72

on bulk purchases of fertiliser, and so on. The groups evolve their own rules and self-regulatory mechanisms, norms, fines, penalties, rewards and sanctions. Such a process takes time, however, and cannot be rushed.

(2) *Implementation of watershed-management activities on private lands*
During this period it is natural for farmers to start with what they can see and relate to closely, such as their own and neighbouring-farmers' land. Each farmer has a choice of performing work (agreed upon in the plan) on his own farm, on an individual basis or with the help of the WMC. Farmers usually negotiate reciprocal arrangements with their neighbours. They are likely to fall back on the WMC only when they run into a conflict which they cannot resolve themselves and which involves two or more farmers. It may also happen that some additional work is required which was not foreseen earlier and needs the approval of the WMC.

(3) *Development and management of common property resources*
Once a rhythm of work has been established in the watershed programme and the micro-watershed group's confidence is enhanced, it is appropriate to address the issue of more intensive treatment and management of common lands, particularly those in the upper reaches.

The treatment plan for common lands will be in line with what was agreed upon in the participatory planning phase. But this may need to be emphasized again through yet another PRA exercise in which technical staff from outside the watershed, either from government, NGOs or other institutions participate to refine the plan further and make it more definite.

Micro-watershed groups may agree to contribute towards the costs of developing common lands, provided they are sure of the benefits and provided their level of confidence in the system is high. This contribution may be in the form of labour, watch and ward, prevention of grazing, or even in terms of agreeing to usufruct rights in favour of landless and women's groups in the watershed. Situations vary, however, and each common property agreement would have to be looked at and negotiated on a case-by-case basis. This also applies to other areas such as check dams and *nullah* (water channel) training. The project should allow enough flexibility for these adjustments to happen. Payments for work done on the common lands would also need to be made, for which a separate work-monitoring groups would be responsible.

(4) *Non-farm income-generating programmes (NFIGPS), gender and equity*
Non-farm income-generating schemes are an important part of the micro-watershed development plan. NFIGPS target the more marginalised groups in the watershed specifically, such as women, landless labourers, rural artisans and marginal farmers. The wealth-ranking exercises carried out in the planning phase will have helped identify these categories of people. NFIGPS are closely linked to the regeneration of natural resources, particularly the perennial biomass such as grasses, shrubs, trees and other vegetation in the upper reaches which serve the function of providing soil cover against the impact of wind and rain erosion.

Such activities also serve to address the issue of equity in the watershed. Most of the activities decided on in the development plan benefit primarily those with land. Resources need to be set aside to enable those without land or with only small portions of land to stabilize their livelihood systems and live with dignity. The issue of equity is also linked to the management of common property resources and the sharing of usufruct as described earlier.

NFIGPS commonly consist of small businesses: trade such as petty shops and tea stalls, services such as laundry and haircutting, and small industries such as smithery and carpentry. The individuals concerned obtain their working capital initially from their respective savings and credit funds, but provisions usually need to be made to supplement these sources.

Throughout the programme, sufficient attention needs to be paid to the practical and strategic needs of women. Women in the watershed should be encouraged to contribute towards the elaboration of the watershed plans. Strong emphasis also needs to be placed on the development of women in the watershed, particularly in terms of their economic condition. This should not, however, be at the cost of their quality of life. Women should not be burdened more than they are with additional jobs and responsibilities even if these are of an income-generating nature. Special care needs to be taken to ensure that women have better access to and control over resources. A few important gender actions are:

- organizing and strengthening women's groups separately;
- setting up savings and credit programmes for women;
- initiating income-generating programmes (of their choice);
- facilitating access and control over portions of common property resources, especially fodder and fuel lots; and
- including suggestions from women for specific watershed activities, such as the selection of tree species, the location of fuel lots and check dams.

Ensuring that women are adequately represented on the WMC is considered crucial. It is also important that the PRAs or planning sessions are not dominated by men. If men far outnumber women, ways should be found to give women a chance to have their say so that their ideas and suggestions can be included in the micro-watershed development plan.

(5) *Monitoring of work*

Monitoring will focus mostly on those tasks and activities which have to be measured physically such as soil and moisture conservation, and forestry activities. The purpose of monitoring will be to assess the quality and quantity of work, whether it is in line with the agreed plan, whether there have been any changes and on what basis, what additional activities are needed, and how payments are to be calculated. The monitoring is usually done by a group nominated by the WMC or by the entire watershed group. In addition there may be one or two representatives from NGOs or government. When the work is on private land, where each individual is expected to contribute according to the agreement reached at the end of the planning phase, the WMC members themselves take the lead in assessing quality, calculating payments and ensuring that contributions are made, usually in the form of labour.

Other aspects connected to the monitoring of activities relate to looking at the way crop trials and demonstrations are progressing, the main-

74

tenance of horticulture and forestry plants, and of soil and conservation works. This is the first step towards achieving asset maintenance and long-term sustainability. One means by which this kind of monitoring is done is in the form of weekly watershed walks or sweeping transects whereby members of the WMC, together with NGO and government partners, walk in the watersheds and look at what is happening, particularly in relation to the treatments that have taken place and their effect on soil and moisture conservation and revegetation. Observations are discussed directly in the field and at the end of the watershed walks. Any issue which cannot be resolved at the individual, group or management-committee level is brought to the Gramsabha, and if it still unresolved, to the Panchayat. Some issues, such as usufruct arrangements of state-controlled land, may require interventions at the district or state level.

Stage 4: withdrawal from the micro-watershed

The withdrawal is a gradual drawn-out process which begins, ideally, as soon as the project starts. This is in order to prevent any dependencies developing, including that of being romantically involved with the project or client communities! That withdrawal must take place is much easier said than done, however, and must be consciously practised. Certain group-strengthening activities such as training in management systems, procedures and planning, bookkeeping and technology generation help ensure a smooth hand-over in the withdrawal process. This is also the time when links are established with other institutions inside and outside the watershed area. By this time, if the community-organizational activities have been effective, the groups should be confident that they can manage their affairs on their own, or with very limited support. This includes the capability and confidence to place legitimate demands on the government to provide resources in the form of schemes and programmes specifically designed for watershed development.

It is also at this stage (once again, if community organizing has been successful) that the established micro-watershed groups will act as promoters for the emergence of new institutions in the adjoining areas of the watershed. These institutions emerge from the micro-watershed groups and management committees, and gradually take on the full responsibility for the management of the watershed's activities. It is the ideal time for a facilitating NGO to withdraw from direct interaction with the group and hand over to the apex institution.

Conclusion

Participatory watershed development does not happen just on its own. It has to be made to happen. What has been described above gives an idea of the complexity of an intervention of this nature. A target or blueprint approach would never work in such a context. To facilitate a process approach successfully requires, however, the right kind of policy and institutional environment. The role of NGOs in the preparation of watershed communities needs to be recognised and enhanced, and government support is needed to enable NGOs to work in more than just a selection of watersheds.

12

Participatory Learning Approaches in the Self-help Support Programme, Sri Lanka[1]

MALLIKA R. SAMARANAYAKE

Chapter 12 reviews and analyses the institutional changes which resulted from the wholesale adoption of PRA in every stage of the programme cycle of the National Development Foundation, an NGO in Sri Lanka specializing in water-tank rehabilitation and irrigation and a partner organization of the Swiss-funded Self-help Support Programme. The chapter shows how over a period of four years (1990–94), substantial changes had to be made in the procedures regarding the following aspects of the programme: site selection (who decides where work should be done); control of implementation, monitoring and evaluation (whose project is it?); funding arrangements (in particular how funds are dispersed and to whom, i.e. who benefits?); progress reporting to donors (whose format counts?); institutional development of farmer organizations (whose power counts?).

The author argues with conviction that 'participation' and 'empowerment' have little meaning unless implementing organizations, together with their partners and donors, are prepared to refashion the programme systems and procedures which often interfere with rather than facilitate participatory processes of development. The chapter warns, however, that the will to change implies, in this case, an acceptance of losing control over the direction, content and evolution of a project in favour of community-based organizations.

Background to the Self-help Support Programme

The Self-help Support Programme (SSP) was introduced in 1988 by Intercooperation (IC) with a small coordination office in Colombo. Intercooperation is a secular non-governmental Swiss organization for development cooperation, with emphasis in the field of rural development.

SSP is operationalized through governmental and non-governmental organizations committed to rural development, in partnership with the rural poor, in the Dry Zone of Sri Lanka (Anuradhapura and adjacent districts). The programme aims to improve the living conditions of the rural poor by:

● promoting capacity for self-organization through self-help groups for sustainable utilization of available resources; and

• enhancing access to services and inputs both existing and newly created.

To this end SSP provides technical and institutional support to partner organizations with a sectoral focus on rural savings and credit, rehabilitation of minor irrigation tanks and the development of self-help groups.

The type of partner organizations associated with SSP – governmental, semi-governmental (statutory bodies), non-governmental and grassroots – differ widely in size, organizational culture, operational focus and field methodology. In analysing how participatory processes and institutional changes are interlinked, it is difficult to generalize: the particular characteristics of each organization will condition the process and make it different in every case. For this reason, I have chosen in this chapter to focus on the case of only one of SSP's partner organizations, the National Development Foundation (NDF) in the hope of sharpening the analysis and making it more meaningful.

National Development Foundation (NDF), partner of SSP

Background of the organization

The NDF is a non-profit making NGO established in 1979 to implement development programmes in rural areas of Sri Lanka. Its present activities are concentrated in Moneragala District (Uva Province) and Kurunelaga and Puttlam districts (North-Western Province).

NDF focuses on technical support to villages in remote rural areas, combined with strengthening the capabilities of farmer organizations. It is responsible for a number of village-based projects with emphasis on minor tank rehabilitation, and support to small farmers dependent on highland crops from rainfed agriculture. In 1994, NDF was working with about 30 farmer organizations. Its organizational structure is composed of a head office in Colombo and regional offices in the project areas of Moneragala and Kurunegala.

NDF has been a partner of SSP since 1988. Other donors of NDF are the Foundation for International Training (FIT) until 1990, the Australian Freedom from Hunger Campaign (1988–93), OXFAM Germany (1988–91), and Community Aid Abroad, Australia (CAA) from 1993 onwards.

NDF's development approach 1985–90

As an NGO, when compared to the governmental and large non-governmental organizations, NDF could be described as an organization that is 'close to the people'. This does not mean that the development strategy NDF adopted then was as participatory as it is today. During its development activities at the field level, 'participation' in this period meant farmer involvement by way of labour contribution for the construction of such things as tank bunds and agrowells. Most of the decisionmaking process was in the hands of the regional-office field staff and the head office. The focus was on minor tank rehabilitation (village reservoirs) for irrigated paddy cultivation.

The tanks to be rehabilitated were chosen from the Small Tanks Register kept by the Agrarian Services Department (ASD). Requests for rehabilitation were then made by the branch offices of the ASD and by members of parliament to NDF.

NDF field officers conducted complex socio-economic surveys of households in selected villages using elaborate questionnaires. Survey reports were eventually produced (delays did not matter significantly as the information was hardly used) and copies sent to donors. Farmers were not actively involved in the process of gathering and systematizing information, nor were they consulted as to the rationale for choosing certain sites as opposed to others. As for the calculation of estimates for the work to be done, this, again, was not considered a responsibility of the farmers but of the field officers.

'Farmer participation' began at the point that farmer groups were to be organized by field officers to carry out construction work. The labour performed by farmers, part paid, part 'contribution', consisted of clearing jungle on the tank beds, clearing tank bunds and uprooting roots when machinery was in use, shaping bunds and turfing. Group funds were set up for maintenance, which was to be a responsibility of the farmers. At the same time, extension-service personnel and some specially trained field officers conducted farmer-awareness sessions on water management and 'scientific' agriculture, basically in lecture mode.

The farmers were involved in the implementation process, but the initiative was not theirs. They did want the tank(s) rehabilitated, but the institutional arrangements for maintenance and follow-up were too loosely defined to hold. In certain cases the field officers had to go house-to-house to persuade people to come to meetings. As a result the completed structures were badly neglected. The organizational capacity of the farmer organizations varied; in most cases, it was active only at the time of construction when the field officers were around.

Institutional changes resulting from the wholesale adoption of participatory methodologies 1990–94

In September 1990, there was a joint evaluation (SSP and NDF) of the functioning of the farmer organizations and the maintenance of the structures completed up to that time. The evaluation revealed the inadequacies of the existing NDF implementation strategy. Although the farmers were involved in construction activities, the process was essentially top-down.

A further joint-reflection session with NDF field and office staff was held in January 1991. It was conducted in a free and open manner, moderated by SSP. Cards were used successfully to help people express ideas and feel relaxed. The final outcome was that NDF as an organization needed to review its implementation strategy, in particular the sharing of responsibilities between head-office and field-office staff, and the monitoring of activities. The strongest recommendation to emerge was that the field staff needed to enhance their competencies in participatory methodologies.

In the period 1990–92, staff were trained in or exposed to participatory methodologies in a series of workshops on participatory appraisal, monitoring and evaluation (principally PRA), as well as self-evaluation techniques; the new skills were subsequently transferred to the partner organizations. As can be seen below, the infusion of skills in participatory methodologies was to lead to widespread institutional changes across the board in NDF.

(1) *Changes at the village level*   The selection of villages is now based on requests from farmers and villagers. Representatives of farmer organizations (FOs) who have been exposed to participatory methods are invited to help determine the selection criteria.

PRA tools and self-evaluation techniques are now widely used by NDF for information generation and analysis, as well for helping to determine specific village interventions. The information related to the specific field locations of tanks, for example, is generated and analysed by villagers themselves. The majority of NDF field staff are farmers from the locality, recruited after working voluntarily with FOs for some time. Given their intimate understanding of local realities, they have proven to be particularly adept at facilitating participatory methods.

Another change at the village level is the preparation of action plans based on participatory problem-identification and options-assessment. The action plans spell out how responsibilities are to be shared, i.e. what the FO can do on its own, and what needs to be supported by NDF or other agencies. Action plans also include activities which do not require funding, and for which FOs take full responsibility.

Finally, participatory monitoring and evaluation activities are carried out by villagers with NDF facilitation. Simple and relevant indicators are agreed upon and the type of information needed to be recorded is identified. Charts, diagrams and other visual techniques are prepared to facilitate ongoing monitoring at the village level. In most cases symbols are used to monitor both quantitative and qualitative data as these do not discriminate between literate and illiterate villagers. FOs also hold regular monitoring meetings in which plans are reviewed, progress assessed, and decisions taken.

(2) *Release of funds and transparency of accounts*   Since 1992, funds are released into accounts held by each FO at the bank. Training in simple account-keeping is provided to farmer leaders, and books are kept by both the FO and the field office. Decisions on how the funds are to be spent are taken in consultation with villagers.

An agreement is signed between the FO and NDF before funds are released and construction commences, so that the responsibilities of each party are clearly defined and understood. A group fund is also set up and held by the FO to ensure future maintenance and meet any emergency credit needs. At the same time, linkages with existing financial institutions are promoted.

Once the construction of the structures is completed, a tripartite agreement between FOs, NDF and the Department of Agrarian Services (DAS) is entered into, whereby the DAS takes responsibility for major repairs and the FOs agree to deal with minor ones.

(3) *Relationship with donors*   Quarterly joint reviews are now the norm. Representatives of NDF, SSP and other donors visit farmer organizations in the field and engage in joint reflection.

Progress reporting has changed. Previously, NDF reports were prepared to meet the specific requirements of different donors for specific activities. Now progress reports are consolidated into a single report for the NDF programme as a whole and sent to all the donors.

Donor accounts have also changed. Separate accounts were previously held for each donor-supported component of the programme. The accounts have now been consolidated and statements are sent to all the donors for the entire programme.

Finally, the way funding is disbursed by donors has been adjusted to fit with the changes described above. Whereas separate projects were once funded by separate donors, funding is now directed at the NDF programme as a whole. The programme budget determines where the money is most needed, and the donors share the costs as partners.

The most significant change is that room has been made for budgets to be readjusted to accommodate the needs identified by the FOs in their participatory analysis. NDF sectoral emphasis continues to lie in minor irrigation facilities (e.g. tanks, anicuts, agro-wells) but is no longer limited to these alone. Other priorities generated by FOs which are not part of NDF's sectoral focus are also considered. Everything is done to ensure that these priorities are communicated to the agencies, NGO or government, with the relevant expertise.

In introducing these changes, NDF has recognized that the introduction of participatory approaches requires a fundamental reordering in the way donor support is conceived. In order to allow the priorities established by the farmers' organizations to determine where, when and what kinds of support are most suitable, a more holistic, demand-oriented vision of development was needed. By dropping activity-focused predetermined interventions, conditioned by narrow donor funding, and requiring that the programme be considered as a whole (and even that priorities unrelated to minor irrigation facilities be considered, and passed on to the relevant agencies), NDF has shifted some of the power from the donors to the FOs.

(4) *Institutional development of farmer organizations*   It is now the priorities established by villagers themselves, as a result of participatory analyses, which largely determine what needs to be funded. As part of the recognized need to strengthen FOs, villagers are required to prepare estimates where technical advice is needed for construction. Proposals are prepared by NDF and sent to the funding agencies, based on these estimates.

The role of facilitators trained in participatory methods is crucial to the strengthening of the FOs. Villagers who display greater interest and capacity for the facilitation of participatory appraisal and analysis are picked out by NDF field officers for further training. They are then asked to help mobilize other village groups. At a later stage, when vacancies occur, the educated youth are particularly likely to be absorbed as field officers of NDF.

NDF has prepared a scale for assessing the institutional strength of FOs based on criteria identified and agreed upon by representatives of different FOs. This innovative measuring scale is now used by FOs and NDF to monitor the progress of the former. The degree of farmer empowerment can thus to some extent be assessed.

80

For the purpose of monitoring the programme as a whole, FO representatives and NDF staff together develop a series of general-impact indicators. The FOs, with NDF field staff as facilitators, formulate their own specific criteria. The indicators cover socio-economic, political and institutional aspects of the programme.

NDF is aware that effective participatory facilitation should place FOs in a position to self-manage their activities. In 1994, NDF, with FO representatives, therefore developed a set of criteria for phasing itself out. True empowerment will only come when the FOs decide that they no longer need NDF.

Box 12.1: Summary of organizational changes resulting from the adoption of participatory approaches in NDF 1990–94

FROM	TO
Infrastructure as output priority	People and their participation and capabilities as priority
Emphasis on project implementation	Going beyond projects
Information collected through socio-economic household surveys	Information generated and analysed with farmers/villagers
NDF as owner of the information collected	Information is shared with farmer organizations. The results of any participatory analysis remains with them
Planning is done at the head office, and at field offices with office staff in control in each case	Planning is done jointly with farmer organizations, facilitated by field officers
Implementation management by field officers	Implementation management by FOs, facilitated by NDF
Funding channelled through field officers	Funding goes direct to FOs
Monitoring by field officers	Joint monitoring by FO/NDF
Monitoring information/data held in field office	Monitoring information/data held by villagers using participatory monitoring techniques. Data is analysed with field office
Separate progress reports for each donor	Common progress reports for all donors
Separate accounts for each donor	Consolidated accounts
Progress review conducted separately with each donor	Joint progress review and reflection with FOs, NDF, and co-funding partners, including field visits
Staff reflection limited to meetings at head office	Field visits followed by joint reflection sessions in the regional office

Key factors emerging from the programme's reorientation

- A degree of role reversal between field officers and NDF staff has been achieved. Officers, to whom a range of decisionmaking powers has been devolved, have become primarily facilitators of processes aimed at the institutional strengthening of FOs. They have notably helped establish links with extension services and credit institutions such that FOs can further develop inter-institutional relationships on their own.
- The significant efforts made towards setting up a system of downwards accountability have also helped strengthen FOs, which now manage their own accounts and have far more say as to how donor money should bespent. Transparency of FO accounts, whether of group funds or donor funds, has helped ensure minimum misuse.
- A more confident leadership, together with new organizational capabilities, is now emerging in the FOs. Among the more notable results are better management of water resources, bulk purchasing of inputs, and local-resource mobilization by groups wishing to free themselves from middle men. Also notable has been the formation of horizontal links between FOs, which have come together in solidarity when affected by injustices committed by the authorities or outsiders, for example unfair land seizures, the felling of trees in the catchment area of tanks, and/or unfair wages.
- Other spin-offs of the institutional changes set in motion since 1990 include: greater gender sensitivity in the generation and analysis of information, and in the planning and implementation of activities; greater environmental consciousness (e.g. concern for the protection of the catchment and interest in tree planting); improved facilitation skills of field staff through ongoing exposure and training in PRA.
- The greatest overall change is that the policymaking and strategymaking process of NDF has become far more sensitive to the needs and priorities expressed by the villagers. NDF is without doubt beginning to institutionalize participatory approaches.

Constraints generally faced by NGOs when attempting to institutionalize participatory approaches

The following do not necessarily apply to NDF, but are considered common constraints facing NGOs interested in going beyond the occasional PRA.

NGOs will face difficulties when adopting participatory approaches if their funding agencies are not sufficiently flexible to accommodate the changes such an adoption entails, and adjust funding policies accordingly. Dislike for consolidated accounting systems is still common. Although there is much lip-service paid to participatory approaches, there is still little understanding of the funding implications at stake. Donors also expect or require given reporting styles, which may jar with the requirements of a participatory approach.

Funding agencies continue to prefer tangible, measurable results (basically infrastructure). When emphasis is placed on process, financial targets are more difficult to meet because it is no longer clear what those targets are. In most planning exercises, process time is not considered. Emphasis is almost always on financial cost, with little consideration for time cost.

There can be resistance by NGO staff who may firmly believe that the implementation approach they have been using is sufficiently participatory, and that further change is unnecessary. The full-blown use of a participatory methodology may be very threatening. For some NGOs it means giving up a comfortable giver-receiver relationship, i.e. it means giving up power.

Resistance can also come from field staff who may feel that the old system was much easier and more convenient. For field staff to adopt wholeheartedly the new system requires a profound change of behaviour and attitude. The experience of NDF shows that training must be ongoing for such a change to take place. The mistake elsewhere has been to imagine that a one-off training event will be sufficient.

Key learnings

- The capacity of an NGO to adopt a participatory approach (or approaches) depends on much more than a one-off training. The training that does take place must be intensive, field-based and ongoing. Training should not be sought until the implications of going participatory are clearly understood. There has to be an ability and openness on the part of the NGO in question to accommodate a series of institutional changes in its procedures, structures and working environment. Critical self-awareness by NGO personnel is indispensable if such changes are to begin to be instituted.
- Once a participatory approach (e.g. PRA) is operational, it must be placed in the context of all the stages of the development cycle. It will not have the desired effect (i.e. greater empowerment of local organizations) if it is limited only to the initial stage of a project (i.e. appraisal). Careful selection of field staff, and the provision of high-quality training, are crucial to ensure high-level facilitation in the field. The long-term success of a participatory project depends more on the skills and enthusiasm of the field staff than on any other single factor.
- The partner funding organizations (donors) must be committed to long-term support of a learning process in which targets evolve, and innovation and experimentation are encouraged. Donors must display sensitivity and consistency in their support of participatory methodologies, and be willing to accept that success may as a result have to be measured in very different terms.

13

Participatory Management or Community-managed Programmes? Reflections from experience in Somaliland

SAM JOSEPH

Chapter 13 explores the institutionalization of participatory approaches from a management perspective, based on experience in Somaliland. It argues that participatory projects have little meaning unless they embrace the broader concept of community management. According to the author, community management implies that decisionmaking on local issues should be left to local collective processes. For development workers to support such programmes, long-term commitment is required, together with the adoption of management styles that coach and facilitate rather than supervise and dictate. The nurturing of local leadership is also considered crucial for community management to succeed. The author recommends a ten-year period of support for each individual community-managed programme, in order to ensure continuity and consistency regardless of changes of staff or structure.

New roles for development managers

In Somaliland we are hoping that the form of management and the type of organizational structure that is prevalent in development projects today will in the future change to one that is more local. There is a growing number of examples of development initiatives around the world where the community, or groups of local people, are being nurtured towards managing their own programmes.

Today, those who are concerned with issues of policy and strategy tend to be development managers in international aid agencies and national development organizations. Their thinking spans questions as broad-ranging as fundraising, operational and strategic thinking, local and international advocacy, and issues of programme/project expansion and withdrawal. These development managers have access to different types of information from multiple sources (plans, reports, regular and innovative work, letters, newsletters, seminars, networks, grapevine) and in contexts which span local, regional, international and corporate domains.

The range of issues discussed at development managers' forums may not be all relevant to locally managed programmes, however. Such programmes may be managed by a group of nationals working closely with the concerned communities, or they may be managed by community representatives themselves. But the motivations and incentives driving externally managed programmes on the one hand, and locally managed schemes on the other, are different. The major distinction is that community-based managers take a long-term view because projects have a direct effect, in terms of livelihoods and opportunities, on them and their children. From their perspective, advocacy and policy issues are of interest only to the extent that they bring about changes which facilitate local management of projects. The development strategies and priorities of funding agencies and development organizations concerned with regional or corporate issues may not be of much interest to such local-management groups. The way external managers conceptualize and define poverty, environmental degradation, the status of women and children, and other similar issues may need to adapt to local perceptions and demands. It may be necessary, as a first step, to hold fora for policy and strategy issues separately. Such fora would in the beginning, I think, have a strong advisory and coaching role. But the key point is that the people involved on behalf of development organizations would then need to commit themselves for at least ten years. This does not mean maintaining a continuous presence on the ground as that would stifle local initiative, but it does mean that all those assuming the role of advisors and coaches must continue to be involved over a decade to see the results face to face.

For any organization, ten years is a long time. Leadership changes which occur at the centre influence issues of organizational efficiency and effectiveness. These in turn have knock-on effects at different levels of the organization. It is often the case, for example, that changes at the centre (e.g. in the UK for UK-based organizations) and country-programme level affect the way a project is managed at the community level. The question then becomes how to ensure continuous, long-term support for local processes of change, regardless of any alterations that may occur at the centre.

Primacy of local management

The primacy of local management is the starting-point of all our work. In any location where we choose to work, we have first to spend time gaining an understanding of how the social capital of the area has evolved, and how in particular individuals have entered into productive relationships that are the basis of group effort. The challenge we then face is to nurture such social capital into appropriate management models.

It seems from case studies on local self-governance that local management is most effective when dealing with a single issue, for example water management in Nepal, road construction in Ethiopia, Erigavo town water supply in Somaliland, and so forth. We have often made the mistake of viewing local management in the context of multi-sectoral project management, for example by trying to get a single local group to manage several local projects at the same time in health, education, agriculture and credit. Such models have created dependencies on NGOs and donor agencies for funds. What is more, the organizational forms and procedures were in these cases imported from outside, and did not last once donor funds ran out. We must work with the principle of 'one group, one issue' and let time and the ideas of local people evolve dynamic, locally responsive forms of management for each issue.

Those from development organizations who are responsible for facilitating a community-managed programme must have the relevant skills. They must be willing to commit seven to ten years to a particular group. Their role is not to supervise and evaluate given project activities but rather to coach, advise and help set up locally appropriate administrative systems in an attitude of nurturing, fostering and caring. This does not mean that a continuous presence on the ground is necessary. What is recommended is a series of visits to the local area, with appropriate gaps, once a specific process has been started and local people have been left to get on with it.

Learning comes from making mistakes. Local people should have the chance to test their own ideas. This testing may sometimes take almost a year. If local people in an agricultural community have to raise resources to finance a teacher, for example, then contributions would be related to seasonal production. It would take a year at least to test the management of such local generation of resources. Project supervisors have to be prepared to wait.

Rethinking project management

In the past we designed programmes in which local people were expected to take over some parts of the programme once we withdrew from a target area. Our energies focused on operational questions, from acquiring information through to implementation and review. The models that the local communities saw us implement required a large infrastructure of staff, equipment, information networks and facilities, and we expected the community to take over and continue that which we had begun, although they had had no part in its design.

We have since learned that in those areas where local management is to assume responsibility for development work, we as outsiders have no right to create liabilities for local management in terms of hiring of staff, purchase of vehicles and setting-up of offices. From a donor-agency point of view, the programme must start small. The funding base should be sufficient to cover the costs of one facilitator/manager from outside and some local costs related to information collection, and coordination. Local planning processes must be nurtured, and additional funding should be sought for specific initiatives only where local management and local resource-mobilization efforts have taken place. This means that local users' groups and local government (including traditional community structures such as councils of elders) have to be brought together in joint ventures.

Efforts to craft strategies for change need to move between two temporal dimensions. One view, 'what do I want my grandchildren to have?', dictates that strategies should span at least 100 years. The other view, 'how can we work effectively now?', dictates that the ability to respond effectively to current situations needs to be strengthened as quickly as possible.

Trust

Effective relationships are built on mutual trust and effective interpersonal communication. The more we trust another person the more we are able to disclose our inner thoughts and feelings, and are able to accept feedback about ourselves. Annual performance appraisals have to be changed into more frequent work-review-and-goal-setting sessions. In this style of distance management, development managers would probably handle several programmes at any one time. They would go into one programme, spend some time to add value, come out, spend some time on administrative and coordinating issues and repeat the cycle in another programme. Each manager should be allowed to choose where s/he wants to base his/her families and the work station should be where the family is based. Such managers would be travelling frequently and would need regular periods to rest, and to be with their families in familiar sociological environments.

All management levels involved in the kind of programmes outlined above would have to work towards creating interdependence. Since there would be almost no formal organizational structure on the ground, and only one agency person, much of the operational work would be based on local agreements, contracts and alliances. Each contract and alliance would last until the objective in hand was achieved, and would dissolve when it had served its purpose. Local management would decide all contracts and alliances, both of local and of external, technical expertise. The policy-advisory group would be consulted on all those issues which are not local.

Long-term commitment

Development managers who are helping to develop locally managed programmes need two levels of corporate support. At the level of immediate reporting and advice they need a policy-advisory group. This would be made up of concerned corporate directors and other temporary members prepared to work in the often-uncertain environment of a community-managed programmes, with its implications for flexibility in terms of planning and reporting timetables. A patrons' group at the corporate level would champion the cause of community-managed programmes and would ensure the working space needed over a period of seven to ten years. As a result community-managed programmes would be nurtured by people with long-term commitments, unaffected by changes of staff, strategy or procedure within development organizations.

14

Participatory Environmental Management: contradiction of process, project and bureaucracy in the Himalayan foothills[1]

ANDREW SHEPHERD

Chapter 14 analyses the experience of the Government of Uttar Pradesh's (UP) European Union (EU)-funded Doon Valley Project. The project has moved from a standard Indian public-sector approach to rural development and environmental management, to a new participatory approach. It has been through a first phase in which a participatory method of village-level planning has been initiated. The chapter addresses the required changes and constraints involved in this first step of transformation. These include issues of organizational structure and procedures, training, gender and other social concerns, and the dynamics of organizational change.

The implications of a participatory approach are far-reaching. Allowing people to decide how they will manage their hillsides requires an ability to facilitate that process. Facilitators need to have the flexibility and creativity to offer a variety of technical and managerial possibilities such that individuals, groups and communities can choose what suits them best. Constraints derive partly from the government's set procedures and schemes in rural development, and from its advocacy of particular well-worn technology packages. Constraints also derive from the way in which the whole project has been handled by the government and the Commission of the European Union (CEU) from the beginning, and from the way in which technical assistance (TA) has been organized.

Recent paradigm shifts

There is a embryonic but significant paradigm shift in the theory and practice of rural development and natural-resource management. The shift can already be seen strongly in practice in the fields of agriculture, project analysis and procedure, and local-level institutional development. The paradigm shift represents a move from an industrial (technical-fix) approach to technology development to an organic or holistic approach; from a technocratic to a participatory approach to environmental management; and from

88

resource control by big organizations to resource management by local institutions.

There are well-known harbingers of the paradigm shift in literature and practice. Chambers (1983) together with Chambers' later writings, raised questions which have become part of the accepted paraphernalia of the rural-development profession, in particular the concern with rural poverty, how to perceive it, and how to address it. These concerns were shared by many, and over the 1980s led to the formulation of a way of talking about and sometimes practising rural development which has come to be known as participatory rural appraisal (PRA). One of the streams of thought contributing to the development of PRA was agro-ecosystems analysis, which lent PRA a strong basis in rural natural-resource issues (Chambers, 1994b: 954–5).

Across the Atlantic this work was echoed by that of the Kortens and others working in the Pacific Rim countries, who focused more on organizational adaptation than on procedures and methods of information collection and planning. This work was also focused explicitly on the quality of relationships between rural-resource managers (i.e. the rural population) and project or agency personnel, insiders and outsiders. The paradigm shift brings these two traditions together, alongside the critique of industrial modernization which always lies close to the heart of rural development, with its essentially populist tradition (Kitching, 1982). Writing on traditional irrigation management and on local-level institutions has bloomed into a new approach to their analysis, and a new advocacy of their usefulness, encapsulated in Curtis (1991). These writings argue the case for 'subsidiarity' (power to the smallest possible unit) in choosing to locate control over development resources.

In the field of project development, the failure of conventional blueprint-project structures (Korten, D.C., 1980, 1990) and the growing predominance of NGOs in the implementation of rural-development projects have led to considerable innovation in project procedures and structures. These have not yet been documented effectively, but have included a move to process approaches, greater interest in environmental and social dimensions of development, and an interest in putting ordinary rural people in control through local institutional development and planning techniques which empower people.

Due to the public-goods character of many rural resources, and the externalities imposed by individual actions on private property, the public sector will continue to retain a substantial role in management. However, the location and nature of the public-management function (government, local government, community, user group) is a live issue. The paradigm shift would suggest that management should be as local as possible, and involve as few external resources as are compatible with operating in a resource-scarce environment where local institutions have often been devalued historically, and are therefore unable to make resources available.

There is a tension between resolving natural resource-management problems in the short or medium term, and building local-management capacity for the longer term. This genuine tension combines with apparent organizational imperatives and the vested bureaucratic interests to thwart participatory development and the devolution of environmental management. In India, currently, there are attempts to devolve greater powers over natural-resource management to communities and local authorities. This chapter will examine the specific case of how these changes are being addressed and managed in the case of the Doon Valley Project in the Himalayas.

Background to the Doon Valley Project

The erosion of the Himalayan foothills has long been a concern, and is now the subject of popular action, government and international intervention, as well as scholarship. There are competing theories about its causes. Implicit in government policy are assumptions that erosion is caused by deforestation and poor land use, in particular by the small farmers who occupy the slopes, and exploit common land and parts of the forest reserves. An historical analysis of forestry policy and the Chipko movement (Guha, 1989) locates the causes in imperial development policy and its consequences for the Himalayan forests. The environmental movement today is as concerned about mining as deforestation, and some mines in the foothills have been closed as a result of popular action. The Doon Valley Project (DVP), though it has nothing to do with mining, was initiated partly to demonstrate that the government was concerned about environmental degradation in the Doon Valley, one of the major mining areas. From observation, this writer would lay much of the blame for the active erosion of today on poor and ubiquitous road construction, military blasting and quarrying. Scientists continue to argue about the degree of natural instability of the Himalayan range and its erosion effects, and about the links between increased incidence of flooding in the plains and degradation of the hillsides.

A series of previous watershed-management projects in the foothills, supported by the Government of India and various donors led by the World Bank, have emphasized the following: the replanting of denuded reserve forest and common land; reduction in use of woodfuel, through promotion of alternatives, especially gobar gas; small-scale concrete-tank irrigation, enabling more rice cultivation and field levelling; high-yielding (crop) varieties (HYVs) and fertilizer; de-stocking and stall feeding.

These more or less standard project activities have been carried out using one of two approaches: (i) public/labour-intensive works, employing contract (often Nepali) labour, through contractors; (ii) subsidies (calculated according to standard Indian rural-development formulae) to individual beneficiaries.

As elsewhere in India, local institutions are thoroughly subordinated to the larger political organizations of party and state. The watershed-management projects have reinforced the consequent degradation of local institutions, and absence of effective local control over and management of resources. As a result, projects are now widely perceived to have proved unsustainable; common assets created have not been maintained, and there is no continuing process of environmental protection without the subsidy and labour employment offered through the projects.

The present need is for village organizations empowered to manage all the fodder and fuel-producing village lands, including panchayat forests and those sections of the reserves which should be allotted to specific villages. Any such organization will require administrative support and technical advice. All villages will need funds... A form of supervision is

90

required to ensure proper utilization of funds without falling into the bureaucratic trap of trying to administer rural affairs by remote control ... A mature government would aim to provide the necessary legislation and hold a watching brief over the people's activities, intervening only where the land was being damaged, funds were misused or panchas were abusing their positions... (Ashish, 1993: 1796)

This is the ideal to which the new generation of watershed-management projects in the foothills subscribe. Policymakers in government and donor-agency personnel appear to have understood the importance of community participation, local institutions and involving the poorer sections of the community, too, in the development of the Himalayan foothills.

Uttar Pradesh (UP) has not been one of the foremost states to move in these directions, however. For example, in forestry, it is the only major state in north India to hold out against the development of Joint Forest Management schemes, which are beginning the process of sharing management of reserve-forest areas with the people who inhabit them. The *gram panchayats* (village governing bodies) have been dormant institutions for a long time, leaving the *gram pradhan* (chief) unaccountable to the community. Corruption is perceived as widespread, and as based on the culture of contract and subsidy. There has been relatively little innovative thinking on the technology of rural development; the schemes which occur throughout India are also those which are made available in the hills, despite radically different geography and varied social organization. A notable few associations have a good record of adapting plains innovations to hill conditions, but most projects have been content unthinkingly to replicate schemes from elsewhere.

The new understanding has combined with political pressures to generate the Doon Valley Project, a nine-year investment with the following objectives:

- arrest and as far as possible reverse ongoing degradation to the Doon Valley eco-systems
- improvement in the living conditions of rural people
- positive involvement of rural people in managing the environment (Doon Valley 1: vii)

The project was also to establish a Watershed Management Directorate in Dehradun capable of providing services and advice to other watershed-management projects which might be in the pipeline.

The original project design was based on previous projects, and contained the same basic components and ideas. The project appraisal, an important document for the Commission of the European Union (CEU) and Government of India (GOI), accepted these as a starting-point, but stressed that a participatory project would have to be much more flexible, and not adhere rigidly to targets. Paradoxically, however, indicative targets were specified very precisely and broken down year by year. It was no doubt the best compromize in the circumstances, but with hindsight appears quite naive in its assumption that participation could somehow be tacked on as an additional component, while leaving other components as they were. Similarly, project documents make declarations about the need to work with women: 'As much of the farming, domestic and family activities are undertaken by women, emphasis must

91

be placed on involving them and ensuring that project activities reduce the current heavy workload imposed on women' (Doon Valley 2: 11), without exploring in either case the need for major strategic, organizational and procedural changes to accommodate this new approach. It is these changes, which the scheme is struggling with in practice, which are the focus of the rest of this chapter.

Participation and Indian bureaucracy

There is a Himalayan contradiction between a participatory, gender-sensitive approach to environmental management and the standard Indian public-sector approach. The DVP inherited a hierarchical way of structuring an organization, a culture which emphasizes hierarchy and the status of office, and a commitment to a huge staff which was to be seconded from parent ministries, and in many cases be transferred from previous watershed-management projects. The workplans for DVP recognized this situation and put training at the centre of its first working plan. However, reversals of attitude and practice were required in so many ways that training alone could not accomplish them. Other supportive processes would also be needed, such as inspiring and innovative leadership, external support in the Government of UP (GOUP), the GOI and the CEU, in the wider constituency in the Doon Valley, the environmental movement and local NGOs. The boundaries of training needs were relatively clear: it was to be for project staff and villagers. It was (wrongly) assumed that GOI, GOUP, the CEU, and associated NGOs were all sufficiently familiar with a participatory approach and the requirements of local institutional development that they could play their parts. The problem was seen to be the project staff, and beyond that the village leadership. In fact as we will see, much of the the problem was precisely located in the organizations nominally committed to and promoting the new approach.

A misapprehension at the CEU was that a participatory approach could be developed whatever the state of administrative culture in UP. Why could the DVP not go as smoothly as the Aravalli Hills Project in next-door Haryana? This would indeed make a valuable comparative study, but two obvious points would be that the Haryana state administration has a somewhat different and more progressive history to that of UP, and that some of the most successful experiments in hill management have been at Sukromajri, in the Haryana Shivalik hills. Projects cannot occur independently of the organizational cultures in which they are embedded. The Haryana project also has much simpler objectives. A different approach would have to be taken in UP.

It was accepted in principle that the DVP had to work with women since adult males migrate out of the hills for significant periods of the year. The environmental organizations were also keen on this aspect of the scheme, as the Chipko movement had been basically a movement in which the grassroots activists are women, if not the leadership. A year-long debate was held about the necessity of employing women fieldworkers, in order to interact successfully with village women, in what was going to be another all-male organization. Finally, in 1994 three women fieldworkers were appointed, after much effort particularly from three women members of the TA team. Some of the male field staff were also beginning to lose their shyness for interacting with rural women.

There was also some debate about how the organization should be structured. Previous watershed-management projects had moved from being implemented through line departments (and consequently being ill-coordinated) to a unified line of command under a project director. This was retained, and a further change was made towards establishing multidisciplinary field teams in each implementation division, with community-participation staff also attached. The major innovation was the establishment of the central-services unit designed to service all future watershed-management projects. Combined with a substantial dose of technical assistance, and considerable interaction with NGOs in the pragmatic wing of the Chipko movement, some energetic individuals were able to raise the level of discussion about issues connected with a participatory, gender-sensitive approach in the organization as a whole, through seminars, meetings and training programmes.

A further debate was about how decentralized the organization should be. Generally, the argument ran, the more decentralized the more responsive it could be. However, seconded officials were posted from field offices where they had a certain level of financial discretion. In DVP they found that their expenditure limits were far lower than in the parent departments, indicating a relatively low level of discretion and responsibility. Senior management reserved the right to increase discretion once the implementation divisions were beginning to prove they could do something useful in the new approach.

The question of targets in participatory projects

Perhaps the most controversial issue of all has been that of targets. Actions on the project are supposed to be governed by the production of annual working plans (AWPs), in phase with GOI/GOUP budgeting and financial-management requirements. In 1993/4, when the basics of the organization were not yet in place, before any serious training could be carried out, there was an expectation in the AWP that physical and financial targets would be achieved. This was reinforced by GOUP, GOI and the CEU, all anxious to demonstrate that the project was well underway. This situation gave the green light to those managers in the project who were sceptical about the new approach and simply wanted to get on with delivering benefits and completing works in the old way. There was thus a premature process of implementation, meaningful in terms of statistics, but meaningless in terms of development in the new sense. There was scope for resisters and saboteurs to chisel away at the new approach. Some of this was not malicious, but arose from anxiety, the insecurity of people confronted with new working methods which were not absolutely clear to them, and which did not become clear for some time. Staff insecurity is a major issue which has to be addressed in any major organizational change.

Implementation according to the old ways allowed the threads of corrupt practices to be picked up. This vital point about corruption was understood by the TA team only 6 months into the project. A participatory approach in principle gives power to communities and groups. Officers are then accountable not only to superiors and village leaders, but also to the wider community. Questions of who should hold the purse strings have arisen: the project or a village institution? All this undermines the ability of officials to earn additional income through the monopoly they hold over certain scarce resources. Once this became clear to some officials they developed a scepticism for the new approach born of self-interest. It remains to be seen whether, once the new arrangements have been bedded down, new structures of corruption will emerge.

The important point about this sensitive issue is that rewards and sanctions in an organization need to be related to its goals. There were (and are) no rewards for the sort of behaviour conducive to a participatory approach, spending long hours in villages, allowing villagers to make decisions, encouraging experimentation and innovation, feeding villagers' ideas and criticisms to management and so on. Confidential reports on staff do not reflect performance on these issues. A formal staff appraisal was not favoured by the project's management, as it is not the basis for any formal decisions. There are no financial rewards. All the project could offer was the hope that good performance might lead to a study tour abroad. Eventually the GOUP Finance Department permitted the introduction of cash prizes for good performance.

Since the beginning of the project the CEU, in standard donor mode of seeking to create a direct line of accountability to itself, had been pushing for autonomous or parastatal status for the project to ensure more effective accountability to it for the funds it was investing. GOUP refused, but eventually established a separate bank account with which CEU was apparently satisfied. Autonomous status would have permitted the project management to get special allowances related to project objectives accepted by the GOUP's treasury. Remaining in the civil service made that very difficult, although it was possible to argue the case for additional allowances for extra hours of fieldwork.

Had the CEU negotiated with GOUP from the start on that basis, rather than using the narrow criterion of financial accountability, it might have had a stronger case. There are, however, well-known problems with detaching project authorities from the civil service: problems of sustainability, termination and reintegration of personnel, and commitment. The Watershed Management Directorate is a halfway house. It is a separate organization, but not detached in terms of powers, which may be the worst of the options.

The dynamics of the new approach itself may well lead, however, to a transformation of this situation over time. There has been a division between senior and junior staff, which also probably coincides with a strong cultural divide, in terms of who actually implements the new approach in the field. Some junior officers (extension officers, foresters etc.) have taken to the painstaking partipatory rural appraisal (PRA) technology the project has started to use with great enthusiasm. They have been the major beneficiaries of training, and have been empowered as a result. Senior staff have to listen to them if they want to know what is going on, and what the new approach involves. PRA technology has created a relationship of much greater equality than ever existed before, where there can be more of a dialogue. The impact of this change has yet to be assessed.

Physical and financial targets remain a potential threat of enormous proportions for the success of the new approach. Conceptually, it is agreed now by the project management that they should emerge from the participatory

94

planning process. It was not clear how far this is supported by GOUP or GOI, or indeed CEU. Targets were also imposed on the participatory planning process. GOI wanted a quite unrealistic target of 30 village plans by June 1994. This would clearly have undermined a serious participatory approach, which at that time was capable of producing two or three plans by the following September, at the most. The request was resisted by the project and the CEU, on the grounds that it would undermine the participatory approach.

All of this demonstrates the importance of building up a coalition of supporters at different levels of the decisionmaking machinery, including the donor organization (Korten and Siy, 1988), and how difficult this can be in India, with its range of personal and sociopolitical interests at each level, and its institutional strength and capacity not to give in to donor demands.

How to merge project activities with people's priorities

Two major debates emerged concerning the substance of the project. The most strident was the frequently expressed worry that participation meant giving way to people's priorities, which would be different from the project's, and that the project would not be able to help them achieve those priorities. There was a general understanding that the project needed to have an ability to respond to people's priorities, from its design onwards. Indeed, in recognition of this, health services appeared as a line item in the budget, as did community participation. However, the implementers, who were mostly foresters, with a smattering of agriculturalists, engineers and animal-husbandry specialists, were quite uncomfortable with this notion. They were much more at ease with the traditional Indian approach of lobbying the Collector or Block Development Officer on behalf of the felt needs of a village where they were working. The alternative idea that an NGO would respond to priorities falling outside the project's scope was also attractive (though many staff had reservations about NGOs too). Clearly, bottom-up planning should not lead agencies to make promises to communities to fulfil all their demands. The boundaries and competences of the agency should always be transparent.

Adopting a participatory approach cannot easily be prevented from leading to the questioning of the use of a particular technology. This was a more subtle, and much more serious problem. For foresters, long-criticized in the Himalayas for focusing exclusively on planting *chir* pine, rather than the people's choice of oak or other more useful species, it has been more straightforward to accept the need to redesign plantations, to be more flexible about species and regimes. But for other professions, the differences between the hills and the plains pose conceptual problems: technologies need to be adapted; the local situation must be analysed to generate an appropriate technology; even the criteria to measure what is appropriate may be different.

The most dramatic example of this was the protest launched by the international ecological thinker and Doon Valley resident Vandana Shiva about the DVP's intention to replace indigenous, adapted hill cattle and buffaloes with exotic stock. The project was undermining biodiversity by this action. In truth it was simply applying a technological solution which appeared to the government to be well-tried and tested: the subsidized provision of 'improved' (exotic) bulls to individuals who would rent them out or use them to service the village animals, combined with a reduction or elimination of 'scrub bulls' which typically graze the open hillside, and are held responsible for much of the environmental degradation of the village commons. This is an assumption which has been challenged on the grounds that villages generally only keep enough bulls to plough. The problem is rather that people do not cooperate over ploughing, since it has to be done in a hurry, and inter-family cooperation is often not strong, so there are far more bulls than would theoretically be needed to plough the cultivated areas (Ashish, 1993). For the project, the point is that it is an issue which is grossly under-researched, and where there is a monopoly of development wisdom deriving from the White Revolution and the Anand model of dairy development, the marketing and veterinary-care aspects of which are quite inappropriate for many areas in the hills. The technical-assistance team failed to consider these issues adequately, though partial rectification was made in response to pressure via the CEU to examine the genetic-conservation issue.

The tradition of agricultural activities in watershed management is also restrictive. The tradition consists of the provision of irrigation water through concrete tanks and canals, distribution of minikits of HYV seed and fertilizer (there must be similar issues of genetic erosion here too), and the renovation of terraces and other soil- and water-conservation structures. All these activities are part of the ancient lore of Indian rural development. The focus on engineering structures rather than on farm practices for soil and water conservation is antiquated practice (Commonwealth Secretariat, 1989); technological advances in irrigation have been made by the Vivekananda Laboratory, using polythene to line an earth tank, far cheaper and more accessible to large numbers of farmers than concrete, but this was rejected by the project (and the TA adviser); minikits in an Indian rural context represent a relatively thoughtless procedure: whatever seeds are available in the local Department of Agriculture store are distributed free or at cost. None of these interventions was preceded by much in the way of investigation. Farm-system analysis is almost unheard of in India; the project has very few agriculturalists anyway. A task for the immediate future is to introduce staff to a farm-system focus, and give them simple analytical tools for identifying potential farm improvements with the farmers. This will be a second stage of training following on from months of preparatory work devoted to learning participatory rural appraisal skills.

If the project were to succeed in interacting more intensively with the women farmers of the hills, it is likely that a whole new range of technical issues in agriculture would arise, since the current prescriptions and activities reflect previous all-male communications. It is not clear whether the flexibility to accommodate changes in project components exists or not.

In order to make a reality of appropriate technology development the project needs to be unusually open to information about possibilities. An attempt has been made to network with research institutions, and to link them up with the project through participatory operational research projects (PORP). Funding a link of any substance may be difficult, however, since no such item was included in the original blueprint, and research institutions, too, have their limitations, sometimes severe. For example, the Central Soil and Water Conservation Research and Training Institute, on the project's doorstep in

Dehradun, is stuck largely in old-fashioned engineering approaches to soil and water conservation, and had only one or two members of staff who could readily use a systems approach. Nevertheless it had previously engaged in a very relevant and rather successful PORP in the nearby Bhagirathi catchment (Kishor and Gupta, nd).

The key link would be with the Vivekananda Laboratory in Almora, the only research organization with a solid foundation and mandate for research in the hills. Again, the way in which the budget had been formulated made it difficult to realize such a link in any more than rudimentary or routine form.

These institutions are all male-dominated, and rarely work directly with women farmers. Their capacity for doing so is untried, but there are likely to be many constraints.

A new role for TA?

The nature of bidding for a TA contract requires that the bidder put sufficient cards on the table to convince the donor that it will do a good job. This involves identifying the consultants who will advise, and working out a timetable for their inputs. Given the pressure on consultancy companies to generate revenue, and on donors to disburse money, so long as it is properly accounted for, most of the inputs are likely to be early in the project. In DVP the majority were over almost before the project was up and running, and certainly before the critical issues had been addressed. It is very important to focus on the key aspects of the project in the early phases, and make sure staff are fully behind any new approach to work before embarking on a wide range of technical developments.

In a new project, where everything starts from scratch, the temptation is to spread the TA thinly over many activities. In this case there were consultancies on everything from hygrogeology to management-information systems during a period of 18 months. Under such circumstances it is difficult for the project to keep its eyes clearly on the main tasks, and difficult to make sure that all the ancillary technical developments link up with and do not contradict the main tasks. In fact, there were apparent contradictions: for example, a sophisticated approach to management information, including geographic-information systems, would not seem to sit easily with a participatory approach, though there do exist attempts to bring the two together.

With any project involving organizational change it is important to focus on the essentials of the change to start with. In this context the role of TA could be to launch the process of change, and provide one set of resources upon which the project can call as it requires additional advice or ideas. TA has to become a process, too; it cannot be overspecified usefully in advance.

Lessons for paradigm shifters

The major lesson is that participation cannot be bolted to an existing project concept simply as an add-on. It has implications for the entire gamut of a scheme's working practices.

At least in the DVP there is no such exclusive focus on any one group. In previous watershed-management projects, however, it seems as though more

97

benefits have gone to the less poor, and especially to the village leadership; it is perceived as critical that the poor do participate and benefit, since they also use the natural resources the management of which the project seeks to improve. Local institutions may not be very good at including the poor, an old truth recently rediscovered with some force. Focusing on the poor, a group which often does not benefit easily from a predetermined package of activities (probably unthinkingly designed for the less poor/rich), should lead to the need to adapt and innovate, to search for appropriate technical interventions, in other words to a demand- rather than supply-led approach to investment.

A project is, furthermore, not something which can be detached or packaged separately from the organizations involved with it. It involves a network; constraints on developing a participatory approach stressing local institutional development can occur at any point in that network, from village through to donor. Associated organizations (scientific research organizations, NGOs) are liable to work with a very different understanding. Nevertheless no process project can do without them. Wherever possible such organizations need involvement in project design as well as execution.

Organization and culture are critical concepts in participatory rural development. Incentives, rewards, sanctions, financing mechanisms, planning procedures, structures of reporting, all are evidently critical to an enabling transformation. The characteristics required of an organization are above all flexibility, analytical capability and membership in information networks which can help to suggest a wide range of options for action. These must be supported by appropriate staffing, administrative systems and, above all, a culture favouring participatory work and continually reinforced by management, outside sympathizers and linked organizations.

Linked organizations are critical: no single body can go it alone successfully. Creating and managing useful links, building up a coalition of support are key management tasks. In environmental work links may be as much with environmental movements and key individuals as with formal groups.

A situation in which there are continual setbacks and obstacles presents too many opportunities for officials who would prefer to carry on in the old ways. Confronting some problems may help to develop an *esprit de corps*, and a sense of common purpose; continual problems distract from the work at hand. In other words, it is important to get the basic parameters of a process approach right from the beginning.

In the DVP the hope would be that NGOs would play a similar role, ensuring greater accountability of government to communities, something which could not be achieved through cost recovery, as the potential for this is much more limited.

The argument over semi-autonomous status for the DVP would be stronger if it were put not only in respect of financing arrangements, but to facilitate organizational change and people's participation. It might be better advocated by DVP's external support network of academic institutions and NGOs, and people's movements interested in seeing government do something significantly innovative in Garhwal.

The implicit logic of institutional development underlying the approach taken by the Doon Valley Project could be stated as follows. Rural environmental management requires considerable local management capacity. The legal basis for this is, at least crudely, laid out in the 73rd Constitutional Amendment (Government of India, 1993) giving considerable powers in the natural resource-management field to district and village Panchayats. However, Panchayats are widely perceived as too remote from the users of natural resources and too corrupt to manage locally critical resources in an effective manner. At the very least more local-level user groups are needed to which the Panchayats can delegate authority. The role of a state bureaucracy (the DVP) is to bring communities and groups to the stage where they can manage these resources more effectively.

In order to play that role effectively, however, the bureaucracy and the donor-assisted financial process must change in significant ways, as outlined in the previous section. Any rural environmental-management effort is likely to require significant organizational development. The project straitjacket needs to be loosened considerably to accommodate organizational change as a major feature, especially in the first few years of a project's existence.

15

Taking on the Challenge of Participatory Development at GTZ: searching for innovation and reflecting on the experience

HEINRICH EYLERS AND REINER FORSTER

Chapter 15 describes how GTZ, the German Technical Cooperation Agency, has responded to the challenges of participatory development. It begins by describing the core elements of three GTZ-supported participation projects that have been considered successful: an urban-upgrading project in Nasriya, Egypt; a watershed-management project in Maharashtra, India; and a rural-support programme in Baluchistan, Pakistan. The authors consider in some detail how GTZ's terms of operation have begun to be modified so as better to support these kinds of projects. Key lessons are that (i) success in participatory projects requires that donors and their agencies be prepared to delegate clearly defined responsibilities and decisionmaking powers to in-country stakeholders from the very start of a project; that (ii) a far broader spectrum of institutions as partner organizations than just the state must be involved; and (iii) donors and their implementing agencies such as GTZ must continuously rethink and adapt their administrative procedures, instruments and strategies to suit the context-specific characteristics of individual participatory projects.

GTZ has set up an internal research and development project, including a number of regional learning groups, to analyse in greater depth the requirements and impacts of participatory projects. GTZ is beginning to see more clearly how planning and monitoring and evaluation methodologies, staff- and policy-evaluation instruments, and funding policies can best be modified to make participatory development more than a pretty concept.

Background to GTZ's experience

The need for a joint learning process to establish and understand the prerequisites and impacts of participatory development approaches has never been greater.

'Participatory development' is a notion that already has more than 25 years' existence: from the early self-help, community-development and popular-education programmes of the 1960s and 1970s, to the instrumental understanding of participation in the 1980s, where participation was seen as an effective mechanism to mobilize local resources for preconceived projects or programmes, to the increasing awareness, finally, that participatory approaches imply the decentralization of decisionmaking power and of control over development resources while at the same time stimulating local capacities for self-determined, responsible development processes.

The 'handing over' of decisionmaking power, together with capacity-building at the grassroots, gives a special meaning to the concept of 'empowerment'. It is no longer the empowerment of target groups that occupies us but that of people, the poor, women, villagers, resource-poor farmers etc. Indeed, the word 'target" may already be part of the problem since it implies that people and social groups are the objects rather than the subjects of development initiatives.

In our search for reasons why so many good ideas from past decades did not materialize, the question of ownership appears fundamental. The commitment and overall responsibility for development processes has to lie with the concerned social groups, institutions and organizations of the partner country, and cannot be substituted by outside interventions or foreign experts.

It is evident that the ownership question cannot be limited to the donor/recipient-country relationship. If applied to the situation within the partner country it leads directly to questions about the roles, responsibilities and control of resources of different actors, institutions and the state. In this perspective, participatory development consciously addresses how the stakeholders negotiate and share control of development processes and, at least normatively, introduces into those processes the more marginalized sectors of society.

Before presenting some of GTZ's experiences in detail we would like to open with three general observations:

Commissioned by the Federal Ministry of Economic Cooperation and Development (BMZ) and other national and international donors, GTZ increasingly supports projects that make use of new participatory methods, learns from and cooperates with NGOs, and is committed to supporting self-help activities and institutional pluralism.

With regard to the concept 'participatory development', we feel that the notion is increasingly falling apart. At present it acts as a kind of umbrella term for a whole array of fashionable notions such as political democratization, decentralization, institutional pluralism, capacity- and institution-building, interactive learning methods, and empowerment. In the examples cited below, more specific terms and concepts are used so as to allow for more precise and unambiguous interpretations.

Although we have been active in encouraging participatory approaches for quite some time, we have yet to carry out systematic analyses of the conditions needed for such approaches to flourish, and their impact on different aspects of political, institutional and administrative life. Of course, we have had some promising evaluations and even unquestionable success stories in individual projects. The actual impact of these approaches on the beneficiaries, and on the broader social power structures, as well as their sustainability, however defined, remain, though, largely unknown. There is a growing need for more systematic feedback from the field.

We are, however, sure of the fact that the concept of participatory development requires organizations and agencies to be willing and able to learn and change, and that does not apply only to partner countries! Both our internal organizational-review processes and our involvement in the international debate on participatory development provided a clear indication that considerable changes are needed in our own organization, in terms of administrative procedures, instruments and flexibility. We will flesh out at the end of the chapter some of the more recent modifications and activities we have made in this regard.

Some lessons from GTZ-supported projects

There are a number of German technical cooperation projects which we consider good examples of how to implement the complex notion of participatory development. These represent learning fields for GTZ as an organization.

Nasriya: participatory bottom-up approaches can work!

As early as 1986, the Nasriya Upgrading Project began in a squatter settlement of about 50 000 inhabitants in the city of Aswan, Upper Egypt, following a participatory urban-upgrading approach. The topdown threat was 'to raze' the settlement. Housing was uncontrolled, there was almost no infrastructure, no schools or community schemes and no public funds or administration to deal with an upgrading concept at the city level.

After learning from experiences of upgrading projects in Nepal (Bhaktapur Development Project) and Latin America, the strategy envisaged was to achieve the active participation of the 6000 households and avoid the new 'demolition and reconstruction' policy. The plan was to improve living conditions and local facilities through financially acceptable and socially tolerable means, mobilize the residents' interest in developing their abilities in self-administration and technical matters, and train them in the operation and maintenance of newly constructed or improved infrastructures.

Both the Egyptian and the German governments and, very importantly, the local administration, headed by a very active and open-minded governor, agreed with the concept of comprehensive participation of the local population stimulated by external guidance in organizational capacity-building. ZOPP proved to be a competent planning tool to organize the planning and monitoring processes, and the way participation was achieved in the project contributed considerably to the reformulation of GTZ's project cycle management (PCM) approach.

In numerous public planning meetings the layout and upgrading activities of the settlement were developed together with representatives of the local population. Improvements included the establishment and organization of a waste disposal system, the rebuilding of the road network, as well as social-sector programmes such as schools, kindergartens, a community-service centre and playgrounds. The highest priority was given to the construction of a waste-water network, a water-supply network with a pumping station and a storage tank. The test case, however, was the waste-water network.

The execution of the work, which required heavy physical labour in a sloping, rocky area, was done by the inhabitants on the basis of fixed rules they had established themselves. The project team consisted of the following:

- the project director, a specialist from the municipality;
- representatives of each quarter of Nasriya who were responsible for mobilizing the inhabitants;
- one German project adviser and short-term experts; and
- Egyptian specialists (architects, engineers, social workers), supported by German financial contributions.

The contribution of Nasriya's population to the construction of the infrastructure reduced costs by at least 25 per cent. Local financing was organized by fundraising or by land sale to the inhabitants, the money being reinvested in the settlement. To some extent, government funds were added. The community's self-confidence was raised to the extent that the considerable tribal differences among the inhabitants were transcended, and a sense of self-reliance and responsibility for the organization and administration of the new structures achieved. From the very beginning, the inhabitants worked through more or less developed formal and informal local institutions, and not government organizations, which played only a supportive role.

The challenge of spreading the experience
This convincing development, the result of a mutual learning process between the local population and the outside support agency, is about to become a model approach in Egypt; after the evident achievements in Nasriya, other governorates showed a vivid interest in adopting this urban-upgrading concept and, currently, two new participatory upgrading projects in Greater Cairo are under preparation.

Special efforts will also be directed towards transferring the learning experiences of Nasriya and other individual upgrading projects to a great number of NGOs representing marginal urban settlements all over Egypt, as well as government services and private companies. The tendency is gradually to influence the national-policy level. For the purpose of disseminating this approach, a special programme is under preparation to strengthen linkages between projects, facilitate inter-institutional networking, build up human resources through training, and support the elaboration of a government policy focusing on self-help and participatory development, as well as institutional pluralism.

Initiating ownership and enhancing the self-organizational capacity of rural communities in Maharashtra, India

Another participatory development project assisted by the GTZ (Financial and Technical Cooperation) is the Indo-German Watershed Management Project in Maharashtra, India. Since the majority of the population in this province earns its living in the biomass-production sector, the project strategy aims to restore the ecological balance of a region plagued by deterioration of soil and water resources, and to increase biomass production on a sustainable and equitable basis through a participatory-watershed development-and-management approach.

103

The project is characterized by its strict adherence to participatory planning and implementation whereby the villagers are the subjects of the project. The major role of the partner institution, the Social Centre, an NGO of Maharashtra, is to secure the training of village facilitators and provide technical expertise on request. Outside support is given only after the villagers who have joined the programme of land reclamation and rehabilitation have agreed unanimously on what to do, have organized themselves in self-reliant community-development committees, and proved their willingness and readiness to do unpaid, voluntary work.

The growing success of the project, which has spread from village to village, proves that environmental and ecological rehabilitation of inhabited areas is possible only when the concerned people see a reason for it and are fully involved in all aspects of decisionmaking, resource-mobilization, management and conservation. Such a strategy is clearly focusing on people, rather than on technical aspects. Foreign expertise, when needed, is financed through the German contribution, but, for the most part, competent local expertise is widely available.

In one typical village, the evaluation of the process of promotion and participation showed that all the activities that were undertaken were based on a discussion of the felt needs of the villagers and a consequent delegation of tasks to the village committee. The Social Centre considered every proposal as long as two conditions were met: (i) a commitment to improve soil conservation and (ii) the development of water resources. Otherwise the villagers' priorities were respected, with only the schedules being modified where necessary. To conclude, one could say that the Social Centre was acting primarily in the role of an assistant and advisor, building up the self-confidence of the villagers and organizing information trips to exchange experiences with other villages. The strategy chosen and the respective delineation of roles resulted in the full ownership by the local population of the activities that were implemented, and an increased capacity on the part of the communities to tackle their own problems and steer their own projects.

Unconventional self-help support, a task for a private company in Pakistan

In Pakistan, the Balochistan Rural Support Programme provides a good example of how the decision to use an NGO as a local implementing agency instead of a government institution improves the chances of achieving a sustainable, participatory regional-development strategy. The interesting feature in this case is that, legally, the NGO operates as a private company. German experts assist in the areas of strategic institutional development, the elaboration of self-organization strategies and concepts, as well as in training in all aspects of self-management and organizational development. With this approach the project is able to support some 800 self-help groups according to their needs (income-generating schemes, village-infrastructural improvement, village committees set up on a self-help basis, the participation of women in planning and organizing development activities, the implementation of small credit systems for the rural poor, and training and institutional development for the participating organizations).

104

Financing for the project still depends on contributions mobilized by government, IFAD and the GTZ. The execution of the labour, however, is organized and implemented completely by village organizations, women's organizations, village specialist organizations and other self-help groups in 12 of the 24 districts of the province. The programme is still growing, under the full responsibility of the Pakistani management group, and assisted by German and local experts.

Such is, in short, some of the 'experience gained'. The few project examples indicate that some answers and lessons can already be drawn and direct us in reorienting our strategies and organization, despite the fact that a systematic analysis of our experiences is still missing.

Reorientations and challenges for GTZ as an organization

Pursuing participatory development approaches does challenge us, the outside support agencies, to continously rethink and adapt our own terms of operation: administrative procedures, instruments, strategies and so forth. Below are set out some of the more recent modifications and activities that GTZ has initiated since 1992, based on the lessons learned so far, in its attempt to improve the ability of our organization to facilitate a more participatory and sustainable development.

When introducing ZOPP as a project-planning procedure about 14 years ago, using the logframe as a tool, we were convinced that this would be a significant step forward in enabling beneficiaries and local staff to carry through well-planned development processes. Today we know that this has been, though important, only a first step. If not used flexibly and in a process-oriented way, the method produces static results that do not take into account daily changes in the conditions, actors, policies and resources available. In addition, the promise that participation meant participation in decisionmaking did not in most cases materialize, either for the beneficiaries of specific projects or for the local population more generally. That is why in an internal GTZ-project, Planning and Sustainablity, it was decided that ZOPP be reformulated as only one of the tools within a broader overall concept of project cycle management (PCM).

PCM is a participatory management approach in which the participation of the different actors, and their respective roles and responsibilities, are clearly defined from the very start of a project (or a programme), that is, from its first planning and designing attempts. Within the PCM framework, ZOPP, formerly often equated with a one-week planning workshop, is now understood as a logical sequence of different steps, in which seminars or workshops, as well as other methods, such as PRA or RRA, can be integrated if appropriate.[1] The crucial difference is that the management tools and instruments are adapted to the stakeholder groups, and not the other way round. The success of PCM depends on our readiness and ability to delegate responsibility and decisionmaking power from the very start of a project to the stakeholders in the country. In order to allow for improved project preparation in the partner country, we have modified our administrative regulations to maximize flexibility so as to support better our partner organizations in elaborating project strategies together with the beneficiaries. Particularly for the preparation of self-help and participatory development projects this may mean that one defines only a loose cooperation framework with ample scope for flexibility and participatory learning processes. These changes and their implementation in our organization have been difficult as they can appear threatening both for headquarters (HQ) people and for project staff.

As we stated in the introduction, the impact of participatory approaches on beneficiaries and institutions in partner countries, and the prerequisites for their success are, at least on a representative level, largely unknown. Systematic analyses and specific evaluations so far have not taken place on a large scale.[2]

What we know are usually individual cases, experiences and snapshots which are almost always (but not all of them) accounts of the early phases of projects entering a participatory mode. Little is known of how participatory methods and approaches are institutionalized in the whole of the project cycle, or which planning, administrative, institutional or political problems emerge in the process of switching to a more participatory approach. It is in this area that project and HQ staff keen to promote participation need greater clarity and conceptual support.

As an important step towards improving our understanding of participatory approaches, GTZ recently initiated a research and development project entitled 'Critical Factors and Preconditions for Success in Participatory Approaches'. Its objective is to analyse and evaluate the insights and experience gained in project practice and to make them available both to the projects themselves and for GTZ-wide discussion. The analysis will include the results of learning groups in Africa and Asia which have examined their experiences on both a regional and national level. These learning groups are attended by national and expatriate project staff with particular experience and interest in participatory approaches. Through this process we hope to gain much clearer insights and answers to some of these five questions:

(1) How do participatory methods fit in with the existing management instruments, regulations and procedures of GTZ, and which modifications emerge as necessary (planning methodology, monitoring and evaluation methods, staff- and policy-evaluation instruments, etc.)?
(2) What experiences in regard to the work and funding requirements of participatory approaches are available, and how can planning and financing requirements be met?
(3) What experience is there with participatory approaches and heterogeneous target groups, in which dominant subgroups attempt to manipulate the process and exclude others?
(4) How have the results from participatory analysis and planning at a local level been linked to regional and/or national decisionmaking processes?
(5) What experience is available concerning supportive or restrictive environments for participatory approaches within partner structures, and how have restrictions been handled?

Another activity to promote participatory development approaches was an unconventional exchange of experiences in participation among NGOs from developing and industrialized countries. Called the 'Dare-to-Share-Fair', this two-day meeting, which took place at GTZ HQ in 1994, raised the public esteem and acceptance of these approaches within GTZ. The fair fostered an intensive exchange between practitioners, GTZ and its non-governmental, sometimes distant partners in development.

Government agencies like GTZ usually enter into a government-to-government agreement[3] as the basis for development cooperation. All too often they find themselves bound as partner organizations to government agencies that frequently follow a top-down approach and have low acceptance and legitimacy with the poorer sections of the population. It is a difficult procedure to break with this automatism, once the crucial role of bottom-up processes for sustainable development is understood. An important lesson concerning what we learned from practice (and it can be found in the project examples above) is that it is imperative to involve a far broader spectrum of institutions as partner organizations than just the state, be they NGOs, chambers of commerce, parent-teacher associations, religious movements or private enterprises. Accepting new and additional partner organizations in a project or programme seems to us a fundamental precondition for a successful participatory development strategy, both on a project and on a societal level.

Needless to say, there are dozens of new problems and hazards that come up when a participatory development approach is adopted. The relevant governments must be ready and committed to decentralize (in the sense of devolving a range of decisionmaking powers to local authorities), and have the political will to cooperate with, rather than control, the various stakeholder groups in a participatory development strategy. They must also understand the institutional consequences this will entail. This is no easy task. We believe, however, that, as far as possible, a precondition for take-off is for sociocultural and sociopolitical relations and conditions at the local level to be transparent in the starting phase of projects and programmes. Mechanisms also have to be developed to resolve conflicting situations that may arise from the different goals and objectives of local, regional and national constituencies. The role, continuity, legitimacy and acceptance of the stakeholders' representatives must therefore be clarified from the very beginning. Existing institutions have to be brought in under terms that are clear. As for foreign experts, they need reliable mediators. In most cases they are not in a position to dip down to the real grassroot level.

There is no other way. The rationale, the soul of participation, its vitality, lies in the conviction that local people have the motivation, the potential and the creativity to solve their own problems and are realistic in their objectives.

Participatory development requires organizational development at all levels. Roles have to be redefined, new tasks drafted and a new understanding of cooperation has to crystallize between the different actors concerned. We are in an ongoing process of adapting our project cycle, our management orientation and our methodology. Continuing the exchange in Learning Groups on Participation on a regional and national basis could help us to get a better understanding of what is really happening at farm, village or town level, where the constraints are, how to adapt our own organization and which kind and type of intervention is the most suitable to promote the process of participation both at project and at a broader societal level.

16

Participatory Approaches in Government Bureaucracies: facilitating institutional change[1]

JOHN THOMPSON

Chapter 16 examines how and why a growing number of government bureaucracies are attempting to develop and integrate participatory research and development approaches into their programme activities. Drawing on empirical studies of three large public agencies[2] that have made significant advances in institutionalizing participatory approaches, the chapter presents a clear strategy for other government bureaucracies keen to do the same. Using a conceptual model of the institutional learning and training cycle, it describes the stages involved in building internal capacity to employ participatory approaches effectively and facilitate the processes of institutional change which must result if the approaches are to be more than a passing fad.

The training of agency personnel in participatory principles, concepts and methods plays an important role in facilitating such transformations, but the author argues that such training is unlikely to have a lasting impact unless it is viewed as part of a broader process of organizational learning. Such a process is likely to require profound changes in an institution's prevailing attitudes, behaviours, norms, skills and procedures. Chapter 16 concludes with ten key elements necessary for institutionalizing participatory approaches within public agencies.

Recognizing the need for institutional change

There is abundant and rapidly growing interest in participatory approaches for research and development in many parts of the world. To date, most of the innovations and accomplishments relating to participatory research and development have emerged out of what David Hulme (1994) calls the 'third sector' (i.e. private organizations that are non-profitmaking but which are not political parties).[3] These organizations normally manage relatively small programmes with limited budgets and areas of coverage and, consequently, achieve limited results. The lessons regarding the activities of third-sector organizations in this area, and attempts to spread and scale-up their successes, have been analysed and documented widely.[4] Less well-known, and less well-understood, is the increasing use of participatory approaches by large, public institutions, especially given the widely-held notion that most state agencies are centralized, authoritarian, formalistic, inefficient bureaucracies incapable of experimentation, self-critical learning or imaginative change (Mouzelis, 1994; Wunsch and Olowu, 1990; Chantornvong, 1988; D. Korten, 1988; F.F. Korten, 1988).

An examination of the literature indicates that there are four main reasons why public-sector agencies are taking an increasing interest in participatory approaches. The first has more to do with attempts by government bureaucracies to ensure their continuing survival than it does with any meaningful embrace of the ideals of good governance, democracy or empowerment. Political-economic exigencies, including rising debt, declining terms of trade, economic liberalization and market integration are forcing many developing countries to reduce the size of their civil services and thus their capacities for direct service provision (Boer and Rooimans, 1994; Due, 1993; Helleiner, 1992). In the drive for efficiency, governments are searching for new ways to do more with less. In some cases, the state is doing this by establishing new partnerships with third-sector organizations, albeit reluctantly, and by adopting new participatory approaches which give local people more control over research and development processes (Farrington and Bebbington, 1993, 1994; Thrupp, Cabarle and Zazueta, 1994).[5]

Second, the international aid community has been instrumental in stimulating Third World governments' growing interest in participatory approaches. With increasing frequency, donors are placing conditions on grants and loans to governments that require them to support participatory research and development programmes and projects (Bowles, 1989; Griffin, 1991; Grounder, 1994). Their stated objective is to create decisionmaking processes in which local organizations and associations have a presence and open those public processes to more scrutiny. In this manner, donors claim to be linking participatory development directly to state accountability, empowerment of local groups and transparency in decisionmaking. In reality, much of this increased accountability is focused upwards (towards the donors), rather than downwards (towards local people), thus placing greater pressure on public agencies to perform to donor-defined standards (Mitlin and Thompson, 1995).

Not all donor involvement has been constraining, however. Some funding agencies are making long-term commitments to supporting public-sector institutions with the specific aim of promoting bureaucratic reorientation.[6] Moreover, some donors have come to recognize the pivotal role that small numbers of outside resource persons can play, not in the traditional positions of technical advisors or financial comptrollers, but as catalysts for change. While it goes without saying that a critical mass of committed agency professionals is essential for initiating and supporting change within an organization, outside perspectives and experiences are also valuable in illuminating internal problems and identifying a range of possible solutions. In some cases, these outside resource persons are university-based researchers, private-sector professionals, or non-government development practitioners, while in others they are programme officers or associates of the donor agencies themselves.[7] Whatever their background, these external facilitators are often in a position to take risks that agency staff cannot and are thus capable of creating political space in which innovative internal advocates for change are able to manoeuvre. Experience suggests that these effective synergies between external facilitators and agency professionals usually happen only through sustained contact and close collaboration on long-term research and development initiatives where trust and a shared set of objectives can be established.

Recognition of the failure of past research and development approaches is a third reason why state agencies have become more amenable to participatory alternatives. Over the past two decades 'blueprint' development strategies have been shown to be ineffective in meeting the basic needs of large numbers of marginalized, vulnerable people (Chambers, 1995a; Doyal and Gough, 1991; Kates and Haarman, 1992; Wisner, 1988; Wisner and Yapa, 1992).[9] From environmental health (Hardoy, Mitlin and Satterthwaite, 1992) to low-cost housing (Hardoy, Cairncross and Satterthwaite, 1990), and from agricultural research and extension (Chambers, Pacey and Thrupp, 1988; Scoones and Thompson, 1994) to water-resource management and irrigation (Guijt and Thompson, 1994; Postel, 1989), standardized, reductionist approaches have been shown to be incapable of addressing the complex realities of poor people, which are locally specific, diverse and dynamic. Although many government bureaucracies have been slower than their third-sector counterparts to recognize and respond to these failures, they too have become aware of the need for fundamental institutional change.

While the failure of past research and development approaches has prompted some government agencies to look for viable alternatives, the successful application of participatory approaches by other organizations has been equally convincing. The manifold achievements of third-sector institutions have begun to attract the attention of government policymakers and planners, especially as official aid disbursements to that sector increase while those to the public sector decline or remain static. It is the positive experiences of other public agencies, however, either through their own efforts or through new alliances with other institutional actors, that have proved most persuasive. These 'success stories' have demonstrated that it is possible for public-sector agencies to develop, implement and institutionalize more people-centered approaches and attain positive results (Cernea, 1991; Pretty and Chambers, 1994; World Bank, 1994a, 1994b).

Training for transformation?

Given these influences, today the question many public-sector institutions are asking is not why to adopt and apply participatory research and development approaches, but how to go about it.[9] For many, the first policy decision is to organize one or a series of training workshops and field activities, often facilitated by external consultants, to expose their staff to the new, people-centred approaches, with little thought given to the long-term management and organizational implications. As a result, public agencies soon encounter the thorny problem of how to build internal capacity in these participatory, process-driven approaches, without fundamentally changing their cumbersome bureaucratic systems and risk-averse management styles. Eventually the contradiction will force the agencies either to abandon their newly adopted participatory methodologies (sometimes while continuing to use the associated rhetoric) or to begin the long, arduous task of reorienting their institutional policies, procedures and norms.

Clearly, training does not take place in an institutional vacuum, it happens within a particular organizational system with its own unique set of management structures, professional norms and field practices (Thompson, 1994b). These influence and are influenced by the set of working rules that individuals use to order particular relationships with one another. These rules determine who is eligible to make decisions in certain areas, what actions are allowed or prohibited, what procedures must be followed, what information must or must not be provided, and what penalties or rewards will be assigned to individuals or groups as a result of the actions (Ostrom, 1986, 1990). Any government agency contemplating adopting a participatory approach soon recognizes that training alone will not convert a conventional, technically-oriented, bureaucratic institution into a more people-centred, learning-oriented, strategic organization.[10] The institution's rules-in-use, financial-management practices, reporting systems and supervisory methods must also be reoriented if its role is to be transformed from that of a primary 'implementor' (i.e. one dictating the terms of research or development work) to an 'enabler' (i.e. one supporting people's own research and/or development efforts). Improving the type and mode of staff training may help this transformation to occur, but it will not of itself bring it about.

Transforming a bureaucracy demands changes to an organization's working rules in order to allow its staff to experiment, make and learn from mistakes, and respond more creatively to changing conditions and new opportunities.[11] Identifying key principles to guide the process of institutional change is a useful starting-point. Functions and objectives must be clarified before new structures can be designed. At the same time, there must be a shift away from the standardized procedures and specialized units responsible for discrete stages in the research or development process, and more emphasis must be placed on interdisciplinary sharing and learning. Finally, a range of incentives for reorienting and restructuring systems and structures needs to be developed for rewarding those who promote and facilitate the process of institutional change.

Training must be linked closely to these internal change processes if it is to have a lasting impact. For this reason, the term 'training' as used here refers to the creation of interactive learning environments and continuous learning opportunities rather than simple classroom-based teaching and instruction. Only by creating space for various actors to interact, question, experiment, share and learn, from one another and from local people, can an implementing organization become a learning organization.

As Richard Bawden (1994: 259–60) has stated:

Learning organizations are collectives or communities of individuals who share experiences and understanding through cooperative learning and genuine participation in those events which affect them. For any organization or community to learn, individuals must not only themselves be active learners, but they must also be committed to sharing that learning in ways which allow consensual understanding or meaning to be reached. Here then is the essence of the participatory process through which 'people-centred development' is made possible through 'social learning concepts and methods'.

In the next section, a conceptual model of the institutional learning and training cycle is presented to aid in understanding the learning process that many centralized government institutions are undergoing currently. This model is used to help analyse the experiences of three large government agencies in Sri Lanka, Kenya and the Philippines, and chart their efforts to institutionalize participatory approaches and become learning organizations. After drawing lessons from their efforts, the chapter concludes with a broad set of policy recommendations on training and the institutionalization of participatory approaches within public-sector agencies.

The institutional learning and training cycle

Many of an agency's most pressing methodological problems will not be solved by a change in policy alone. In many instances, donor and government policies already mandate, either implicitly or explicitly, that local people should be actively engaged in development and research. For various reasons, however, true interactive participation is not occurring. What is needed is a learning process that develops and promotes new methodologies and changes the prevailing attitudes, behaviour, norms, skills and procedures within the agency. This process of institutional transformation will, of necessity, be gradual, based on trial and error, combined with self-critical reflection and further experimentation and innovation.[12]

According to Frances F. Korten (1988), institutionalizing a participatory process involves five inter-related learning stages or phases, each of which can last a number of years (Fig. 16.1).

Through these five phases, the identification of a need for institutional reorientation and innovation leads gradually to improved practices on an agency-wide level. However, a linear conception of those phases represents only part of the learning process. Equally important are the feedback loops within the cycle. The small-scale, site-specific experiments, the process of systematizing the lessons, the interactions between internal innovators and external facilitators, and the broader-scale applications are all used to identify additional programme elements needing modification and improvement, which then initiate new learning cycles. Similarly, lessons are not drawn only from small-scale field tests, but from experiences and insights drawn from other institutions, thus enriching the lessons and increasing their applicability.

Training is an integral element in this process of organizational learning. As part of the first phase of the cycle, an agency reviews its existing training policies and procedures and identifies aspects that need to be altered or redesigned to support the new participatory approach. During the second phase, after the new participatory approach has been adequately conceptualized, a small group of mostly senior staff is exposed to the new approach, sometimes with support from one or a number of outside agencies with substantial practical experience in training in participatory approaches.

The reason for concentrating initially on higher-ranking officials rather than more junior personnel is that these senior officers will determine whether the new approach receives further testing and institutional support. If they give their approval in these early stages, then there is a good chance that the new approach will receive broader acceptance.[13] If they do not, then its proponents

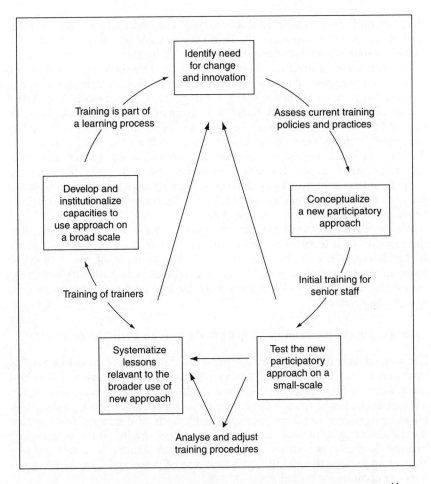

Figure 16.1: The institutional learning process and training cycle[14]

will face an uphill struggle to obtain institutional backing. However, it is the mid-level officers, with their detailed knowledge of the agency's operational problems and their understanding of how new strategies may be integrated effectively into existing systems and policies, who will eventually carry the responsibility for developing and institutionalizing the new participatory approach. Once approval from senior management is received, the focus shifts to building a working team of well-trained, well-motivated and well-resourced mid-level advocates capable of building a coalition for change within the agency and formally representing the change process to the outside world.

In the third phase, the new participatory approach is tested under diverse field conditions (e.g. different production systems, social settings and so on). Following these early field trials, the methodology's strengths and weaknesses are assessed, after which the method is modified and amended further. During this phase, lessons are also learned about the procedures used to train the working teams.[15] These, too, are analysed and adjusted according to feedback from the team members, the field coordinators and, in some cases, the outside resource persons who are supporting the agency.

This process of testing and modification, both of methodology and training procedures, continues until the agency feels confident enough to attempt to apply the approach on a broad scale. At this point, a greater number of skilled trainer-facilitators, especially those with extensive field experience, will be required to train large numbers of agency staff. This may be accomplished by employing trainers from other organizations, such as NGOs or universities. This has the advantage of maintaining links between the agency and third-sector organizations which can take a more independent view and give local people's interests high priority. However, such an approach can be prone to budget cutbacks, internal resistance to outsider involvement and outsider resistance to collaboration with the state.[16]

For these reasons, most government agencies will identify and strengthen the capacity of a team of trainer-facilitators within their own organizations in the later phases of the training cycle. The training of these in-house facilitators serves two purposes: it builds a cadre of skilled trainers within the institution, and it enables the agency to shape future training to meet its own specific requirements.[17]

Charting the course from participatory rhetoric to participatory reality

For more than a decade a growing number of public-sector institutions has been experimenting with participatory approaches for research and development, and remained hopeful that these might be employed on a wide scale. Such sentiments are frequently expressed in the national plans produced by planning agencies, in the project-appraisal reports of donor agencies and by the heads of government agencies themselves. Sadly, this participatory rhetoric is rarely backed by more than the introduction of a few training courses or perhaps the addition of a new type of personnel (e.g. social mobilizers or community organizers).

To implement participatory approaches successfully, an agency must examine every aspect of its work and determine whether its policies and procedures are capable of responding to the needs and priorities of local people. Does an agency's staff have any reason to care whether they are providing an effective service, and if so, whether it is valued by local people? Do participatory approaches for analysis, planning, implementation, and monitoring and evaluation result in the selection of viable projects, programmes and processes that strengthen local capacities and support local livelihoods? Do internal structures and management systems facilitate effective problem-solving and active learning? Do existing budgetary procedures allow local adaptation and flexibility in investment and disbursement?

The typical mode of investment and expenditure followed by most government agencies and their donors continues to make it difficult for programmes to employ participatory approaches effectively. Their emphasis is on disbursing funds and showing measurable results quickly. By contrast, constructive dialogue, joint analysis, participatory planning, all of the critical elements of participatory approaches, run counter to this way of thinking. Instead of 'front-end loading' of capital investments and expenditures, there would be a more gradual release of funds only after a substantial period of interaction with local groups and institutions (Fig. 16.2). This would mean that the initial investment would be quite small in terms of capital improvements, but significant in terms of human-resources development, including training. Such a strategy would require the development of new indicators for assessing performance and measuring success. It would also necessitate a reduction in or elimination of rigid, predefined targets for expenditure and investment.

Co-ordinating expansion temporally and spatially is critical to the success of the institutional reorientation process. Expansion and integration that proceeds too slowly will leave the agency little changed, while rapid expansion could outpace the organization's ability to train staff and adjust internal procedures to facilitate implementation. The same is true at the project or community level, as a substantial amount of time will be required for community facilitators to gain local people's trust, understand their problems and priorities, and help support the development and strengthening of representative local organizations. Several strategically selected, low-risk, high-profile, tangible projects could, however, be undertaken in the early stages of the new programme. These would have the advantage of making the participatory process visible at relatively low cost, and thus placate impatient politicians, reassure anxious donors and government officials, and strengthen local people's self-confidence and capacities.

Particular attention needs to be given to creating learning mechanisms within an agency and facilitating transitions to successive phases of the institutional learning cycle. The Badulla Integrated Rural Development Programme in Sri Lanka, the Soil and Water Conservation Branch in Kenya and the National Irrigation Administration in the Philippines (analysed in detail in Thompson, 1995) provide important lessons regarding the need to facilitate transitions to successive phases of the institutional learning cycle. All three

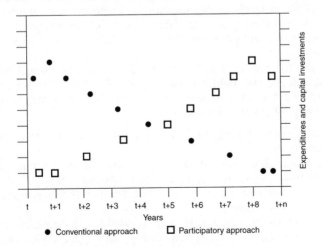

Fig. 16.2: Conflicting patterns of expenditure and investment

115

agencies mentioned above used pilot projects as learning laboratories for testing, modifying and refining their new participatory approaches. These lessons were analysed and discussed in great detail by key decisionmakers from the agency and, in some instances, other external resource persons in a variety of workshops, review meetings and working groups. The emphasis in all of these sessions was on critical reflection, open sharing, constructive dialogue and learning. Various forms of process documentation were also initiated, including regular village reports, catchment reports, process reports and socio-technical profiles. All of these forms of documentation were distributed and discussed by a wide array of key stakeholders on a regular basis.

These and other conditions that determine whether a particular institution's programmes and policies can be effective at all, irrespective of whether 'participation' is involved, will need to be examined concurrently with efforts to introduce a new participatory approach to any development or research activity. Each of these changes must constitute an integral part of the whole, all contributing to change involved in an organizational learning process in which errors are detected and embraced, alternative solutions examined and tested, adjustments made, and competing interests confronted and negotiated.

Training is only one of many components that shape and influence the institutionalization of participatory approaches, albeit an important one. For it to have a lasting impact, training must be viewed as a social learning process, not simply teaching and instruction, and must be integrated into a wider programme of human-resources development. Such a programme would focus not only on preparing agency personnel to use certain innovative field methods, but also improve their communication, analytical and facilitation skills. It would encourage staff at all levels to take increased responsibility for their own learning, support the development of competencies such as adaptable, transferable skills, and focus on learning how to learn rather than absorbing facts (Bawden, 1989; Ison, 1990; Macadam and Packham, 1989). This kind of training process would help to foster a relaxed and open environment in which staff from different levels in the institutional hierarchy felt comfortable and thus able to work together constructively. This would mean concentrating on attitudes, behaviour and principles, as well as key methodological concepts and techniques.

It is possible to alter the operational procedures and institutional cultures of centralized, bureaucratic, public agencies, but a transformation is neither easily nor quickly achieved. For public agencies to become strategic, enabling institutions require ten key elements:

(1) a policy framework supportive of a clear role for local people in research and development;
(2) strong leadership committed to the task of developing learning-organizational systems, capacities and working rules;
(3) long-term financial commitments and flexible funding arrangements from key donor agencies;
(4) better systems of monitoring and evaluating performance, and new mechanisms for ensuring accountability, both to the donors and senior decisionmakers, and to the local people;

116

(5) careful attention to and patience in working out the details of systems and procedures, each involving careful analysis of lessons learned from small-scale pilot tests, and the negotiation and accommodation of different interests and perceptions;

(6) creative management, so that improved policies, procedures and field practices, once developed, can be scaled-up and implemented effectively;

(7) an open, supportive, yet challenging organizational climate in which it is safe to experiment and safe to fail;

(8) small, interdisciplinary teams or working groups of innovative and committed agency professionals working in collaboration with external resource persons capable of acting as catalysts for change;

(9) regular documentation and analysis of lessons for improving practice and building an institutional memory;

(10) a flexible, integrated, phased training programme over a sustained period of time, involving key actors at different levels.

Institutionalizing and operationalizing participatory approaches is undoubtedly an extremely complex and problematic business. Change and stability are inextricably linked to any open management system; the challenge for large public institutions attempting to employ participatory approaches is to facilitate the emergence of new ways of knowing and behaving so as to manage change creatively. This will offset growing concerns over the coopting of the term 'participatory' by those with short time horizons and narrow agendas who may be promoting stasis and the status quo rather than change, innovation and, eventually, transformation.

PART 3

WHERE DO WE GO FROM HERE?

17
Introduction to Part 3

In parts 1 and 2 of the book, we were presented with 11 rich case studies exploring the challenges of scaling-up and of organizational change in countries as diverse as Ethiopia, Vietnam, Bolivia, Indonesia and Estonia, and institutions as diverse as community-based organizations (CBOs), non-governmental organizations (NGOs), government bureaucracies, and donors. The lessons learned from these diverse cases are in many ways strikingly similar. In Part 3, an attempt is made to synthesize such lessons and determine the most appropriate courses for future action.

Chapter 18, by Robert Leurs, analyses succinctly the current challenges facing PRA, as well as the changes implied by some these challenges. With insights based on an extensive review of the available literature on PRA, as well as from a series of workshops held with the staff of six NGOs promoting PRA in South Asia, Leurs considers the challenges at six levels, namely the individual, community, organizational, project and programme, donor and policy levels. The author argues that the challenges in all cases can be attributed to five cross-cutting factors: differences in power, culture, knowledge, money and time. The overall conclusion is that the success of PRA, in terms of its capacity to produce significant outcomes, is highly context-dependent, and that insufficient attention paid to the five factors listed above is likely to lead to frustration.

Chapters 19 and 20 are summaries of the discussions held by 26 participants at the IDS workshop, Institutionalization of Participatory Approaches, held in May 1996. The first focuses on issues specifically related to scaling-up; the second on questions of organizational change thought to be essential to launch and sustain participatory initiatives. For practitioners and policy-makers considering a scaling-up strategy, and the concomitant organizational changes such a strategy invariably implies, chapters 19 and 20 are highly recommended. They represent key learnings from the combined efforts of some of the most experienced and knowledgeable people in these fields.

Chapter 19 begins by considering three enabling conditions which the workshop participants agreed are needed to ensure maximum success in the scaling-up of participatory approaches: a policy context in which democratization and decentralization are genuinely embraced as necessary governance reforms; the support of high-level government figures; and the existence of an in-country critical mass of people with training experience. Certain dangers of rapid scaling-up are then pinpointed, notably routinization, duplication and abuse in the application of PRA and related methodologies. Recommendations are consequently made for quality PRA training and field practice to

121

avoid the poor standards noted in some scaling-up experiences. The need to overcome cascade training, and to include in PRA practice transparency as a general principle, the honouring of commitments and the production of user-friendly documentation and other ways of recording experience are all explored. The chapter ends with a list of recommended actions, agreed upon by the workshop participants, for communities and local groups, NGOs and donors involved in the implementation of participatory projects.

Chapter 20 explores in greater depth the concept of the learning organization as a useful model for making development agencies more participatory from the inside. The consensus at the workshop was that much more research is needed to understand the kind of internal organizational changes needed to maximize the impact of participatory projects. These changes were grouped under three headings: personal skills and attributes; procedures; and systems and structures, each of which explored a number of key characteristics as essential attributes of a participatory organization.

In terms of personal skills and attributes, the following points are highlighted and developed: the ability to listen and engage in dialogue and mutual learning, the ability to be reflexive, and a capacity for vision. In terms of organizational procedures, particular emphasis is paid to the question of moving from product to process to avoid the tyranny of pre-set targets; establishing new incentive mechanisms to reward participatory behaviour in-house as well as in the field; setting up multiple feedback mechanisms to trace more effectively the progress of different initiatives; and the will to be evaluated by different stakeholders, especially the proposed beneficiaries of projects. Finally, in terms of systems and structures, calls are made to set up flexible, ad hoc, innovative learning units to foment a task culture inside development agencies, as opposed to one centred on rigidly defined roles. The need for more flexible forms of budgeting and, concomitantly, for the piloting of new systems of downwards accountability, was also recognized. Chapter 20 concludes by making useful comparisons with the optimal-management characteristics of the so-called post-Fordist flat management model developed first in Japan.

In Chapter 21, John Gaventa draws on the 11 individual cases in the book to argue that the success of scaling-up depends largely on linking the quantity of participation (the number of people involved and the geographical scope of projects, programmes and policies), its quality (moving from appraisal to the involvement of people throughout the whole development process in a way that increases their empowerment), and the organizational changes required for both to work simultaneously and effectively. Gaventa is adamant that such changes must occur not only intra-institutionally but also inter-institutionally, looking at how organizations link and collaborate across sectoral and power differences, an area he feels is given insufficient weight in the book. He concludes by pointing to a number of areas for future research. Of particular urgency, he argues, is the need to explore further how to link personal and institutional change to broader issues of political economy such as race, class and gender relations, and the current trend in the governance arena towards democratization and decentralization; how to define the expected outcomes of participatory processes with greater clarity, measure actual impacts and so increase our understanding of the relationship between participation as a means and participation as an end; and, finally, how to improve the tools and better define the indicators to monitor participation, and ensure that local people are centrally involved in evaluating both the impacts of projects and the professionalism of the implementing agencies.

18

Current Challenges facing Participatory Rural Appraisal

ROBERT LEURS

Chapter 18 provides a summary of the major challenges currently facing PRA, as well as the changes implied by some of those challenges. The challenges are considered at six different levels, namely the individual, community, organizational, project and programme, donor and policy levels. The challenges identified are drawn from the literature on PRA, as well as from a recent series of workshops held by the author with the staff of six NGOs that are promoting PRA in South Asia. The chapter concludes by attributing these challenges to five cross-cutting factors: differences in power, culture, knowledge, money and time.

Introduction

While other contributions to the literature on PRA have already focused on the challenges facing PRA at particular levels (e.g. Mosse, 1993 on community-level challenges, and Thompson, 1995 on institutional challenges), no other writing has, as yet, to the best of the author's knowledge, provided an overall contextual summary.

The author believes that it would be useful for existing or intending future practitioners of PRA to have access to such a summary overview of the challenges facing PRA (and some of the associated changes) so that they can take account of these in the design of their own approaches or relate these to their own experience and make any changes they believe to be required as a result.

This summary is, however, by no means intended as a substitute for a local analysis of the challenges facing PRA in any given situation. Indeed, the author believes that such local analysis by community members themselves should be encouraged everywhere and that this is likely to lead to the identification of many more locally specific challenges, as well as corresponding and more appropriate local-community recommendations for action.

Challenges facing PRA at the individual level

Training

One of the major challenges at the level of the individual PRA facilitator is training. Most of the PRA training conducted up to now has been short term (anything from a few days to a few weeks) and one off, with varying combinations of classroom- and field-based learning. In addition, most PRA training to date has concentrated on methods rather than behaviour, attitudes and principles, for the simple reason that this has been much easier (and less threatening) to do. Finally, much of the PRA training has been cascaded, i.e. provided to others by participants of initial training programmes even though these were not conceived as training-of-trainer programmes.

The results of this approach have been that:

- PRA is still often practised as a one-off exercise (or a series of these), even though it is now increasingly being conceived as an ongoing process or culture (e.g. Chambers, 1994a).
- much PRA has been reduced to the increasingly mechanical application and standardized sequences and combinations of methods (e.g. Kar and Backhaus, 1994).
- the quality of PRA training has suffered, with the lowest levels of PRA support-agency staff often receiving the poorest quality training (personal observation).

Consequently, there is now an urgent need to rethink the approach to, and design of, PRA training.

Drinkwater (1994) has described one possible alternative approach and design, which focuses on the role of the PRA facilitator and his or her relationships with different community members. These are then regularly reviewed and updated in the light of ongoing experience. Another interesting innovation of this approach has been that participants generate their own training/learning materials and are required to start analysing their own experience right from the outset of the process.

As such, this approach concentrates much more on some of the principles of participatory learning methods (such as critical awareness and self-awareness), as opposed to the means. It also helps ensure that resource persons of future training sessions have themselves learnt about the role and relationships of facilitators through ongoing personal experience. It is alarming that many current PRA trainers continue to work as such despite their own lack of experience with these methods as part of an ongoing process of learning with communities. Finally, the self-generation of materials avoids the dependency and lack of local training materials, a problem inherent in the current approach to PRA training.

Cultural barriers

Many PRA facilitators are young educated professionals, whose experience, language and values are quite different to those of the community members with whom they are working. The language barriers cannot be overcome unless the local languages are learnt. Similarly, the experiential and resulting cultural differences can be transcended only if each side learns to understand and respect such differences.

The question is whether such understanding (and linguistic fluency) can be achieved, even over an ongoing series of infrequent and short-term visits (which seems to be the pattern for many externally based PRA facilitators).

If not, does the answer lie in more community-based facilitation (by community-PRA facilitators) or in more frequent and longer visits? Would not the same cultural barriers be present in the communication between community-based facilitators and the field-based representatives of external development agencies, who are initiating and supporting their community-based PRA facilitation skills?

How to integrate the role of PRA facilitator with other roles, both public and private, is another major challenge. This can be a particularly acute problem for women in male-dominated societies, both in the home and at the office (Leurs, 1995)

Power differentials

A PRA facilitator implicitly represents the benefits (funds, technical expertise etc.) which his or her organization is perceived to be able to offer, even if s/he explicitly offers only to facilitate a community-based process of PRA. This power differential will inevitably influence the facilitator–community relationship, with community members highlighting their own relative poverty, needs and problems in the context of what they hope to be able to get from the external organization.

It can, consequently, be difficult to get community members to accept that the process itself is the benefit, especially if it is presented as a means for securing other benefits. Even in the (relatively few) cases where facilitating the PRA process is the only benefit on offer, those struggling to gain their livelihood may not wish to risk investing a lot of time in an untried process for what may seem to be mainly non-livelihood rewards.

Changing attitudes and behaviour

One of the great strengths of PRA is that its facilitation causes many PRA facilitators to undergo a process of reversals. However, some PRA facilitators can continue this kind of work without undergoing such reversals (Leurs, 1995) and some PRA facilitators will make more and/or deeper reversals than others. The question therefore arises, should PRA facilitators be monitored for the quality of their work and supported, promoted or dismissed accordingly? Ideally, PRA facilitators should be self-monitoring and self-improving, but is this happening in practice?

The challenge then is continuously to develop and apply an agreed PRA quality standard, with associated indicators, for monitoring, including self-monitoring, purposes. This has not yet been done by anybody or any organization as far as the author is aware.

Accountability

Although the philosophy of PRA would suggest that the PRA facilitator should be accountable to the community, s/he is in practice accountable to her or his project or organization. The best way of changing this accountability would be for the community to pay for the services rendered by PRA facilitators. In practice, however, not many communities are prepared to pay for an externally proposed service, whose benefits are yet to be demonstrated. This takes time. PRA facilitators may, therefore, need to be paid externally during this period. In such a situation, however, both they and the community may be reluctant to change matters, for obvious reasons. Therein lies the paradox.

Transport

Lack of transport facilities is a major constraint (and cost in terms of time and fatigue) for most externally based PRA facilitators. The associated challenges are for organizations to become more aware of the logistical implications (budgeting accordingly), or for them to provide for lower facilitator/community ratios.

Challenges facing PRA at the community level

Existing social relationships

PRA is assumed to improve the quality (representation, analysis, decision-making) and quantity (numbers) of participation in the development process. This is mainly because of the visual character of many of the PRA methods and the collective forums in which these usually take place. In practice, however, the quality and quantity of participation has been thoroughly documented only in a few field-based PRA training exercises (e.g. the IIED PRA training reports).

Theory would suggest that, as Mosse (1995) points out, PRAs involve public social events which construct local knowledge in ways that are strongly influenced by existing social relationships, in particular by relations of gender, power and by the PRA facilitators themselves. This is borne out by recent reflections on the constraints facing PRA at the community level by the field staff of several NGOs in South Asia, who are facilitating PRA in the communities with which they work (Leurs, 1995).

The following were some of the challenges identified (Leurs, 1995):

- hierarchical culture;
- raised expectations (see also Edwards, 1994);
- poor initial participation in terms of quality and quantity;
- public-domain biases;
- gender biases;
- power-inequality biases (dealing with influential people);
- difficulty of sustaining participation;
- heterogeneity of the community (conflict resolution);
- local participation in outsiders' programmes;
- seasonal variations; and
- groupism, castism, gender inequalities, vested interests.

Feedback

The absence of feedback about the constraints perceived by community members themselves about the PRA process is another challenge, given the philosophy of the approach. The available literature does not contain any feedback

127

from different community members of what PRA is all about or how it compares with other existing approaches to problem analysis, problem-solving and decisionmaking. The question 'whose perception counts?' needs to be raised in this context and more community analysis of the perceived challenges, and their possible solutions, to be encouraged by PRA facilitators.

Another major challenge at the community level is how to sustain a network of community-based PRA facilitators. This challenge is addressed in the next section on the organizational challenges facing PRA because such community-based networks are likely to be initiated by external development organizations using the PRA approach.

Institutional development

What PRA can do in terms of institutional development is to create the realization that participation is about the building of local institutions managing resources according to their own rules, as opposed to local contributions in kind or in cash, to outsiders' programmes. Beyond that, it can create and sustain fora for collective discussion, analysis and decisionmaking, as well as for subsequent action. However, PRA does not provide many of the other skills necessary for the implementation of development activities such as financial management, for example.

The challenge now is to reflect on, document and share what contribution PRA has actually made to institutional development, as defined above. If this is not done, PRA runs the risk of being perceived (and used) mainly as a tool for project planning, monitoring and evaluation.

Challenges facing PRA at the organizational level

Hierarchical organizational cultures

The message still seems to be that PRA is something for the field (communities) and does not apply to the organizations initiating it themselves (Leurs, 1995). Howes and Roche (1995) have shown that PRA can also be useful for organizational appraisal, although many of its methods have their limitations in this context. The challenge is therefore to experiment with various forms of participatory organizational appraisal.

On the other hand, where PRA has been taken seriously in the organizational context, it can lead to perceived confusion over levels and lines of authority (Leurs, 1995). Perhaps the biggest challenge facing PRA at this level is the hierarchical organizational culture which is still so pervasive in non-governmental (including aid-funded projects) as well as government organizations. PRA can help to change this indirectly, through the changes in attitudes and behaviour that exposure to fieldwork helps to bring about (Chambers and Blackburn, 1996).

A major challenge here, however, is that senior staff often only have time for short familiarization training. Even when this involves field visits, their staff and community members will often revert to the pre-PRA deferential behaviour, while they themselves will revert to theirs (i.e. making speeches exhorting others to do certain things).

Rigidity in government organizations

The organizational challenges facing PRA are particularly severe in the case of government organizations. Staff-recruitment criteria, based on age, qualifications and years of experience, do not take account of the all-important attitudinal and behavioural characteristics of the candidates. Low salary scales also make it difficult to attract good candidates (Kar and Backhaus, 1994). Similar promotional criteria provide no incentive to work overtime promoting participatory approaches (Kar and Backhaus, 1994), and high rates of staff turnover (transfers) make it difficult to build the intra-organizational and community relationships required for quality PRA work (Kar and Backhaus, 1994).

Training the numbers of staff involved in large organizations also presents a major challenge, given the scarcity of good PRA trainers (Kar and Backhaus, 1994). Different levels of understanding, between technical and non-technical staff, and between different levels of staff, represent another challenge (Leurs, 1994). Lack of sharing of experience between staff further compounds the problem (Leurs 1995), as does lack of inter-organizational cooperation.

A final major challenge at the organizational level is how to build up and sustain a network of community-based PRA facilitators. To the best of the author's knowledge, there is, as yet, almost no literature about how such facilitators have been or should be selected, whether and how their training and support has or should differ from project-based PRA facilitators, whether and by whom they should be remunerated, what their relationship has or should be with the communities where they work, as well as with external development organizations, how this should change as time goes by, and according to what kinds of criteria.

Challenges facing PRA at the project/programme level

Whose project?

Despite its many limitations (Cernea, 1991), the project/programme remains the dominant vehicle for development assistance or intervention, depending upon one's point of view, despite the recent emphasis on sectoral and policy development. The major reason for the project/programme approach is the need for development-funding agencies to account to their political authorities for monies spent. Projects and programmes provide a framework for accountability, and a mechanism for influence and control over development policy and practice in other countries. They also provide a way for funding agencies to recycle much of their development funding back into their own economies through the use of development agencies from their own country.

Targets and accountability

The continuing emphasis on financial and physical targets within short-term time frames (3–5 years) in development projects and programmes can be explained by bilateral donors' need for political accountability. Financial and physical targets are easier to measure and monitor. They are also less threatening politically. The short time horizons are similarly, explained by the short-term nature of the political (electoral) cycle, with its consequent changes in accountability requirements.

Projects and programmes are attractive instruments to development agencies for similar reasons, i.e. control and upwards accountability. Moreover, agencies need to apply and legitimize the professional education and training which their staff have received, in project or programme packages which they design, implement, manage, monitor and evaluate (either themselves or through the project beneficiaries). These needs have continued to override a growing realization amongst agency staff that development is an ongoing process with uncertain outcomes, as opposed to a planned product, which has to be owned and controlled locally.

Reversals

This realization has been reflected in the shift from blueprint to process projects, a shift in which RRA and PRA have played an important part (Jamieson, 1987). Such projects have recognized the need for greater flexibility required in development work. They have not, however, changed the fundamental organizing principles of funding (power) and control (accountability). PRA does challenge both of these principles, because it calls for reversals of accountability and, ultimately, power. It has, however, been much more effective at bringing about reversals of professional knowledge than it has been in shifting the balance of power (funding) and accountability (control).

The fundamental challenge facing PRA at the development-project and -programme level is, therefore, about access to and control over funding and the power inequalities which this generates.

Funding

It is almost always the service providers, whether government or NGO, that are funded in the development project or programme context, as opposed to the users. Even where users are subsidized, the subsidy is usually tied to the provision of certain services which the funding agency has determined as being necessary. In this situation the funding agency and providers have all the power to determine and insist on the agendas, the priorities and the ways of working. This can happen in many subtle ways, even with approaches such as PRA.

Although PRA has the potential to raise awareness within both the community and the development organization, and to identify mutually acceptable priorities and agendas for work, thereby building a more equal partnership between them, the temptation for the funding organization will be to use PRA to collect information for its own planning monitoring/evaluation purposes, an approach sometimes referred to as information-mining (Wright 1995). The latter use of PRA has been observed to be more common than the former (Absalom 1995, Mwayaya and Johnson, 1994).

130

The solution is to change the way in which development work at the community level is funded. The users/beneficiaries of development programmes and projects, whether both individuals or collective organizations, should receive funding, which they can then use to pay for development services provided by government, NGOs and the private sector. Such a system has already been tried and shown to work (Okurut, 1995; Arube-Wani and Kafuko, 1994).

PRA could be used to help development-funding agencies identify relative needs, both within and between communities, as perceived by different community members. As such, external funding agencies would remain able to reflect their political agendas in terms of poverty alleviation, greater gender equality and so on through their distribution of funds. It would, however, be the beneficiaries of these funds who would decide what this money should be spent on and who should be asked to provide the associated services required.

Funding agencies would, no doubt, still keep the right to demand accountability for the spending of their monies. If such accountability could be framed in terms of long-term process objectives, however, excluding how things should be done and who should do them (the agenda which the development agencies have controlled so far), this would represent a major advance.

The question this raises is whether PRA has the potential to bring about such reversals amongst agency staff, especially the senior personnel of large government bodies and NGOs, that they will press funding agencies for direct release of monies to community members and organizations identified by them as suitable beneficiaries.

Challenges facing PRA at the policy level

Most PRA experience to date has been at the micro, i.e. project or programme, level, usually in small rural communities. PRA is, however, being increasingly used at the macro level by governments, aid agencies and NGOs for policy formulation and analysis purposes. This is in response to the growing realization that one of the major constraints facing micro-level PRA work is that it often conflicts with the wider policy environment, e.g. the country and sector reviews and priorities of aid agencies and northern NGOs, or the public-expenditure reviews and allocation formulae of governments.

The logic and spirit of PRA, if taken seriously, demands that such an approach should contribute to information-gathering, analysis and decision-making for development at all levels. Tamang (1994) has reviewed the limited experience with RRA/PRA for policy research and concludes that the current major challenges at this level are as follows:

- generalizing (synthesizing) the information generated by a large number of village level PRAs;
- sampling; the PRA approach tends to emphasize the importance of identifying poor, marginalized and vulnerable people and giving them a voice, as opposed to seeking maximum representation;
- combining PRA with existing secondary information;
- the quantitative bias of many researchers and end-users of policy research;
- the lack of local contextual understanding by external researchers;
- changing attitudes and behaviour; and

131

- trustworthiness of PRA findings compared to those of other methodological approaches (various references).

These challenges are internal to the process of using PRA for policy-formulation purposes. There are, however, wider contextual challenges, the most important of which is probably the continuing centralization of power in terms of funding, decisionmaking and policy formulation.

For PRA to become more than just another source of information and knowledge for policy formulation (a major achievement in itself), the entire structure and distribution of political power would have to change. This will probably only happen as a result of a gradual and long-term process of change from the bottom up. PRA can contribute to such an outcome most effectively if it is used as part of a process of participatory development at all the levels described above. That requires the application of PRA principles, and perhaps some methods, to development organizations and donors, as well as projects. It also requires the widespread introduction, acceptance and ongoing practice of PRA principles and methods in communities all over the countries concerned.

The use of PRA in development projects and programmes (many of which do not even aim to change existing power relationships at the community level, let alone at higher levels) will only contribute to policy making in so far as such projects and programmes themselves influence the policy formulation process.

Challenges facing PRA at the donor level

Accountability

Most PRA takes place within the project context, where project staff, including PRA facilitators, are accountable to the scheme rather than to the communities which they serve. The project is, similarly, answerable to the implementing organization, which in turn answers to the government and the donors. Lying behind the question of accountability is the question of control (power), and behind that is the question of who pays. Moving from upwards to downwards accountability is, therefore, a question of shifting control over resources to the community.

In practice, however, the shift described above does not take place because the external agency has its own development agenda which is different to that of the various sections of the community.

Upwards acountability, as a system, is also reinforced by other parallel donor requirements. Reporting needs, for example, are set by those who pay the piper to play their tune: donors continue to determine what is worthy of being reported, and how. Donors also continue to prefer output as opposed to process orientation. Physical development targets are much easier to account for than intangible processes of self and collective development.

Sectoral orientation

Organizations are geared to offer what their staff are able to provide. The disciplinary education and training of development staff converts, therefore, into corresponding sectoral approaches to development and a top-down generation of priorities.

Conclusions

There are four key challenges to PRA, which cross-cut all the above-mentioned levels, at which PRA operates. These are inequalities in power, knowledge, time/money or the access to these and cultural differences.

Power

The key elements to power in development are influence, authority and decisionmaking over other people, and access to, control or ownership of money and other assets such as land and animals. Although PRA inherently challenges many existing power structures at all the levels identified in this chapter, it may not necessarily change them.

Existing social, economic, political and cultural relations within communities and between communities and government or NGOs are often highly resistant to change, precisely because they serve the interests of those who play a key role in defining and maintaining these relations. The same applies to the current hierarchical procedures, structures and relations within and between various government and non-governmental organizations, from the community level upwards. The language itself reflects this hierarchical thinking and practice; similarly, most individuals, communities, projects and organizations fear change because of the potential for conflict, as well as the possible attendant loss of power, which this involves.

PRA has undoubtedly changed the attitudes of many of its practitioners, making the approach to their work less power oriented. The extent to which the participatory procedure has significantly changed existing power relationships within the communities where it has been practised, or within the organizations, government or NGO, which have been practising, promoting or supporting it, is more difficult to assess given the newness of the approach. Evidence is accumulating, however, to indicate that the consistent application of PRA over time can, and is likely to, change power relations significantly (see, for example, Blackburn and de Toma, Chapter 6, this volume; Scoones and Thompson, 1994; Welbourne, 1993).

Knowledge

Those with less power also tend to have less access to knowledge and information or less power in defining what sorts of knowledge and information are useful in development. Such relative ignorance makes them objects rather than subjects of development. Many in this position also accept the superiority of the knowledge of those in more powerful situations, while many of the latter feel confident about the superiority of their own knowledge (e.g. Chambers, 1993).

The biggest contribution of PRA to date may have been to challenge the superiority of professional (development worker) knowledge over that of the non-professional (indigenous/community), in the minds of many of the

133

development professionals who are using a PRA approach. There is, however, much less evidence about the extent to which PRA has increased the self-confidence of community members in their knowledge, particularly in relation to that of professional outsider knowledge.

Cultural differences

Culture is here defined to mean all the ideas, beliefs, values and traditions that guide people in their relations with others. These can be different, often conflicting, between the various stakeholders of any PRA process.

In particular, those initiating PRA often value individual initiative and grassroots action. Such values may be completely opposed to those practised in the receiving culture, even amongst sections of it which outside development professionals regard as oppressed. Developing skills in cross-cultural communication is, therefore, a key challenge for PRA. Although visualization makes this process more participatory, it is still subject to cultural misinterpretation.

PRA facilitators should, according to the principles of PRA itself, be humble about the extent of their knowledge and understanding of the communities where they facilitate such a process, remembering that they remain outsiders. In practice, however, the perceived advantages of PRA over other approaches has, in the author's opinion, sometimes led to exaggerated claims about the learning and understanding achieved (on both sides).

Time and money

This is a key issue for all the stakeholders in the PRA process. PRA is a time-intensive process. Although PRA is poverty and gender sensitive, as well as sensitive to local time preferences and availability, those with the least amount of free time (e.g. the poorest, particularly women) are still likely to be left out of the public forums where much PRA activity (analysis and decision-making) is carried out.

Much of the participation in PRA may also result from the expected benefits from the organization or project initiating the process. Once again, however, those most in a position to capture such benefits are usually not those for whom they were intended.

Finally, many donors and development organizations remain to be convinced that participation pays. Although there have been studies of the long-term economic benefits of a participatory approach (Cernea, 1991), no one has as yet looked at the costs and benefits of participation through the whole life-cycle of a project.

The task ahead is immense. For PRA to be really effective, further reversals of power, such as control over funding, decisionmaking and analysis, will be necessary, not only at the community levels but, perhaps even more importantly, at the agency, donor, and policy levels.

19

Reflections and Recommendations on Scaling-up and Organizational Change

IDS WORKSHOP

The lessons learned from the diverse cases presented in parts 1 and 2 about the dangers and optimal conditions for scaling-up, and the requirements needed for better practice in the future, are in many ways strikingly similar. Chapter 19 presents a synthesis of the discusssions held on scaling-up and organizational change[1] at the IDS Workshop held in May 1996. For practitioners and policymakers considering a scaling-up strategy, this chapter is highly recommended. It summarises key lessons and recommendations from the combined efforts of some of the most experienced and knowledgeable people in this field.

The chapter begins by considering three enabling conditions which the workshop participants agreed are needed to ensure maximum success in the scaling-up of participatory approaches: a policy context in which democratization and decentralization are genuinely embraced as necessary governance reforms; the support of high-level government figures; and the existence of an in-country critical mass of people with training experience. Certain dangers of rapid scaling-up are then pinpointed, notably routinization, duplication and abuse in the application of PRA and related methodologies. Recommendations are, consequently, made for quality PRA training and field practice to avoid the poor standards noted in some scaling-up experiences. The need to overcome cascade training, and to include transparency as a general principle in PRA practice, as well as the honouring of commitments, and the production of user-friendly documentation and other ways of recording experience, are all explored. Chapter 19 ends with a list of recommended actions, agreed upon by the workshop participants, for communities and local groups, NGOs and donors involved in the implementation of participatory projects.

Enabling conditions for scaling-up

Decentralization

Decentralization can provide a policy context in which participatory approaches are more likely to spread. It is now a policy priority for governments seeking new ways of reducing public expenditure. Decentralization can take many forms (Manor, 1995), and is not necessarily democratic nor participatory. Local authorities to whom a range of powers have been devolved, in the fields of finance, policy design, and resource management, for example, can choose to accumulate rather than share power with those who live inside local authority boundaries.

In some cases, however, central governments are encouraging local authorities to use PRA and related methodologies to involve local people in research, planning and resource-management activities that are part of the process of implementing democratic decentralization. In Bolivia (Chapter 6, this volume), NGOs have started training municipal authorities in PRA and related approaches to assist in the implementation of the country's most radical decentralization law to date, the Law of Popular Participation. In Uganda, a range of administrative powers has been devolved to the parish level, and participatory approaches are also being used to assist in the decentralization process (pers. com., Ben Osuga). Similar changes are taking place in India, the Philippines, Colombia and Mexico. The scaling-down of government may be one of the keys to the scaling-up of participatory approaches.

High-level government support

Evidence suggests that for participatory approaches to scale-up, support in the higher echelons of government is indispensable. The PRA take-off that took place in India from 1990–91 onwards, for example, would not have been possible without the involvement of senior government staff from the very beginning. PRA has now become a multi-institutional, multi-sectoral phenomenon in many parts of India. There has been movement up, down and across.

One strategy for making PRA 'official' is to introduce the approach into formal bureaucratic training programmes as has occurred, again, in some Indian states, where government officials have since commented that they wished they had been trained in PRA from the start of their careers. It is more difficult to train senior officials, given the constraints on their time. Even short field exposures can be difficult to organize; nevertheless, taking senior people into the field, even for just half a day to witness a mapping, can have a dramatic effect. Pressure must be maintained. People will tend to settle back into non-participatory office routine once the enthusiasm is past.

The challenge is to make prolonged periods in the field, or successive short visits, integral to government staff-training programmes at all levels. World Bank executives have moved in this direction recently by issuing recommendations for Bank staff to spend time in villages as part of their training programmes.

> Government people can easily play PRA, but are they willing to make the sacrifices to change themselves?
>
> *IDS Workshop participant, May 1996*

In-country critical mass of people with training experience

Decentralization and high-level government support are not sufficient enabling conditions on their own for scaling-up to proceed, let alone succeed. More fundamental is an in-country critical mass of experienced individuals capable of ensuring and maintaining quality in PRA training and practice. Such expertise is likely to come initially mainly from the NGO sector, particularly from people who have worked in community development and have been influenced by previous and/or parallel currents of participatory research and action. Such people are likely to be very responsive to PRA because they will already have been imbued by a participatory working culture. In countries in which such an NGO culture does not exist, or is marginal, suitable trainers in sufficient numbers are unlikely to be found. It is questionable whether scaling-up, on whatever scale, should even be attempted in such a setting.

Dangers of rapid scaling-up for PRA practice

Routinization

Experience shows that when done *en masse*, PRA becomes routinized. When the same group is required to facilitate one PRA after another over a substantial period of time, the initial enthusiasm wanes. Tired facilitators begin to direct the PRA process, often unconsciously, and highlight those aspects of village or urban reality that have already become apparent in other localities. The approach can then become little more than a 'quick and dirty toolkit' to kick-start predefined projects.

Too many standardized outputs are a sure sign that the scaling-up process is going badly wrong. Local realities are too complex, multi-dimensional and situation-specific to be uniform across entire regions (Corwall and Fleming, 1995, Thompson and Scoones, 1994).

Duplication

It is not uncommon for two or more development organizations to facilitate PRAs in the same village or urban district at different times. Unnecessary duplication may be an important cause of the participatory fatigue now being observed among villagers, and the urban poor, in some parts of the world (Richards, 1995). In areas where PRAs have already been facilitated by NGOs, governments are strongly advised not to repeat the process. It is wise, also, for NGOs operating in the same area to be kept informed about each other's activities, and to coordinate these more closely.

Abuse

There has been much abuse of PRA by outsiders keen only to extract information quickly and use it for their own purposes. Such practice is unethical because local people are brought into a process in which expectations are raised, and then frustrated, if no action or follow-up results. PRA should not be used purely for research purposes unless researchers are completely transparent about what they are doing. Development organizations which request PRA training must do their best to support, if requested to do so, the actions that local people decide on in the communities where field practice takes place.

PRA abuse is likely to increase when a scaling-up strategy is launched. When PRA is scaled up quickly, as in the case of Indonesia (Chapter 5, this volume), there is a danger that roles are wrongly reversed: a process which is supposed to be directed by local people with outside support ends up being directed by outside organizations with the support of local people.

Taking 'community' for granted

Some of those who practise or promote PRA speak of the 'community' as some kind of ideal cohesive unit which outsiders can penetrate and empower. It cannot be assumed that poor people living in rural or urban areas, in tightly-knit villages and districts, or more spread out, will move fast in response to a participatory stimulus, producing participatory plans on demand, as it were. Dramatic differences in wealth, status, gender, ethnicity, race and education within communities are more often the norm than the exception (Cornwall and Fleming, 1995; Mosse, 1993; Mosse *et al.*, 1995; Scoones and Thompson, 1994; Welbourn, 1993). Different groups in the same locality perceive and (re)construct different realities over time.

PRA should never be thought of as a quick fix. At best it is a solid foundation on which to build what cannot but be a long and often arduous process (chapters 11 and 13, this volume; Richards, 1995).

Recommendations for quality PRA training and field practice

Quality training

High-quality training is a core component of the process of institutionalizing a participatory approach. The demand for good PRA trainers has far exceeded the supply. In consequence, some trainers have put themselves forward who have not had the opportunity for exposure to PRA field experience or philosophy. Poor PRA training and practice risks discrediting the approach and other related methodologies. The IDS workshop participants called on donors to support more South–South training workshops to maintain the high standards of innovation and ongoing learning that have characterized PRA training since the beginning. It was also suggested that good trainers be released from other duties so that they can commit themselves full-time to training activities. 'One-off' trainings were also identified as leading to low-quality PRA practice over time. Some have recommended that trainers and training institutions only be employed by organizations or programmes with long-term commitments in order to guarantee adequate follow-up and review. At the same time, the selection of trainers should as far as possible be based on consultation and on their ability to follow up the processes their training will have set in motion.[2]

As PRA has scaled up, the composition of trainees has changed from a relatively narrow range of people (e.g. agricultural extensionists) to professionals of all kinds and all levels. This has been a major challenge for PRA trainers, in particular when addressing the question of behaviour and attitudes. Short training cycles cannot hope to change deep-set behaviour and attitudes. PRA trainers need more sophisticated tools to explore this delicate domain. One suggestion is for specific training modules and exercises to be developed from the work of behavioural psychologists.

The growth of cascading workshops to speed up training was identified as a disturbing by-product of scaling-up. By cascading workshops is meant a process in which a small group of seasoned trainers begin by training people who subsequently become trainers themselves of yet more future trainers, and so on. Quality can be maintained in such workshops only if trainees are allowed to build up enough experience to become good trainers in their own right. Trainees do not always spend time in the field as part of their training, however (see Chapter 5, this volume), and quality can seriously suffer as result.

PRA has been criticized by anthropologists and practitioners of other currents of participatory research for being too rapid and project focused (Chauvau, 1994; Mosse, 1995; Cornwall and Fleming, 1995). Speeding it up even more is neither possible nor desirable. Training should neither be rushed nor mass produced. Participation takes time. Experience in India (see box below) and elsewhere shows that many of the problems associated with training can

---

Box 19.1:   WIN-WIN training in Uttar Pradesh, India

The idea of a WIN-WIN training is that villagers trained in PRA tools and processes then function as co-trainers for outsiders who want to learn about village and rural conditions. Outsiders pay the villagers for the training, and villagers decide on the use of the money.

One such training was conducted in Uttar Pradesh in a village called Panahpur near Shahjahanpur for staff from CARE, OXFAM, SCF, Sabhagi Shikshan Kendra and PRADAN. Participants learnt not only how to apply the tools of PRA, they also took part in many village activities. They endured the cold, slept on the floor, fetched their own water ... As one of them remarked at the end of the training session: 'I thought that rooms and chairs and tables were necessary for running a training session. Now I know that you can do it under a tree, under a tent, or on a threshing floor'.

The village trainers read out on the last day the expenses that had been incurred so that everyone knew how much money had been spent from the fees collected. Money was left over after all the costs had been met. The farmer trainers in consultation with other people in the village agreed that some of this money would be spent to install a drinking-water hand pump on a public location near the main road. In the height of the summer months of May and June every passer-by on the road drank from this pump and was vocal in their appreciation of the farmers' group.

Things did not stop here. When the Government Irrigation Department heard of the effort of the five villages in the area in desilting the local canal, an activity considered high priority in the early PRAs conducted in the area, they took their responsibility of the annual cleaning of the canal more seriously. So, too, did the contractor who was awarded the work. Together they desilted the canal further. Local people say that they have not seen the canal so deep in the past 20 years! So there have been some knock-on effects on the large system.

---

be resolved by turning villagers into trainers. This form of training has been called 'Win-Win' because villagers gain (in cash as well as experience) as much as outside trainees.

Specific recommendations for training practice agreed upon at the IDS workshop were to:

- always include fieldwork in any PRA training, especially if it is to be cascaded;
- place as much emphasis (or more) on exploring behaviour and attitudes as on learning the methods of the approach;
- develop multiple approaches to training and familiarization workshops, tailored to fit the needs and opportunities of each sort of organization and context;
- integrate community action and institutional development concerns. PRA may have begun as an appraisal methodology but now includes aspects of project/programme planning, implementation, and monitoring and evaluation. It is as much concerned with *action* as it is with *appraisal*, and this must be reflected in the training.

Transparency in the field

Transparency has long been a concern of seasoned PRA practitioners. When outsiders first approach a community or group with the intention of setting in motion a PRA process, it is imperative they be open regarding their motives and expected outcomes, not only to the community itself but also to any collaborating organizations (Edwards, 1994). There are strong ethical reasons why transparency is crucial. Communities and local groups may see PRA as leading to immediate material benefits and ongoing external support, but this is often not part of the facilitating organization's agenda.

Local people must be clearly informed of what they can and cannot expect from the time the initial contacts are made. If there has been no previous relationship with the outsiders who wish to facilitate the PRA, local inhabitants will need time to reflect and come to their own conclusion about whether or not they wish to proceed. They will need as much information as possible in order to make the appropriate decision. There is nothing more heartbreaking than a rushed PRA in which a local group is carried on a wave of enthusiasm, expecting benefits which will never arrive.

Honouring commitments

In the heat of PRA, it is common that outsiders will make commitments which they find they cannot honour once the PRA is over, and office reality sets in once again. Those agencies responsible for facilitating PRAs should be very clear what they can commit themselves to before engaging with a local group. It is helpful to have possible commitments planned, costed, and agreed upon *before* the first contacts are made. Some in Vietnam enter into formal contracts with communities about what each party will do and by when.

Documentation and other ways of recording experience

Local people should be encouraged to participate, not just in the methods of PRA, but also in any writing that takes place during the exercise, or in the production of video, audio tapes, art or any other medium which captures the experience. The visuals from the methods themselves should be left with the community in good condition. A specific recommendation from experience in Bolivia is to cover the papers on which diagrams have been drawn with plastic so that they can be used in schools as educational material and/or in future community- and regional-planning meetings.

Courtesy requires that support organizations also leave a written document of the PRA process with the community or groups concerned, if possible as soon as the process ends.

Too much good PRA does not get documented. The ideal is to have a 'scribe' who is part of the PRA field team, but whose sole role is to gather up the evidence and write it up as the process unfolds. It is recommended that donor agencies make a trained 'scribe' part of their funding criteria for PRA. Well-presented documents can be invaluable to communities when it comes to negotiating with support agencies, especially government staff who value such resources very highly. It is also important to ensure that several copies of the document are produced and passed on to the relevant agencies, particularly when scaling-up is being envisaged.

After the initial PRAs, support organizations should build on the analytical and documentation skills of community-resource people. Involving the local inhabitants in the production of documentation can help ensure that participation does not stop at the appraisal stage. It is also part of the broader process of local institutional development which is indispensable to long-term empowerment.

Recommended actions for communities and local groups, NGOs and donors

Communities and groups on the receiving end of participatory interventions

(1) Ensure that outside agencies keen to implement participatory projects pay proper respect to existing local knowledge and community/group-management systems.
(2) Demand that externally funded projects include a pre-project preparatory period to help recover or build anew local confidence and capacity.
(3) Negotiate from the outset with donors, support organizations and/or government as to the content, time scale and resources needed to implement a project.
(4) Insist to implementing agency and donors that 'participation' and 'empowerment' also mean (i) participating in decisionmaking processes and (ii) acquiring greater control of project resources (power); at the very least, establish with the implementing agency a corpus fund at the community/group level to increase security and potential for project success.

(5) Press for the training in PRA and/or related methodologies of village (or urban district) analysts/facilitators to enable (i) more local analysis without the need for outside intervention, and (ii) local people to offer their training skills, for a suitable fee, in PRA and/or related methodologies to outside trainees.

NGOs engaged in implementing participatory projects and programmes

(1) Seek alternative sources of income (self-generated if possible) to avoid over-dependence on donors.
(2) Avoid criticism by encouraging social audits by donors, performance evaluations by communities and local groups, and by continuously improving technical and managerial competence.
(3) Support, strengthen and delegate to community-based organizations from the outset of a project; never plan to stay.
(4) Network with other NGOs, government and academic institutions etc. to keep up to date with the latest developments in participatory methodology and process.
(5) Collaborate with other NGOs in the project area to avoid duplication of activities.
(6) Devote more resources to learning about the way government works, how policies are formulated, and how inter-organizational links can be made, especially if scaling-up is on the agenda.

Donors engaged in supporting the implementation of participatory programmes and projects

(1) Provide resources and allow time for a preproject-preparation period to help communities and local groups undertake thorough local analyses, using PRA and/or related methodologies, before committing themselves to a programme/project.
(2) Inform 'beneficiaries'' representatives of the donor(s)' agenda(s): philosophy, range of expertise, available resources, constraints, etc.
(3) Ensure that intended beneficiaries participate in the design of the programme/project, and that participatory monitoring and evaluation procedures include the beneficiaries' evaluations of the performance of implementing agencies.
(4) Allow for the time and flexibility which participatory processes require. Long-term project commitment (e.g. ten years) is preferable. This implies reducing project expenditure in its early phases. Participatory programmes/projects need time more than they need money.
(5) Demand that NGOs and other implementing agencies involve the beneficiaries in establishing locally relevant indicators of process performance.
(6) Encourage experimentation with systems of downwards accountability and flexible budgeting.
(7) Encourage social audits of NGOs and other organizations which receive donor funding.

(8) When PRAs have been done, demand of the facilitating organization(s) that the end product of a PRA process be made available to people in communities and local groups in the local vernacular language.

PRA could turn out to be an option to save their faces (the donors). Who are we empowering?

IDS Workshop participant, May 1996

Recommended actions for those involved in shifting organizations to more people-centred and participatory approaches[4]

Catalysing phase

Be prepared to take risks and suffer the consequences (scorn, marginalization, jealousy) if institutional resistance is strong. Begin by building alliances with like-minded people within the organization. Choose strategic moments to put participation on the agenda – media events, governing council meetings, policy reviews, the arrival (or departure) of top staff, etc. Bring out any contradictions in existing mission statements, rules and procedures, to justify mainstreaming participatory approaches. Gradually move 'participation' from periphery to core activities, e.g. from lunchtime meetings and weekend events to official working time. Beware, however, of saboteurs, even like-minded individuals who at key moments feel too threatened by the implications of their personal involvement in the process of change.

Gradually create the conditions for the realization of a need for change, by raising, for example, questions about the rationale for development work, or encouraging surveys of community perceptions about agency performance. Encourage or directly facilititate in-house appraisals by people at different levels within the organization, as well as across levels, in a non-threatening, dialogical way. Encourage face-to-face interaction – avoid at all costs memo wars – and informal networking. Draw on the support of individuals in organizations which are one step ahead in the process of change.

Spreading and reflection phase

Hand over the process of change to those within the organization whose job it is (personnel officers, training officers etc.) Secure visible and explicit support from top and middle managers for change. Using participatory tools whenever possible, promote the internalization, personal and institutional, of a people-centred and participatory philosophy and praxis. Among the specific changes (see Chapter 20 for more detail) required are: appropriate reward systems; appropriate resource allocation; autonomy and freedom to experiment and make mistakes and learn from them; linking individual and professional aspirations to institutional mission statements which refer to participatory approaches; valuing cultural and gender diversity in processes of decisionmaking; redesigning and restructuring departments and organizational procedures.

Build on incremental success through a continuous, progressive process of coalition-building within and across organizations. Encourage learning workshops, inviting other organizations to share their experience. Consider establishing a code of conduct to determine precisely what is and what is not participatory.

20

Towards a Learning Organization: making developmental agencies more participatory from the inside

IDS WORKSHOP

It has been suggested elsewhere in this volume (see, for example, chapters 14, 16 and 19) that the kind of organization best able to adapt to the requirements of implementing and sustaining a participatory approach in its programmes or projects can be defined as a learning organization. As a management concept, the learning organization has been applied principally to the world of business (Senge, 1990), but is now gaining ground among development academics and practitioners (Thompson, 1995; chapters 14 and 16, this volume). It has long been a concern that development organizations, and NGOs in particular, often lack the management tools to put into practice what they preach. As more and more development organizations are expected to implement 'participatory' projects in response to the recent boom in such methodologies, it is emerging that these bodies' internal systems, structures, procedures, and values more generally, are far from participatory.

Understanding the issue

The tendency for development organizations wishing to go participatory has been to focus immediately on the operational dimensions of participatory projects (participation *out there)* rather than consider the internal organizational changes that such projects require in order to succeed (participation *in here)* (see chapters 4, 5, 12 and 14, this volume). A common strategy, particularly in the case of large public institutions, has been to start by requesting PRA training, usually from foreign consultants, and hope that participation will unfold as a result. The pitfalls of such an approach have been many. PRA is stuck on to existing programmes as an appendage. The priorities thrown up thereafter by PRAs often contradict those already fixed by the programme, and the organization may be unable or unwilling to make the necessary changes. Resistance by those in comfortable, hierarchically established positions leads to friction, and field staff, who are often the only people to receive training, can easily become disillusioned. The quality of PRA then drops as staff begin to apply the approach mechanistically, without the creative enthusiasm needed to make a real difference (see Chapter 9, this volume).

The consensus at the IDS workshop was that 'going participatory' means moving beyond PRA and related methodologies as the central concern of implementing a more participatory form of development, and exploring in greater depth questions of organizational development without which methodologies such as PRA are unlikely to have a lasting impact. Below are set out the characteristics of the kind of organizational development which the IDS workshop participants considered important to facilitate an effective institutionalization of participatory approaches. They have been grouped under three subheadings: personal skills and attributes, procedures, and systems and structures.

Personal skills and attributes

The ability to listen and engage in dialogue and mutual learning

The first skill needed to begin to build a learning organization is the ability to listen, and in particular to recognize that other people's perceptions are usually different, though no less valid, than one's own.

The creation of a mutually enabling environment in which people are encouraged to think and learn together requires facilitation as well as listening skills. Not everybody has the personality to be a good facilitator, however. Some prefer more passive roles, while others enjoy activity that does not necessarily involve facilitation.

Good facilitation brings out the particular skills of each person. At the same time, it brings individuals together in complementary roles. The enthusiast may need to be tempered by a more cautious or reserved person who, in turn, may need to be pushed now and again. Recognizing complementary attributes in others can have a synergic effect, helping to build effective teams. People learn faster when they feel part of a group which is learning together.

Reflexivity

Individuals who are part of a learning organization must be open and willing to change. Such an attitude requires a high degree of critical self-awareness, as well as a capacity for self-evaluation, i.e. the recognition of one's own limits and the ability and willingness to embrace error. The latter is perhaps the most difficult personal attribute to develop. Professional insecurity and/or career pressures usually lead people to hide or minimize the errors they commit, be they of judgement or of action. Openly to admit one's errors takes some courage. It can be liberating, however, and lead to improved professional relationships. Others are made to feel comfortable that they are not alone in making mistakes. They also recognize the courage needed to admit an error, and are eventually more likely to be open about their own errors.

Capacity for vision

Another personal attribute, perhaps less easy to define, is the capacity for vision. This is particularly important when people are engaged in participatory projects – there has to be an awareness of what participation is for and where it is leading. Part of such awareness is the recognition that one of

146

the goals of such a project is to make oneself redundant, to 'hand over the stick' to local people once they have gained the core competencies needed to manage their own projects. It is not easy to have a vision of oneself as 'no longer there', but there can be no greater achievement than to depart in the knowledge that local institutions are now strong enough to manage projects on their own.

The joint production of mission statements can help articulate such vision. It also leads to a 'bonding' of individuals into a team.

Procedures

Moving from product to process

Donors and governments (see chapters 9 and 15, this volume) remain unwilling to let go of the quantifiable product, usually a physical target, as the most appropriate measure of project success. Participatory initiatives demand, however, a much greater appreciation of process and capacity-building as relevant qualitative indicators of success.

Emphasizing process implies being willing to change the time scale of a project. A prolonged pre-project preparatory period may be necessary to allow local institutions to grow. Process also implies allowing local people to define their own indicators and criteria for success, which may differ substantially from those seen as relevant by donors and implementing agencies. Finally, encouraging local people to establish their own indicators implies that they be actively involved in a project from the design stage. As far as possible, the proposed beneficiaries must feel they own the project, that it is, in effect, their product. How this can begin to be achieved is discussed below.

New incentive mechanisms to reward 'participatory' behaviour in-house as well as in the field

Project managers must be able to identify and reward staff for displaying certain attitudes and behaviours which make participation work better in practice.

Particularly worthy of reward are some of the personal attributes outlined above, namely:

- *tolerance and mutual respect* – the willingness to accept and value that the perceptions of others may not agree with one's own;
- *openness and adaptability* – the willingness to talk about mistakes and to embrace change; and
- *wisdom* – acknowledging that experience, and in particular the development of initiative in the field, i.e. methodological experimentation and innovation, should be encouraged as it creates opportunities for learning.

The question, however, is not so much *what* should be rewarded as much as *how*. In certain small, tightly-knit organizations, e.g. of a religious kind, belief or faith may be sufficient to keep individuals motivated to sustain a participatory ethic. In most organizations, however, a system of material and professional rewards and incentives, e.g. bonuses, privileges, promotion, etc., is needed if people are to be encouraged to adopt a more participatory style. Exactly what these incentives will be, and how they are to work in practice, will largely depend on the specific institutional culture of the organization in question. In all cases, however, it is recommended that the incentive system be devised in consultation with every category of employee. One way to do this is to conduct in-house participatory appraisals. Once a group has been trained in PRA, for example, it can practice the approach as part of an internal assessment before applying it in the field. This kind of organizational appraisal has been attempted elsewhere with some success (Howes and Roche, 1995; Ben Osuga pers. com.).

Multiple feedback mechanisms

Different departments within an organization often guard information from each other rather than share it. Making information easy and fun to share is essential to inter- and intra-unit learning and trust. Too much information, however, can have a counterproductive effect, as no one will have enough time to digest it. Hence the importance of original presentations, and summary reports that contain only the most pressing issues.

Documenting and presenting experience, particularly that from the field, helps to build up a rich institutional memory, and is an important part of the learning process of an organization. Creative ways of documenting field experience should be encouraged. Most organizations still rely on the bland report, which nobody reads, unless absolutely required to do so. If feedback is to contribute to planning processes, it must draw attention and excite. The use of videos, often made by project beneficiaries themselves, has become increasingly popular as a way of reporting experience. In some cases, local people have been encouraged to make their own presentations in agency offices, using PRA methods (Chambers and Blackburn, 1996). With the staggering developments in the world of computer software and CD Roms, it is possible to envisage a future in which presentations will combine text, image and sound. The day academics move in that direction should prove exciting: impenetrable texts will hopefully become more accessible to more people.

Willingness to be evaluated by different stakeholders

A learning organization has to be willing to be evaluated, not only by external consultants or donor representatives, as is usually the case for implementing agencies, but also by different units inside the organization as well as by the beneficiaries it claims to serve. This implies an acceptance that different stakeholders can generate their own indicators to assess the organization's performance. Self-evaluations using self-generated indicators should also be encouraged across the institution's units. Evaluation is not about judging others, it is about creating a space in which to systematize and learn from experience, to reflect on a programme's activities to see how these might be improved.

Systems and structures

Changing the procedures of an organization may be severely constrained by the continued existence of non-participatory systems and structures. Below are set out the systemic and structural characteristics identified by the IDS workshop participants as fundamental to the building of a participation-friendly learning organization.

Allowance for flexible, ad hoc, innovative learning units

Certain organizations are composed of different units whose functions are so absolutely defined that communication across units is difficult, with innovative practices and individual initiative difficult to introduce or sustain (Handy, 1989). Handy uses the image of the ancient Greek temple to describe the structure of so-called 'Appolinian' organizations in which each department is the equivalent of a column (Handy, 1995). The only link between the temple's different columns is across the top, i.e. through executive channels in the organization. Initiatives launched in one column are often blocked before they can reach others, and the separate units cannot easily combine forces and respond flexibly to the unplanned events and outcomes that are, by definition, the stuff of participatory programmes.

Hence the need for a *task culture* made up of a network of loosely connected 'commando' units with a high-learning potential. Each unit is composed of a team with a strong sense of purpose and clearly defined tasks. Units move across the organization as if they were on a grid, helping information move more rapidly and ad hoc decisions to be made when necessary.

Choosing the right people to form a learning unit is crucial. They must be communicators and strategists, capable of making decisions quickly and dealing with problems as and when they occur without in many cases having to wait for official approval from above.

Ideally, the offices of an organization promoting or implementing participatory projects should by their very design foster a learning and enabling environment. Different units should not be isolated from each other more than is necessary. Face-to-face interaction of people in the building should be encouraged through common spaces where interaction need not be formal. The most interesting ideas, initiatives and plans are often born in those relaxed, creative moments that come in informal conversation. A relaxing place to have a cup of coffee can make all the difference!

Flexible accounts

It is difficult to plan ahead exactly what will be needed in a participatory development project. The particular requirements will depend largely on what local people identify as important, and how project staff decide they can best respond to their needs.

The point is that rigid, pre-set budgets, in which specific amounts are tied to particular activities (to be done within a set time-scale, usually far too short), do not allow for the unplanned requirements of participatory projects. Participatory projects involve added preparation and organizational costs which are usually overlooked in more conventional schemes: a pre-project preparation period of at least six months (as recommended by Mascarenhas, in Chapter 11, this volume); training in participatory methodologies for the field; organizational restructuring and development, such as creating new task-oriented learning units, conducting in-house organizational development training; and training project staff in very specific new skills, such as report-writing and basic accountancy.

What is more, participatory projects by their very nature will involve activities which could not possibly have been planned in advance; for example, activities overlooked by donors and project staff but determined by local people to be important.

For staff to respond adequately to the unexpected requirements of participatory schemes, the following minimum changes in accounting procedures are needed:

- increasing the number of people entrusted with the handling of accounts (minor staff should be trusted as much as possible to draw from accounts without having to wait for the appropriate signatures if the need is urgent);
- the ability to switch money from one budget heading to another; and
- the ability to roll unspent balances forward.

Donors have always required that budgets be planned, but increasingly, they are showing flexibility in allowing for contingency funds, or what some have called 'unexpected opportunities'. What this amounts to is the ability to switch money between budget headings, and/or to have a special contingency fund set apart for emergencies and activities not specified in any particular budget but which are relevant to the project or programme as a whole. This is without doubt a step in the right direction which can help nurture a participatory project. NGOs, government bureaucracies and other spending organizations are also urged, however, to do their bit to reduce red tape. Drawing funds from any one account should not be dependent, for example, on the presence of any one person. A wider range of people needs to be trusted to handle accounts so that crisis situations can be dealt with quickly.

The extent to which an organization can institutionalize a system of flexible accounts will, however, largely depend on the broader accountability framework within which it operates. Accountability, traditionally, is secured by legal norms and regulations, and by bureaucracy. A donor or the spending organization may abide by national accounting rules, or governing trust documents which require that money be spent only in some specified way. In either case, the rules should leave enough room for manoeuvre for flexible accounts to be set up. Bureaucracy can be more of a problem in this respect, however, especially in large organizations where there is often excessive administration under the banner of accountability. Judging the border line between required procedures and excessive procedures is difficult, and requires full consultation with everyone concerned. The ideal to be pursued is a system of downwards accountability.

Towards downwards accountability and transparency based on trust

At present, lines of accountability in the great majority of development organizations move upwards. The procedure is for reports on monies spent to be passed from field staff to the local office, on to head office, and finally to donors. Upwards accountability assumes that people in the higher levels of the hierarchy have already determined how much money is to be spent, on what, and by when (unless a system of flexible accounts has been set up). The further down the line, the fewer people are trusted; there is always someone above with power, control over and/or access to funds ready to judge and criticize. The intended beneficiaries usually find themselves at the end of the line.

The challenge in a learning organization, or indeed in a learning project, is to make accountability work *downwards*. When this happens, not only are local people informed of the monies that have been spent in their name (horizontal as opposed to vertical transparency), they are also more likely to have a say on how future monies should be spent. In certain cases, it may be appropriate to extend monies directly to community-based organizations, and let them pay for external services as and when they see fit.

A more or less rigid system of upwards accountability – the norm in most development projects – is to a large degree incompatible with the spirit of participation. If beneficiaries are effectively to participate in a project and make it their own, common sense dictates that they must be shown how the monies are being spent. Since it is now common in most projects for local people to be trained in credit management, bookkeeping, and other basic financial skills, it is not unrealistic to expect those who hold the scheme's purse strings to be accountable, or at least more transparent, to those in whose name they have obtained funding.

For such a system to work ultimately depends on trust. A profound change in the behaviour and attitudes of those in positions of power, those who control accounts, may be necessary. Such change can begin to occur when policymakers, donors and other office people are taken to the field (see Holland with Blackburn, 1998) to see for themselves why flexibility is required.

Flat management and organizational structure: tips from the East

Much has been written of the Japanese post-Fordist management model (Kaplinski, 1994; Womack *et al.*, 1990). The Toyota company's capacity to respond flexibly with new models almost as soon as the market changes, to take a well-known example, may seem far from the concerns of projects keen to encourage the participation of people whose life income in many cases would be insufficient to buy a new car. In fact the Toyota management model is highly relevant to what concerns us in this book. Demand in the car market may be for a more fuel-efficient model; demand in a participatory project consists of the priorities established by the proposed beneficiaries as a result of PRA and related methodologies. The common feature of both is the question of how the organization (NGO in one case, say, and the Toyota factory in the other) responds to such demand.

The premise of the Japanese model is that to respond quickly, effectively and efficiently to changes in demand (i.e. produce the required car as cheaply as possible and make it available to the customer as quickly as possible), communication across hierarchies in the company must be allowed to flow with minimum interruption. Some have called this a 'flat management' structure. Not only can workers assembling cars communicate ideas directly to the executive and R&D staff, they are also rewarded for taking initiative and for-

151

mulating ideas on the spot. They do not work as isolated individuals on the production line, but as part of a team.

Just as PRA is predicated on the idea that local people are experts in their own field, that they have profound knowledge of their situations, and that such knowledge should be respected and elicited to help design relevant projects, so flat management is predicated on the idea that each unit has expert knowledge of the particular kind of tasks it performs. In both systems, respect for local knowledge introduces an element of egalitarianism. No longer is it possible for 'the boss' to assume s/he knows best. As Japanese managers have had to adapt and respect that the worker often knows more that is important, so the NGO director, government or donor representative will increasingly have to adapt to the fact that it is the field staff who have relevant knowledge of what is really going on out there, and, in turn, that it is the knowledge of the proposed beneficiaries which holds the key to the success of a project. Not only are they articulating the project's demands, they are also the ones who will eventually, it is hoped, take over project-management responsibilities.

21

The Scaling-up and Institutionalization of PRA: lessons and challenges

JOHN GAVENTA

Micro–macro linkages

For over two decades, participatory methods of research have proven their usefulness for development at the local or micro level. Much has been learned about the value of these methods for the development of local knowledge, for strengthening local action and for empowerment of the poor.

As this book documents well, PRA and other participatory approaches are now being adopted and promoted by larger organizations – governments, agencies, large NGOs, universities and others. The rapidity of these developments is astounding.

The challenge that is before us now is how to build upon the successes of participatory development that have occurred at the micro and local levels to take them to a larger scale – to incorporate participation into the development and implementation of national policies and in large-scale institutions. On the one hand, such 'scaling-up' of PRA offers tremendous opportunities for expanding the participation of the poor in development. On the other hand, there are serious dangers of misuse and abuse which ultimately could discredit the concept of participation as a critical ingredient for development.

Despite the rapidity of the developments, up until now we have actually known very little as researchers about the experiences of taking participation to scale, especially that which is grounded in participatory research (e.g. PRA, PAR, etc.) as a basis for action. In fact, a number of authors have pointed to the urgent need for further research and learning on the challenges and processes involved.

For instance, Stiefel and Wolf (1994) summarize many lessons and experiences, learned from the research programme on participation conducted in the 1980s by UNRISD. They review several attempts to institutionalize participation through government programmes. Among their conclusions:

> A basic question regarding participatory grassroots action is the relationship between the 'genuineness' of the participatory efforts (i.e. the participatory, autonomous and self-reliant character of the organizations), their relative size and rate of expansion, and their real effectiveness

over time (i.e. their capacity to negotiate their claims with powerholders, parties, unions and the state). Past experiences, confirmed by the findings of the UNRISD programme . . . tend to reject claims that small can be both beautiful and effective in the long run. To what extent 'scaling-up' through co-ordination and 'networking' of grassroots organizations and local participatory efforts can overcome the inevitable contradictions between smallness and effectiveness and between largeness and participatory authenticity is a question which in the present political post-democratization context is of burning interest. (Stiefel and Wolfe, 1994: 203–4)

More specifically, in relationship to the scaling-up of PRA, Robert Chambers has observed that 'those of us engaged in the development and spread of PRA and related approaches and methods are now confronted with choices. These are where to act on the continuum between the small, safe and beautiful, and the big, risky and patchy' (Chambers, pers. comm.).

Similarly, Barbara P. Thomas–Slayter, has pointed to the challenge of forging micro-macro linkages to move successes with small-scale projects to a broader scale of activity. She cites earlier work by Goulet, who argues that 'micro-macro linkage thus emerges as the key research and strategy issue...the research task is to conceptualize and theoretically validate the possibility of such linkage. And the strategy task is to illustrate this possibility and elaborate the methods and instrumentalities for achieving it' (Thomas-Slayter, 1992:137; quoting Goulet (1989:8). Drawing from case studies in Zimbabwe and Kenya she observes in specific reference to PRA that

The question of micro–macro linkages is of paramount importance to the satisfactory execution of PRAs. It is of little use to an impoverished community to be invited to discuss its development needs and to establish priorities, if there is no way to support efforts to address them. The PRA team cannot simply do the assessment without helping the community make the linkage to external resources that can provide capital, material inputs for projects, or technical expertise...the next question for PRA is whether or not it can systematize these linkages. (Thomas-Slayter, 1992:141)

The chapters in this book and the experiences shared at the May 1996 workshop at IDS contribute a great deal to our knowledge base about the challenges of scaling up participation, and the related importance of both institutional as well as personal change. We have been provided with 11 rich examples, as well as several overviews. Here, I will suggest a framework for linking these cases, as well as to point to areas for future research and learning.

The dimensions of scaling-up

While both the literature on participation and the experiences of the practitioners gathered at the May workshop suggest the importance of taking local practice to a larger scale, there is not a common understanding of what is meant by scaling-up, or of how its differing aspects relate to one another.[1] In the general introduction to this book, Blackburn defines scaling-up similarly

154

as 'an expansion, which has a cumulative impact'. In the book, however, we find examples of differing types of expansions. Some refer to expansion of the types of participation, others to the geographic scope of PRA work, others to the spread of PRA activities from smaller organizations to larger institutions.

For our purposes, I believe that it is useful to group discussion of cases in this book along three important dimensions of change (see Figure 21.1):

(1) *Scaling-out, or increase in the types and quality of participation*   This refers to the expansion of participation from one activity, such as appraisal, to the involvement of people throughout the whole development process in a way that increases their empowerment;

(2) *Scaling-up, or expansion of the quantity of participation*   This refers to an increase in the number of participants or places where participation, especially PRA, will occur; and

(3) *Institutional change*   This refers to the shifts required in and among larger-scale institutions for scaling-out and scaling-up to occur effectively. More specifically, it refers to the ways in which larger-scale institutions in government or the civil society will interact with smaller-scale organizations or communities in the participatory-development process.

These dimensions are inter-related, if quality participation on a large quantitative scale is to be achieved. In particular, I will argue, the cases here have demonstrated that in order to increase the types and quality of participation

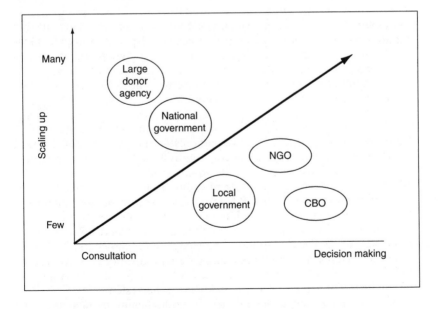

Fig. 21.1: Scaling-out: types and quality of participation

155

with more people and places significant institutional change will be required. The inter-relationships may be understood further by focusing on each dimension in turn.

Scaling-out: increasing the types or quality of participation

The case studies in this volume suggest at least two important ways in which we can think about strengthening the quality of participation, growing from PRA processes:

(1) In several of the cases, we find arguments for the use of PRA and peoples' participation throughout the whole project cycle i.e. appraisal, planning, implementation, monitoring and evaluation. This represents an important expansion of PRA from a tool for appraisal to an approach to development, which insists on participation at every stage.

One of the strongest examples of this type of expansion is found in the Sri Lanka case, in which PRA was adopted in every stage of the cycle in a water and irrigation programme. Participation involved 'site selection (who decides where work should be done); control of implementation and monitoring and evaluation (whose project is it?); funding arrangements (in particular how funds are dispersed and to whom, i.e. who benefits?) progress reporting to donors (whose format counts?); institutional development of farmer organizations (whose power counts?)' (Samaranayake, see Chapter 12, this volume).

However, full involvement in this expanded sense, also involves a shift in the level of participation, from consultation to real decisionmaking and mobilization. In this sense, the case studies suggest that participation in most cases is not something which you either have or don't have; it's not a zero-sum game. Rather, participation needs to be seen as a scale, ranging from token participation on the one hand to full participation and empowerment on the other. Social scientists have over the years developed a number of such scales. A very useful scale is that developed by Pretty and others (1994) as seen in Box 21.1.

In general, to say that we want to increase participation could mean that we want to move the quality of participation up this scale, so that participation involves at least interactive participation amongst all partners and stakeholders – government, local community-based organizations, donors or NGOs – and moves towards self-mobilization.

(2) We find in this volume, a number of examples of such expansion in the level of participation, from PRA for consultation to broader empowerment and decisionmaking. In addition to the Sri Lanka case, cited above, another very good example is that found in Estonia, where PRA, designed originally to ascertain farmers' knowledge and perceptions of field-drainage systems, set into motion an entire participatory process, leading to the formation of an organization, the Voluntary Society for Amelioration, which will actually manage and operate the systems.

If we are interested as practitioners in strengthening participation, that is in increasing its quality, then we must not only recognize that the levels of participation are interrelated, but we must also ask, 'What are the

156

Box 21.1: A typology of participation

1. *Passive participation* — People participate by being told what is going to happen or has already happened. It is a unilateral announcement by an administration or project management without listening to people's responses. The information being shared belongs only to external professionals.

2. *Participation in information giving* — People participate by answering questions posed by extractive researchers using questionnaire surveys or similar approaches. People do not have the opportunity to influence proceedings, as the findings of the research are neither shared nor checked for accuracy.

3. *Participation by consultation* — People participate by being consulted, and external people listen to their views. These external professionals define both problems and solutions, and may modify these in the light of people's responses. Such a consultative process does not concede any share in decision making, and professionals are under no obligation to take on board people's views.

4. *Participation for material incentives* — People participate by providing resources, for example labour, in return for food, cash or other material incentives. Much on-farm research falls in this category, as farmers provide the fields but are not involved in the experimentation or the process of learning. It is very common to see this called participation, yet people have no stake in prolonging activities when the incentives end.

5. *Functional participation* — People participate by forming groups to meet predetermined objectives related to the project, which can involve the development or promotion of externally initiated social organization. Such involvement does not tend to be at early stages of project cycles or planning, but rather after major decisions have been made. These institutions tend to be dependent on external initiators and facilitators, but may become self dependent.

6. *Interactive participation* — People participate in joint analysis, which leads to action plans and the formation of new local institutions or the strengthening of existing ones. It tends to involve interdisciplinary methodologies that seek multiple perspectives and make use of systematic and structured learning processes. These groups take control over local decisions, and so people have a stake in maintaining structures or practices.

7. *Self-mobilization* — People participate by taking initiatives independent of external institutions to change systems. They develop contacts with external institutions for resources and technical advice they need, but retain control over how resources are used. Such self-initiated mobilization and collective action may or may not challenge existing inequitable distributions of wealth and power.

Source: Pretty *et al.* (1994)

conditions or requirements for moving participation from one level to another?' Again, the cases in this book give us some valuable insights.

The link to participatory learning

One clear lesson is the importance of developing learning processes that allow participants to reflect on their experience, and to develop the awareness and knowledge necessary for the next steps in the process. Though there is often an assumption in PRA that it will lead to self-learning and analysis for action, one cannot assume that it will necessarily do so. Rather, such learning must be included as a deliberate and conscious part of the empowerment process.

This insight involves a convergence of PRA with other methods of participatory education, such as those pioneered by Paulo Freire and other popular adult educators around the world. For instance, in the Zimbabwe case, Training for Transformation (TFT) methods (which adapted a Freirean approach to Southern Africa) were linked with PRA methods of documenting farmers' own knowledge systems, as well as to changes in the extension system. As the authors point out, 'Our experience has shown that the concept of strengthening local organizations, in particular its component of stimulating leadership and co-operation, requires more than a number of practical PRA-tools to set in motion . . . A broader philosophical framework for the participatory development process was required and introduced in the form of Training for Transformation' . . . TFT was found to help 'to empower local people to gain greater control over their circumstances by participating actively in their own development through the sharing and joint construction of ideas and knowledge'(Hagmann *et al.*)

Though not explicitly using Freirean approaches, in the South India case Mascarenhas also points to the importance of giving groups the opportunity to learn and to grow, even if such learning opportunities have to be created deliberately. The strengthening of participation, he reminds us, is a progressive growth process over the stages of a project, and may take at least eight to ten years to achieve.

The link to capacity building

Not only must PRA be consciously linked to deliberate learning, but if it is to lead to empowerment, it must also be linked to the increase of the organizational capacity to act. Mascanrenhas points out that if an organized self-help group is not in place which can help provide the basis for local mobilization, then time must be taken to build this capacity, before moving to the stage of generating information and research. In turn, the participatory research process can become the catalyst to lead to greater organizational capacity and action, as we found in the examples from Estonia, Somaliland and Zimbabwe. However, as in the case of participatory learning, this linkage to building organizational capacity does not happen automatically. As is discussed elsewhere, one of the current challenges for PRA is how it can help to create and build local institutions managing resources according to their own rules.

158

Tying PRA activities to processes of learning and organizational capacity to act calls for a reconceptualization of the term PRA, to the term PLA (participatory learning and action), as some have argued, or the renaming of the same acronym to participatory reflection and action, as suggested in Chapter 1. Regardless of the labelling issues, the point here is clear: when participatory research, learning and capacity building are linked consciously and successfully, they can lead to progressive empowerment along the participation scale. On the other hand, when these links are not present or are not made successfully, then PRA methods can also have negative affects, leading down the scale from consultation to pseudo or manipulative participation. Attempts to increase the level of participation must be understood in the context of the previous history in a given community. Prior, positive, inclusive experiences of participation may have created the environment for future collective learning and action. Negative experiences may have simply reinforced a sense of powerlessness or futility.

This understanding about the necessary conditions for strengthening participation along the quality scale, and the dangers of negative participatory experiences, are critical as we move to a discussion of how to scale up participation along the quantitative scale. Linking the steps to increased participation even at the micro level is a complex process, in which each step impacts upon the other. To do so in many places is even more challenging, but it must begin with the recognition that the quality of 'scaled-out' participation at the grassroots is also critical to the success of the quantitative scaling-up process.

Scaling-up: increasing the quantity of participation

However difficult the process of building quality participation at the micro level, there is also the pressure, as we have seen in this volume, to expand quantitatively, to use PRA methodologies to address problems on a larger and larger geographical or numerical scale. There are perhaps many reasons for the drive to higher quantities, not least of which is the growth in the scale of the problems to be addressed. As Uvin (1995: 927) observes:

It is often recognized that most of these grassroots initiatives are small, underfunded, poorly staffed, slow and localized in the face of poverty, hunger and environmental degradation on a vast scale. They are thus considered to be only actions at the margin, capable of providing local relief and empowerment, but not of tackling the real issues of the eradication of hunger and poverty of millions of people.

In this volume we find a number of attempts to take PRA processes developed at a local level to a larger regional or national level. The largest in scope is that of Indonesia, which involved some 60 000 villages in a pre-determined set of PRA activities, but there are others as well, including Vietnam, Ethiopia, Bolivia and South India.

Often when we talk about national or large-scale plans for participation, we mean doing the same thing (a set of PRA activities) in a large number of places very quickly, as in the case of Indonesia. The temptation is to mandate from above that 'participation shall occur', and then expect a uniform response from around the region or nation.

159

As we have seen, however, this approach is fraught with difficulty, for participation cannot be imposed from above, it will develop differently and at differing paces, depending upon local contexts. In this sense, participation is like a growing process: the seeds may be sowed widely, but whether they will take root depends upon the local conditions. In some cases they might, but only if the local conditions have developed appropriately; in other places they will be choked out by non-participatory weeds, or die for lack of nourishment. As in the case of increasing the quality of participation, we need to ask 'what are the conditions which allow large-scale participatory processes to take root and grow?' The case studies suggest several.

The importance of prior participatory experience

Several of the case studies in this volume point to the need for local successful examples of participatory experiences in place from which to scale up more broadly. For instance, in India, Kar and Phillips (Chapter 9) point to the need for successful sustained community action in several small places, before replicating the strategy more broadly. Similarly in Bolivia, Blackburn and De Toma (Chapter 6) argue for linking national scaling-up processes to processes of decentralization and scaling-down, and in Vietnam, Paul (Chapter 4) argues for the importance of local context, especially the existence of local organizations. Where a prior set of successful small-scale experiences have not been developed, there may simply not be the base from which to grow and expand.

The importance of training

Prior experience is critical when it comes to the need for training, a second important pre-condition for successful quantitative scaling-up. For participatory processes, training works best to the extent that it is horizontal, that is that groups and trainers who have had successful experiences in one case can then spread those outwards to other communities. Unless a critical mass of experience and capacity exists, training can simply become routinized and top-down, as seems to be the case with the rush to scale in Indonesia. To gain quality training capacity over a large area may also mean changing traditional large-scale training organizations, such as extension services, or universities, as Wordofa argues in the case of Ethiopia (Chapter 3).

There are other pre-conditions as well: a readiness and willingness at the local level to act; strong leadership at the local level, prior trust and relationship between the locality and external agents, or what some refer to as social capital; time and other resources; and enough political stability and democratic space for participation freely to occur.

All of the cases suggest that participation can occur gradually on a large scale, but that to do so requires starting with an assessment of local conditions and building upwards. Top-down standardized approaches, especially where they are imposed quickly and without adequate training and preparation, may lead to manipulation or pseudo-participation at best. What change agents can do is prepare the ground (through building local capacities for participation), provide the seeds and inputs (through training, resources and support structures), and support and nurture the process (through strengthening support networks, resolving the inevitable conflicts, and responding to the needs that unexpected changes in conditions might bring).

The conditions for successful scaling-up are not only at the local level. To play the role of developing and nurturing these local conditions, large-scale organizations must themselves adopt approaches to work that are more catalysing and facilitating, rather than directive and imposing. Moreover, links and networks must exist between local organizations and larger-scale ones. These needs take us to the issue of institutional change.

Institutional change

Participation at a large scale rather than a local scale cannot occur without the involvement of large-scale institutions, be they national governments, large NGOs, donor agencies or others. But for a large institution to support increased and higher-quality participation in more places means more than focusing on communities, it also means changing the institutions themselves. Whereas large institutions like governments have an advantage of scale over local groups, they have the disadvantage in that they are usually not very participatory. Institutions tend to work on standardized, bureaucratic procedures which often inhibit more flexible, innovative practices. People who have worked in large institutions for many years bring sets of attitudes and behaviours which may have served them well in a more traditional 'blueprint' approach to development but which will have to adapt to be supportive of more participatory approaches (see Chambers, 1994).

At a recent meeting of PRA practitioners in India, a group of trainers and practitioners from the South discussed their experiences with the increased emphasis on mainstreaming participation by governments and donors. While they welcomed these efforts, they also outlined what they saw as the dangers of abuse and bad practice.

Again and again, in different countries and contexts, with different donors and governments, we have found dependency created and participation destroyed by:

- failure to understand the philosophy of participation and PRA;
- pressures to scale up PRA rapidly, sometimes on a national level;
- demand for instant PRA training one-off and on a large scale;
- low-quality PRA training, limited to routine methods;
- the rush to prepare projects and programmes;
- top-down procedure;
- drives to disburse funds;
- time-bound targets for products, neglecting process;
- inflexible programmes and projects;
- neglect and underestimation of the knowledge and capabilities of local people;
- neglect of local capacity-building and institutional development;
- lack of staff continuity;
- penalization of participatory staff; and above all

- failure to recognize the ABC of PRA, namely the primacy of personal behaviour. (Kumar, 1996)

Similarly, the case studies in this volume point to the need for institutional change if the scaling-up of participation is to be effective. In Zimbabwe, for instance, Hagmann *et al.* (Chapter 8) found that in addition to PRA and participatory learning and organization processes, changes were needed in planning, implementation and monitoring procedures, requiring a strong commitment by staff at all levels, including donors. The Sri Lanka case (Chapter 12) reminds us that participation and empowerment 'have little meaning unless implementing organizations, together with their partners and donors, are prepared to refashion the programme systems and procedures which often interfere with rather than facilitate participatory processes of development'.

The case study of the Himalayas (Chapter 14) also illustrates the point. Where there was a more participatory institutional culture in place in the governmental bureaucracy, then the expansion of participatory processes in the community was more likely to be successful. Leurs (Chapter 18) provides challenges facing PRA not only at the individual and community levels, but also for organizations, programmes, policies and donors.

The importance of organizational and institutional collaboration

It is also important to observe that such change is to be made in many types of institutions and organizations – universities, donors, national governments, local governments, larger NGOs, local community-based organizations. Each of these types of bodies may have differing comparative advantages – a national government may rank high on the ability to implement programmes high on the quantitative scale, while a smaller community-based organization may rank higher on the ability to carry out high qualitative participation but in fewer places.

The institutional challenge, however, is not only how to make single institutions more participatory through internal organizational change, but also how to develop more collaboration and linkages between and among organizations, which historically may not have worked together.

Though few of the case studies highlight this point explicitly, a number refer to the importance of inter-sectoral or inter-institutional collaboration. In the Somaliland case, Sam Joseph (Chapter 13) writes of the need to build mutual trust, interpersonal communication and interdependence across the various levels of a project or a programme. The Zimbabwe case (Chapter 8) points to the need for networks of organizations, if local projects are to be replicated or disseminated more broadly. The Bolivian case (Chapter 6) is one which will necessarily involve new collaboration between national government, local government and the civil society. The GTZ case (Chapter 15) argues that it is imperative to involve a broader number of institutions than just the state in the development process, be they 'NGOs, Chambers of Commerce, parent-teacher associations, religious movements or private enterprises.' Projects need to learn to accept new and additional partner organizations, and mechanisms need to be established for resolution of conflicts which will inevitably arise as new organizations learn to work together.

These examples pose a fundamental challenge for the practice of PRA, one of whose fundamental tenets has been that of 'handing over the stick' to the local people (insiders) to develop analysis, learning and action themselves. Yet, these examples point to the recognition that in an age of globalization, local communities cannot necessarily solve poverty at the local level – they must build links with other communities, and with government, donors and other institutions. Participatory development on a large scale requires, therefore, another ingredient – learning to build cross-sector partnerships at all levels, especially between local and external organizations, as well as between civil society, governmental and private institutions.[2]

Such partnerships must begin with the respect for people's knowledge and actions that has been informed by the PRA paradigm. At some point, however, the new holders of the stick will need to join their sticks with others or hold them jointly with external actors for action to grow more broadly. When and how to develop such coalitions or partnerships is a critical strategic question, and how to do so without disempowering the new stickholders is a difficult challenge. Lack of trust arising from differences of power, culture, style, capacity etc. may all interfere with the development of effective collaboration. To overcome these obstacles, changes must be made in at all levels to create new ways of working together across institutional and power differences, and in a way that keeps the participation of the grassroots communities at the centre of the process.

Summary and questions for future research

The cases in this volume have contributed a great deal to our understanding of the dimensions of the scaling-up of participatory processes, and particularly to the types of institutional change that will need to occur for it to be done effectively.

In general, we have found that the dimensions of scaling-out, scaling-up and institutional change must be inter-related. If there is a rush to scale up quantitatively without a concern for the quality of the participation involved, then critical questions of institutional change may not arise. Neither is the expansion likely to be effective or empowering. Similarly, if the concern is with improving the quality of participation only at a micro level, then there may be less attention given to the issue of institutional change of larger organizations necessary to reach more places and people. (The Estonia case, for instance, focuses primarily on the qualitative dimension.) However, when the concern is both for increasing the quality and nature of participation as well as its quantitative scope, then, the cases remind us, institutional change is not only desirable but required. Such change is both intra-institutional, i.e. within the culture and procedures of the organization; and inter-institutional i.e. in how organizations link and collaborate across sectoral and power differences.

There are many challenges to linking quality, quantity and institutional change simultaneously and successfully. The important point is that there must be change along all three dimensions if participation is to be widely

163

achieved. Even with learning, there are still, of course, enormous questions as yet unanswered. Four areas appear to be critical both for future research and for improvement of practice:

What are the appropriate strategies and interventions for personal, institutional and social change?

While this volume has pointed again and again to the need for institutional change, that is to the need to create more participatory organizations, cultures and collaborations, getting from here to there is not an easy task. We need better road maps that will point us in the direction we need to go, and help us understand what we do when we reach new crossroads. What types of change are needed? Where are the leverage points, that allow us to raise the lessons and experiences of the micro to the macro?

A number of chapters in this volume point to the need for attitude and behaviour change. As Robert Chambers' Foreword makes clear, personal change of development professionals and institutional staff is as important as the methods that PRA has introduced, if not more so. This is an essential starting-point, and we need to learn much more about how such change occurs with large numbers of people, through training, field exposure and the like.

While starting with the personal, we need also to look beyond it, to ask questions about necessary changes at the institutional and social levels as well. What happens when individuals change but institutional practices remain the same? How can organizations and institutions be redesigned and re-oriented as more participatory structures? Here a great deal of work is being done within the organizational development field on how to change cultures, procedures, reward systems, budgeting processes and the like.

However, as changes occur personally and institutionally, we can expect that they will in turn encounter broader barriers of power, entrenched interests and resource inequalities. What sorts of changes in the broader political economy are necessary for larger-scale participatory development to occur? Here we must examine the links of personal and institutional change to broader issues such as race, class and gender relations, as well as economic and political forces.

These are important questions. Many of our strategies for community empowerment and organization developed in a time when there were clearer sets of differences between those on the outside of large institutions and those on the inside, between 'us' and 'them'. Now, with the adoption of participation by large institutions, the boundaries between 'us' and 'them' have become less clear. When is institutional change an opportunity for new collaboration and partnership to strengthen previously marginal voices? How do we ensure that as voices on the margin move to the centre cooptation does not occur? When are the moments that perhaps require conflict and pressure from without for change to occur, and when do the opportunities for change arise through collaboration and institutional participation? As both practitioners and researchers, we need much more learning about the dynamics of linking personal, institutional and broader social change in this new climate of openness towards popular participation.

What are the conditions under which these changes will occur?

The first set of questions takes us to the second. While this volume suggests an individual and organizational requirement of increased participation, there are broader social and political conditions to be analysed as well. What levels of openness and readiness need to exist for participation to grow at the state or political level in the civil society/in the cultural arena? The scaling-up of participation will be different in Indonesia, or Estonia, or Zimbabwe, not for institutional reasons only, but for historical, political, cultural and social reasons. We need to understand far better the links between these levels of analysis in order to determine the necessary conditions for our strategies of personal and institutional change to be effective.

Related to this is the question 'why is participation emerging as a key issue for large-scale, traditionally more powerful institutions at this point in history?' How does participation at the community level, growing from a trajectory of community appraisal and action, link to the current trends in the governance arena towards democratization and decentralization? How are both of these developments affected by simultaneous trends towards greater inequality in the economy, greater globalization of economic forces and an increasing concern with social exclusion?

What difference does it make?

A third critical set of questions has to do with the impact of expanded participation and institutional change upon the nature and outcome of development itself. What is the impact of expanded participation in terms of actually solving problems more effectively and urgently? A debate in the participation literature has involved whether participation is seen as a means to development or an end in itself. Are we talking about differing means to the same ends, or a change of ends as well?

Surely we must talk about both. On the one hand, to open up institutions to a process of greater participation without expecting or hoping for a change in the ends/outcomes seems futile and ultimately manipulative. On the other hand, to work only towards participation as an end in itself, without being able to demonstrate impact in other conditions that affect people's lives as a result (or at least a by-product) also seems short-sighted. The challenge is to pursue participation as both means and ends, and to hope that each pursuit affects the other, i.e. that a more participatory process leads to more desirable outcomes, and that the desire for greater participation affects the means and strategies for getting there.

The monitoring of participation and participatory monitoring and evaluation

As participation becomes more and more accepted, the new debate is less about means or ends but about monitoring and measuring whether participation is occurring, and with what results. What are the indicators for success in participatory development?

This issue has at least two important inter-related dimensions:

(1) On the one hand, as participation is accepted in principle we must evolve indicators and ways to know if it is in fact occurring in practice. While researchers have developed earlier methods of monitoring and evaluating more traditional forms of development, such as infrastructure, job creation or education, the tools and indicators do not exist when it comes to measuring potentially more fuzzy concepts of participation. This is a matter not only of academic concern; ultimately being able to monitor and document the degree in which participation is actually being achieved will be one of the few vehicles for maintaining quality as the concept is taken to a larger and larger scale.

(2) The second dimension relates to the question of who measures? Whose indicators of success are used and who uses them? As institutions become more inclusive in the front-end of project development, that is, in promoting participation in appraisal and implementation, then the question of 'who measures?' the results also becomes critical. The rapid evolution of PRA has taught us a great deal about the importance of peoples' knowledge and has provided sets of tools that can be used for implementing that knowledge in the appraisal and development of projects. The next step is to involve people centrally in evaluating their success and impact. 'Who counts reality?' may prove as significant as 'whose reality counts?'. (See Chambers, 1996).

The question of who measures is important not only for improved quality but also for improved accountability. The scaling-up of participation into the realm of large institutions risks the concept of participation being taken out of the hands of the poorer and powerless whom these institutions claim to serve.

In this sense, participatory monitoring by grassroots, local people themselves of whether participation is being achieved is a critical way of evaluating how the institutions are doing. This implies another reversal: for decades, community-based projects have been at the receiving end of evaluation by larger institutions. If we are now arguing for institutional change rather than change of poor and local people, as Robert Chambers' Foreword suggests, then why not have them become the judges of whether the institutions are meeting their participation goals? 'Handing over the stick' also means relinquishing the 'measuring rod'!

Ultimately, of course, the purpose of taking participation to a greater scale is to increase the quality of people's lives, be it in greater self-reliance and autonomy or in the ability to meet the basic human needs necessary for survival and personal development. Unless these fundamental goals are met, then the basic hopes for expanded participation will not have been achieved.

22

Conclusion

JAMES BLACKBURN

Never had I abandoned the conviction that only by working with the people could I achieve anything authentic on their behalf.

Paulo Freire

'Who Changes?' shows us that we have covered considerable ground in understanding how participatory approaches in development are best scaled up, and what resulting organizational changes are needed in order to increase both the scope and the impact of participation in development. PRA and related methodologies, the nuts and bolts of turning the concepts of participation into practice, were, until only a few years ago, the preferred domain of NGOs in small, often site-specific projects. Now they are being promoted with growing vigour by government bureaucracies, bilateral donors and large international organizations such as the World Bank. Participatory approaches appear to have gained a new legitimacy, even, some would say, an orthodoxy. Success has conferred respectability: what was radical yesterday has become conventional today. For better or for worse, participation in development is in the process of being institutionalized.

The theorists and practitioners of participation, who were until recently on the margins, and are now at the centre of development debates, have reason to celebrate. The changes over the last decade in the way development has been conceived and practised can only be described as momentous. Participation as a social energy, to borrow the term from Albert Hirschman, is gaining ground. Those familiar with the spectacular spread of approaches such as PRA will recognize the colour, creativity, boundless enthusiasm and innovative spirit which is possible when people feel they have seized on something that can make a difference. The scaling-up of such approaches, and the concomitant organizational changes such scaling-up implies, are now taking place in a growing number of settings throughout the world, and we are learning to do both better. Partly as a result of this process, donors, governments, NGOs and popular organizations are working more closely than perhaps ever before, each learning from the experience of the other, and as an ever wider variety of development professionals gains exposure to participatory approaches, a kind of 'benign virus' appears to be spreading, affecting the design and implementation of a growing range of programmes and policies, as well as the procedures of organizations engaged in development practice.

Few would deny that many of those working in participatory development today are continuing to clear new roads which lead away from the repetition, mediocrity or cynicism which has characterized some of the interventions of development, into new horizons of continuous innovation and experimentation. The patient work of organizations such as OUTREACH in India, or the National Development Foundation in Sri Lanka (see chapters 11 and 12, this volume), attest to a painstaking and creative search to test the most appropriate ways of building up local participation, with 'success' defined as the moment when the NGO is no longer needed and local organizations can take over and manage their own projects. Equally, the efforts of government bureaucracies in the Philippines, Kenya, Bolivia, Vietnam and elsewhere, to respond to the challenge of adopting more participatory practices provide us with ground for hope (chapters 4, 6 and 7, this volume).

The book shows us that enthusiasm for increased participation should be tempered, however, with careful thinking about its implications for the way development projects, programmes and policies are designed, implemented and evaluated. While the expansion with a cumulative impact (or scaling-up) of participatory approaches should be seen as a progressive step in the history of development intervention, many of the book's authors have also pointed out the pitfalls of a scaling-up strategy that is too rapid and ill-conceived. When such a strategy is being considered, nothing can replace careful preparation, unhurried training and the use of smaller pilot projects to act as learning laboratories before large-scale action is initiated. We are also learning that the macro-political context in which scaling-up occurs is fundamental to its success. A government committed to democratic decentralization is more likely to be responsive to the spread of approaches such as PRA. Local processes of democratization, including 'good' local government, go hand in hand with increased community or popular participation in which methodologies such as PRA can play an important part. The scaling-up of participatory approaches may thus depend increasingly in the future on the scaling-down of government, with the implementation of increasingly sophisticated policies of democratic decentralization, as is occurring in Bolivia.

It is, nevertheless, disturbing that governments with a strong authoritarian streak are also showing enthusiasm for the participatory approach. It has to be assumed that their understanding of participation is essentially opportunistic and manipulative. Because such approaches are relatively cheap to apply and can bring considerable benefits, authoritarian governments may speak the language of participation without endorsing its underlying democratic philosophy. It cannot be stated with sufficient force that participation as it is used in the development enterprise must be part of a progressive political agenda, and cannot be justified if it is to prop up regimes known to be corrupt and essentially anti-democratic.

The institutionalization of participation does not depend only on exogenous policy factors. It also involves changing the organizational characteristics of development organizations, whatever their size and specific remit. The book indicates that as such organizations learn to operationalize processes of participatory development in rural communities and urban neighbourhoods across entire districts and regions, or even nationwide, they are realizing that the true challenge of participation lies in transforming themselves. But the kind of internal organizational changes which are needed, as part of a government-sponsored scaling-up strategy or on a much more modest scale, for example in a small, site-specific NGO, are as yet little understood.

The latest developments in ethical business-management practice may provide us with the most useful practical lessons yet as how best to institutionalize participation in the practices of development organizations. The ability to respond rapidly to changes in developmental needs, with the procedural flexibility such changes require, together with the commitment to devolve management tasks and responsibilities to the proposed beneficiaries of projects (what some authors in the book have called 'downwards accountability'), are practices which already have some legitimacy in the world of progressive business management. Such practices need further testing in development settings, however. What is clear is that the kind of donor pressure commonly applied on implementing agencies, for example to abide by unrealistic time constraints, pre-set targets and measurable outcomes, would be seen as archaic by the more progressive business managers of today. More importantly, such practices are in several ways incompatible with both the philosophical basis and the operational implications of participatory development projects. To dangle the carrot of participation, on the one hand, while continuing to apply the stick, on the other, by maintaining a strict control over resources, time, procedures, as well as the methods and criteria for evaluation, is plainly unacceptable. The heart of participation means allowing the proposed beneficiaries to increase their stake in the design, implementation and review of a project, whatever its nature. It is for them now to wield the stick.

Another dimension inherent in the institutionalization of participation which is easily overlooked is that for participatory approaches to scale up successfully, they must also be *scaled out*, that is, they must be applied consistently throughout the life cycle of the specific projects and programmes to which they are tied, not only at the beginning. Approaches such as PRA are still primarily used only at the appraisal and early planning phase of projects. True, the use of PRA in monitoring and evaluation is also on the increase, often as the logical outcome of a participatory baseline study aimed at generating relevant indicators which can be compared and explored further as the project's life extends. But we are still a long way from understanding how to devise appropriate mechanisms to sustain participation in the difficult and often arduous processes of negotiation, and resulting conflicts of interest, which invariably arise in the day-to-day management of a project. We also need to learn more about how best to build up local or popular organizations to ensure that 'projects' are as much theirs as ours.

It is relatively easy to engage a local population in conducting its own research through participatory appraisal techniques. But to follow through the consequences of such facilitation is considerably harder. By then, the consultants will have gone (until they return to evaluate), while the messy business of turning the glossy rhetoric of participation into nitty-gritty practice must still be done by those who are left behind. Only rarely are such processes written about. 'Who Changes?' goes some way towards plugging that gap. Several of the authors suggest that the real challenge is to ensure that the commitment of donors to a particular region, programme or policy stretches over a period of at least ten years. Only in such a way, they argue, can it be ensured that *going participatory* does not result in pseudo-participation or manipulation (chapters 11, 13, 14, 15, 18, 21, this volume). The key is to nurture local leadership and popular organizations until organized outside intervention is no longer needed. Too many projects try to do too much too quickly, failing to recognize that building up local institutions needs time and considerable personal and institutional commitment more than it needs money.

For the institutionalization of participatory approaches to have a lasting impact in the practice of development, we need also to build a common vision of where the changes we are setting in motion are leading. We should not be content only with the instrumental benefits of participation. The sensitive use of participatory methodologies may make projects more 'efficient', organizations more responsive to people's needs and, even, perhaps, policies more in tune with people's realities. Participation, however, also requires its advocates to be good social critics, to move beyond the instrumental into the realm of the philosophical and political, and back again. To institutionalize participation in development is about much more than adopting a number of new procedures and methodologies. It is about recognizing that those who were 'targets' of *our* development (our priorities, categories, formats, time constraints, etc.) must now become 'subjects' of *their* development, even if the course they choose turns out to be radically different from the one we would have wanted them to choose. Contained in such an assertion are the seeds of a truly radical and alternative way of thinking about development. It implies nothing less than revolutionary changes in the way 'development' is conceived and translated into practice. 'Who Changes?' show us some of the practical ways such changes can be applied in real-world situations.

We cannot afford to be complacent at a time when the banner of participation is being taken up by people of conflicting ideologies. In a world in which ideology has been replaced with efficiency, and in which politics has become a dirty word, it is crucial for those using participatory approaches in development to be aware of the existing social and political dynamics in those places in which intervention is being considered, and the changes that such interventions are likely to set in motion. Learning how to use participatory methods is only a small part of a highly complex equation. The true test of engagement with participation has more to do with one's personal commitment than with one's desire to learn a set of new tools. It is about vision, not only about methodology.

Participation is more a set of principles than an ideology, an ethic more than a model. If it is to have a lasting impact, not only in development, but more broadly in politics and society, participation must uphold a vision that is personal as well as societal. Rediscovering the Freirean notion of 'dialogue' and the Chambersian notion of 'sharing' reminds us that, deep down, participation is about learning to respect and listen to the opinions, feelings and knowledge of those we have in the past 'targeted'; being transparent regarding our intention to intervene in their lives, while at the same time being careful to decentralize and delegate, allowing the less powerful to manage greater resources and assume more responsibility; sharing our knowledge and expertise, our humanity, taking time to partake in people's lives and not being afraid to reveal one's weaknesses; in short, it is about opening up, taking risks and

170

showing trust. Such changes do not come easily to those weighed down with the baggage of long years in formal education and hierarchical cultures. Change will not occur unless we recognize that we too have to change.

Dialogue and sharing also have to do with bridging the gaps which exist between ourselves as development professionals. Many of this book's authors reveal that we are so keen to spread the message of participation to others that we forget to do ourselves what we preach. The finger is often pointed at government bureaucracies where work cultures, steeped in hierarchy and set procedures, are easily criticized for excessive anti-participatoriness. But the same accusations can often just as easily be made of NGOs, despite the progressive rhetoric in which they revel. As for academics, too few are those less concerned with the need to publish in obscure journals than with the desire to share their findings with a wider audience.

To expand and have greater impact, the commitment to participation requires the building of alliances between theorists, between practitioners and between both. It is about the realization that we can do very little on our own, and that we need others as they need us. Policymakers, project managers, extensionists and others in the field have too little time to reflect systematically on their activities. Academics can perhaps offer new perspectives and concepts to help them view reality in a new light, with new lenses. Those 'on the ground' have an even more important role to play: it is their intimate knowledge of development practice, their perceptions, which should form the basis of the kind of academic thinking which will have the most useful outcomes.

Considerable social energy is also released when practitioners from different realities who work in the same vein come together. For those who work in PRA, the knowledge of being 'linked' to a loose system of networks which now extends worldwide has provided strength and inspiration, as well as continuous innovation and creativity. Such doors must be kept open if we are to maintain the momentum of change and gradually build a movement which can do better than what has been done before. The challenges facing us in the future remain as momentous as ever, but new spaces have opened up, and alliances been built, through which the voices of the excluded can be heard more clearly, cautioning us on how to do a better job in the future. Donors are urged to continue to support the regular exchange of experience by those experimenting with participatory approaches in different settings and countries. The learning that takes place in such exchanges is invaluable in further refining the tools we use and deepening our understanding of what we are doing and what it implies.

Finally, a word of caution concerning the term 'institutionalize'. That participation in development should be institutionalized may be interpreted by some as meaning that participation can somehow be mandated. First, participation will not 'happen' as the result of a government decree or of an NGO mission statement; it is something that can be built up only slowly and nurtured carefully over time. The particular forms it will assume will vary according to the setting. There is no magic formula which can be universally applied. 'Perfect' participation does not exist. It is an ideal to be constantly sought, with its tools and techniques to be continuously improved. The danger is that for some, once institutionalized, participation will lose its meaning

171

and vigour. Those engaged in the task of mainstreaming participation are therefore urged to be critical and self-critical. The task does not 'end' with institutionalization; rather it begins anew, with fresh challenges ahead.

Those of us pressing for a more participatory approach to development are living intensely, breaking new ground every day, and gaining more and more supporters. We are no longer mere observers of a process of change; we are also makers of it. 'Who changes?' shows us how to be better crafters of change.

Notes

Chapter 1

1. The acronym PRA has long been known to mean participatory rural appraisal. A consensus has been building up that rural and appraisal are no longer adequate words to describe an approach whose applications are (i) no longer only rural but also urban, not only geographically determined but also organizational, and (ii) no longer limited to appraisal but extending into implementation, monitoring and evaluation, and related actions.

2. The International Institute for the Environment and Development (IIED), London, publishes and disseminates widely a three-monthly publication, *PLA Notes*, which brings together articles reporting on the use of different approaches in different contexts. Until 1994, the publication was called *Rapid Rural Appraisal (RRA) Notes*. Strangely, it was never called PRA Notes, despite the fact that PRA remains the most widely used of participatory research approach. In this volume PRA is referred to specifically as such, unless a quite different approach is being described.

Chapter 6

1. The law has also forced the state to redraw municipal boundaries in several Bolivian departments. The law's 'territorial' dimension has been much criticized in some sectors. It has revealed the illogicality of much of Bolivia's territorial make-up: most municipal boundaries were established arbitrarily by the government in La Paz soon after Independence, and have in many cases not been recognized or respected by local populations. The controversial redrawing of municipal boundaries, especially in the Lowlands, has been criticized by indigenous groups in particular as yet another 'imposition' by central government.

2. In La Paz and El Alto, CONDEPA has succeeded so far in dissuading neighbourhood organizations under its influence from registering as OTBs.

3. The *Movimiento Nacionalista Revolucionaria* (MNR – National Revolutionary Movement) has been the dominant party in Bolivian politics since 1985. Its ideological roots spring from the Revolution of 1952 which saw sweeping land reforms and the nationalization of the mining industry. Today, however, the MNR has embraced neo-liberal thinking in its economic policies, but remains a 'social' party through its alliance with the indigenist Katarista party.

4. Of Bolivia's 7.5 million inhabitants, about 4 million are defined as 'indigenous' – people whose first language is not Spanish and who distinguish themselves from the dominant Hispanic society usually in dress, custom, and world-view. The main groups are based in the highlands (Quechua, almost 3 million; and Aymara, almost 1 million). There is also a number of smaller, more scattered groups based in the lowlands.

5. The CORDES are government-funded Regional Development Corporations active in each Department.

173

6. These have now been renamed POAs (*Programas Operativos Anuales*) because there was some confusion about the use of the word 'Plan' in the previous name.
7. This is a question one of the coauthors of this article, James Blackburn, is at present exploring as part of his DPhil. research.
8. It is a concern of the authors that the kind of PRA being promoted by World Bank consultants in Potosi, Bolivia's poorest department (to take but one example), falls short of the rigorous approach developed by some at the Institute of Development Studies, Sussex University and many others in the field. The concern is also shared by the 'old timers' of Bolivian PRA, notably Fernando Dick of Nur University, who deplores what he sees as the growth of PRA abuse in the country.
9. Funding for the translations was provided by the Institute of Development Studies at Sussex University and by the International Institute for the Environment and Development.

Chapter 7

1. The work was coordinated by John Thompson, Associate Director of the Sustainable Agriculture Programme, IIED, London, and Carolyn Jones, Independent Consultant and PRA trainer, Edinburgh, Scotland.

Chapter 8

1. Consultant, Talstrasse 129, D-79194 Gundelfingen, Germany.
2. Institute of Environmental Studies, University of Zimbabwe, PO Box MP 167, Harare, Zimbabwe.
3. Intermediate Technology Development Group, PO Box 1744, Harare, Zimbabwe.

Chapter 14

1. This chapter is an abridged version of the following article, reproduced with kind permission of John Wiley and Sons: 'Participatory Environmental Management: contradiction of process, project and administration and development', *Public Administration and Development*, Vol. 15, No. 4 (Dec. 1995).

Chapter 15

1. Compare for further reading, GTZ (1996) and GTZ (1995b).
2. One positive example worth mentioning is the Deepa Narayan's World Bank ESD Paper No.1 'The Contribution of People's Participation – Evidence from 121 Rural Water Supply Projects', August 1995. This presents promising results for those projects which gave special attention to users' participation.
3. Compare GTZ (1995a).

Chapter 16

1. A longer version of this chapter is available under the title 'Participatory Approaches in Government Bureaucracies: facilitating the process of institutional change', *World Development*, Vol. 23, No. 9: 1251–554, 1995.
2. These are the Badulla Integrated Rural Development Programme in Sri Lanka, the Soil and Water Conservation Branch in Kenya and the National Irrigation

Administration in the Philippines. Each case study is dealt with in some detail in the author's *World Development* article (see n. 1). For the purposes of this chapter, however, these institutions are mentioned only briefly.

3. 'Third-sector' organizations include local non-governmental organizations (NGOs), international NGOs, community-based organizations (CBOs), including slum-dwellers associations, farmers' federations and church organizations, and social movements. See Hulme (1994) for a typology of these third-sector actors and their interactions.

4. See, for example, Edwards and Hulme, 1992; Farrington and Bebbington, 1994, 1993; Fowler, 1994, 1993, 1992; Hulme, 1994; Kaimowitz, 1993; D. Korten, 1990, and Uphoff, 1993, 1992; Clark, 1991, for empirical evidence and detailed discussions on the strengths, limitations, diversity, activities and influence of NGOs.

5. Some central governments accept the necessity and even the desirability of third-sector organizations, but only if those bodies can be controlled adequately by the state or the official party. They are not willing to tolerate associations that can operate independently of central tutelage, make claims for resources that may strain or embarrass the government, or become instruments of opposition groups. To prevent such unwelcome contingencies, some governments effectively proscribe certain third-sector organizations or suffocate them with surveillance and attention so paternalistic as to undermine all local initiative (cf., D.C. Korten and Alfonso, 1983).

6. The Scandinavian bilateral agencies, in particular, have attempted to provide more flexible, long-term funding arrangements while continuing to promote accountability and transparency in decisionmaking (David Satterthwaite, pers. com., 1995).

7. Among large foundations, the Ford Foundation has been one of the most proactive and engaged in the internal management discussions of large, public institutions, from the Philippines (cf. F.F. Korten and R.Y. Siy, Jr., 1988), to India (Gordon Conway, pers. com., 1994) to East Africa (Alan Fowler, pers. com., 1994).

8. Using data drawn from the Worldwatch Institute, USA, on various social and economic indicators of well-being by country, Kates and Haarman (1992) estimate that there are a total of approximately 1225 million people living in absolute poverty, half of whom live in Asia and a quarter of whom reside in Africa.

9. The concept of institutions is fundamental in understanding why many government organizations established for the provision of public services and management of resources create obstacles or disincentives to the sustainability of development projects and programmes. In the social-science literature, the term 'institution' refers often to established social relations, such as the institution of marriage or family. In the development literature, it may be used to describe a particular organization in a specific country, such as the Ministry of Agriculture, or to denote the set of 'working rules' that individuals use to order to organize repetitive activities that produce outcomes and create particular relationships with one another and others. This chapter uses the term 'institution' in these second and third senses, as both public organization and as rules-in-use. The term 'agency' is used interchangeably with institution.

10. For a useful discussion of the distinction between bureaucratic and strategic organizational forms, see D.C. Korten, 1984. For an insightful analysis of the differing theoretical and epistemological bases of these two basic organizational types, see Lincoln, 1985.

11. This holds true for large organizations in both the public and private sectors. The parallels between debates about organizational learning in the two sectors are striking. For more than a decade the corporate world has been engrossed in discussions

about 'corporate cultures' (cf. Peters and Waterman, 1982), 'learning organizations' (cf. Pedler, et al., 1991; Senge et al., 1994; Senge, 1990), 'leadership as stewardship' (cf. Block, 1993) and 'management revolutions' (cf. Peters, 1987, 1994). Many of the same concepts and principles can be found in the emerging public sector literature with regard to the management of large government agencies (cf. Godfrey, in Senge et al., 1994: 493–9), consensus-building and conflict resolution (cf. Kahane, 1994), communities as learning organizations (Weisbord, 1992) and the design of participatory research processes (Webber and Ison, 1995).

12. Over the past 15 years, there has been a convergence of opinion that has called for the rethinking of management systems and policies. This has been a recurrent theme in the development administration literature, particularly with respect to 'process-oriented planning' and 'the learning process approach' (cf. Blair, 1985; D. Korten, 1980, 1984, 1990; F.F. Korten and Siy, Jr., 1988; Hage and Finsterbusch, 1987; Honadle and VanSant, 1985; Johnston and Clark, 1982; Moris, 1981; Pretty and Chambers, 1994; Rondinelli, 1983). Similar sentiments have been expressed in the soft-systems literature, especially with regard to agriculture, development education and extension science (cf. Bawden, 1989, 1994; Bawden et al., 1984; Bawden and Ison, 1990; Checkland, 1984, 1985; Ison, 1990; Kolb, 1984; Macadam and Packham, 1989; Röling, 1994).

13. This strategy was used recently in a series of high-level workshops organized to assist in the process of designing and implementing the new Government of South Africa's participatory rural development, agriculture and land-reform policies (Cousins, 1994). A similar approach was employed for exposing senior government officers to PRA in an FAO-supported programme aimed at promoting participatory artisanal fishing-port development in Guinea (Reusen and Johnson, 1994).

14. Adapted from F.F. Korten, 1988, with additions from Bawden, 1989; Checkland, 1984; Kolb, 1984; and Macadam and Packham, 1989.

15. The recognition of the need for systematic institutional reorientation is frequently driven by individuals within the agency who perceive problems and opportunities and take action. Hence, change occurs through policy decisions by senior members of management. 'Pen-stroke' decisions by senior officials can be effective in changing such policies as training practices and helping decide whether a particular research or development approach is to be adopted and promoted. These policies may do little, however, to change the agency's incentive systems, norms or working rules, or develop better management procedures. Learning-based change is more likely to occur through the sustained interaction and experimentation of small teams of internal and external professionals representing different perspectives and priorities, who help programmes navigate through a phased series of expansions. Frances F. Korten (1988) refers to these teams of facilitators as 'working groups'.

16. Although government–third sector collaboration is occurring with increasing frequency, there is still a tendency among government staff to view the non-government 'outsiders' with a degree of suspicion ('They are a bunch of leftists, so what do you think their real agenda is?'), envy ('They are just like us, only they get paid more') and even disdain ('It's easy for them, they get plenty of money from the donors, are not accountable to the people and are not responsible for servicing the entire country'). I have heard senior government officers utter these and other similar statements on several occasions when the subject of government–NGO collaboration was raised. The reverse is also true, as many third-sector organizations fear that by becoming associated closely with a government-led initiative they will either lose their reputa-

176

tion as independent advocates for the poor or be manipulated and exploited by the state for its own dissolute ends. A third, separate shortcoming is that most third-sector agencies are small and, hence, unable to provide the kind of large-scale, long-term support necessary to train large numbers of government staff. For example, in 1994, the newly-elected Government of Sri Lanka abolished its *Janasaviya* programme, which was designed to identify and channel resources to the poorest sectors of the community, when it was discovered that those resources were not reaching their intended 'target groups'. An alternative programme is now being developed that would employ a modified form of participatory rural appraisal. The Sri Lankan authorities have estimated that they will need to train 10 000–15 000 staff in the new approach over the next one to two years in order to implement the participatory poverty assessments across the country. The combined resources of the entire third sector in Sri Lanka would have difficulty training that number of field staff (Mallika Samaranayake, pers. com., 1994).
17. For examples within irrigation bureaucracies, see Bruns, 1993; Korten and Siy, Jr., 1988; and Uphoff, 1986. For examples within forestry bureaucracies, see Poffenberger, 1990 and Someshwar, 1993.

Chapter 18

1. This chapter is an abridged version of the following article, and is published with kind permission from John Wiley and Sons: 'Current Challenges facing Participatory Rural Appraisal', *Public Administration and Development*, Vol. 16, No. 1 (Feb. 1996).

Chapter 19

1. Chapter 20, 'The Learning Organization: making development agencies more participatory from the inside', provides more detail on the specifics of how to make institutions more participatory.
2. In part drawn from 'Going to Scale with PRA: reflections and recommendations', by 26 trainers in participatory approaches mainly from South Asia, Calcutta, May 1997.
3. The following is drawn from Issue No. 5 of the *Participation in Action Newsletter*.
4. These recommendations are partly drawn from those established at the IDS workshop on 'Institutionalization of Participatory Approaches', and partly from the conclusions reached at the 'Dare-to-Share' conference convened by GTZ in 1994.

Chapter 21

1. Peter Uvin (1995) also points to a general lack of unanimity in the literature about the meaning of scaling-up. While generally the term is used to refer to 'increasing the impact of grassroots organizations and their programmes,' Uvin provides a review of the literature and presents a typology of four types of scaling-up: (928–99). These include quantitative scaling-up, functional scaling-up, political scaling-up and organizational scaling-up. While examples of these are found in this book, our focus is more on the scaling-up of methods, while Uvin focuses on the scaling-up

of NGOs. I am grateful to David Brown and his colleagues at the Institute for Development Reseach, Boston, for pointing me to Uvin's work.
2. Some important lessons regarding building partnerships across differing kinds of organizations and institutions are found in a series of case studies in Asia and Africa which have been coordinated by the Synergos Institute in New York. The lessons are summarized in L.David Brown and Darcy Ashman, 'Participation, Social Capital and Intersectoral Problem-Solving: African and Asian Cases', IDR Reports (12:2), 1996.
3. For discussion of 'Whose Reality Counts', see Chambers (1996).

References and Sources

Absalom, E., Okurut and Anube (1995) Personal communication, in K. Wright (1995).

Adepoju, A. (1993) *The Impact of Structural Adjustment on the Population of Africa: the implications for education, health and employment*, London: James Currey Ltd.

Admassie, Y. (1992) 'The Catchment Approach to Soil Conservation in Kenya', *Regional Soil Conservation Unit Report*, No. 6, Nairobi: Regional Soil Conservation Unit, Swedish International Development Authority.

AGRITEX (Department of Agriculture and Technical and Extension Services) (1995) *Organisational Development (Pilot Programme)*, Masvingo, Zimbabwe: AGRITEX.

Alfonso, F.B. (1983) 'Assisting Farmer-controlled Development of Communal Irrigation Systems', in D.C. Korten and F.B. Alfonso (ed.), *Bureaucracy and the Poor: closing the gap*, West Hartford, CA: Kumarian Press, 44–52.

Ardaya Salinas, R. (1996) 'El Fortalecimiento Municipal para la Participación Popular', in *Apre(hen)diendo la Participación Popular: análisis y reflexiones sobre el modelo Boliviano de descentralización*, Bolivia: SNPP, UNDP.

Arrieta, M. (1995) 'La Participación Popular y las Tendencias del Desarrollo', in *Participación Popular y Desarrollo Rural*, M. Arrieta et al. (eds), Colección Debate de Políticas Agropecuarias, Bolivia: Club de Economía Agrícola y Sociología Rural.

Ashish, M. (1993) 'Decentralised Management of Natural Resources in the UP Hills', *Economic and Political Weekly*, 28 August.

Bagadion, B.U. and F.F. Korten, (1991) 'Developing Irrigators' Organizations: a learning process approach,' in M. Cernea (ed.), *Putting People First: sociological variables in rural development*, Oxford: Oxford University Press.

Bagadion, B.U. (1988) 'The Evolution of the Policy Context: an Historical Overview', in F.F. Korten and R.Y. Siy, Jr. (ed.), *Transforming a Bureaucracy: the experience of the Philippine national irrigation administration*, West Hartford, CA: Kumarian Press, 1–19.

Bagadion, B.U. (1987) 'Government Intervention in Farmer-Managed Irrigation Systems in the Philippines: how research contributed to improving the process', in E.D. Martin and R. Yoder (ed.), *Public Intervention in Farmer-Managed Irrigation Systems*, Colombo: International Irrigation Management Institute, 265–76.

Bawden, R.J. (1989) *Systems Agriculture: learning to deal with complexity,* New York: MacMillan.

Bawden, R.J. (1994) 'Creating Learning Systems: a metaphor for institutional reform for development', in I. Scoones and J. Thompson (ed.), *Beyond Farmer First: rural people's knowledge, agricultural research and extension practice,* London: Intermediate Technology Publications, Ltd., 258–63.

Bawden, R.J. and R.L. Ison, (1990) 'The Purpose of Field Crop Ecosystems: Social and Economic Aspects', in C.J. Pearson (ed.) *Field Crop Ecosystems,* London: Elsevier.

Bawden, R.J., R.D. Macadam, R.G. Packham and I. Valentine (1984) 'Systems Thinking and Practices in the Education of Agriculturalists', *Agricultural Systems,* Vol. 13: 205–25.

Bebbington, A. and G. Thiele *et al.* (1993) *Non-Governmental Organisations and the State in Latin America,* Overseas Development Institute, London and New York: Routledge.

Blair, H.W. (1985) 'Reorienting Development Administration', *Journal of Development Studies,* Vol. 21, No. 3: 447–57.

Block, P. (1993) *Stewardship,* San Francisco, CA: Berret-Koehler.

Boer, L. and J. Rooimans (ed.) (1994) *The World Bank and Poverty Reduction,* Development Cooperation Information Department, Ministry of Foreign Affairs, The Hague: Government of The Netherlands.

Booth, D. (ed.) (1994) *Rethinking Social Development: theory, research and practice,* London: Earthscan.

Booth, D. *et al.* (1996) *Empowering the Poor through Institutional Reform? An inititial appraisal of the Bolivian experience,* Report to SIDA by the Development Studies Unit, Department of Social Anthropology, University of Stockholm.

Booth, D. *et al.* (1997): *Popular Participation: democratising the state in rural Bolivia,* Report to SIDA, commissioned through Development Studies Unit, Department of Social Anthropology, University of Stockholm.

Bowles, P. (1989) 'Recipient Needs and Donor Interests in the Allocation of EEC Aid to Developing Countries', *Canadian Journal of Development Studies,* Vol. 10, No. 1: 7–19.

Bruns, B. (1993) 'Promoting Participation in Irrigation: reflections on experience in Southeast Asia', *World Development,* Vol. 21, No. 11: 1837–49.

Cablayan, C.M. (1990) 'The Role of Social Organizers in Communal Irrigation Development in the Philippines', in S. Manor and M. Olin (ed.), *Role of Social Organizers in Assisting Farmer-Managed Irrigation Systems: proceedings of a regional workshop of the farmer-managed irrigation systems network,* Colombo: International Irrigation Management Institute, 81–90.

Cernea, M. (1991) *Putting People First: sociological variables in rural development,* Oxford: Oxford University Press.

Cernea, M. (1992) *The Building Blocks of Participation: testing bottom-up planning,* World Bank Discussion Papers, No. 166, Washington: World Bank.

Chambers, R. (1983) *Rural Development: putting the last first,* Harlow: Longmans.

Chambers, R., A. Pacey and L.A. Thrupp (ed.) (1989) *Farmer First: farmer innovation and agricultural research,* London: Intermediate Technology Publications, Ltd.

Chambers, R. (1992) 'Rural Appraisal: rapid, relaxed and participatory', *IDS Discussion Paper 311*, Brighton: Institute of Development Studies.

Chambers, R. (1993*) Challenging the Professions: frontiers for rural development*, London: Intermediate Technology Publications.

Chambers, R. (1994a) 'A Note for the Staff of Bilateral and Multilateral Aid Agencies and of Northern NGOs on Participatory Rural Appraisal, (PRA)', unpublished paper, available from the author at the Institute for Development Studies, University of Sussex, Falmer, Brighton, UK.

Chambers, R. (1994b) 'The Origins and Practice of Participatory Rural Appraisal', *World Development*, Vol 22, No. 7: 953–69.

Chambers, R. (1994c) 'Participatory Rural Appraisal (PRA): challenges, potentials and paradigm', *World Development*, Vol 22, 10: 1437–54.

Chambers, R. (1994d) 'Participatory Rural Appraisal (PRA): analysis of experience', *World Development*, Vol 22, 9: 1253–68.

Chambers, R. (1995a) 'Sharing Our Concerns and Looking to the Future', *PLA Notes 22*, London: IIED.

Chambers, R. (1995b) 'Making the Best of Going to Scale', *PLA Notes*, London: IIED, 24.

Chambers, R. (1995c) 'Poverty and Livelihoods: Whose Reality Counts?,' *IDS Discussion Paper*, No. 347, Brighton: Institute of Development Studies.

Chambers, R. *et al.* (1996) 'Sharing Our Experiences: an appeal to donors and governments', in *Participation, Policy and Institutionalisation, PLA Notes 27*, London: IIED.

Chambers, R. (1997) *Whose Reality Counts?*, Intermediate Technology Publications.

Chambers, R. and J. Blackburn (1996) 'The Power of Participation: PRA and policy', *IDS Policy Briefing*, Issue No. 7, Brighton: Institute of Development Studies.

Chantornvong, S. (1988) 'Tocqueville's *Democracy in America* and the Third World', in V. Ostrom, D. Feeny and H. Picht (ed.) *Rethinking Institutional Analysis and Development*, San Francisco, CA: International Center for Economic Growth, 69–99.

Chauvau, J.P. (1994) 'Participation Paysanne et Populisme Bureaucratique: essai d'histoire et de sociologie de la culture de développement', in J.P. Jacob and P. Lavigne Delville (ed.), *Les Associations Paysannes en Afrique*, APAD-IUD-CARTHALA.

Checkland, P.B. (1984) *Systems Thinking, Systems Practice*, Chichester, UK: John Wiley & Sons.

Checkland, P.B. (1985) 'From Optimizing to Learning: a development of systems thinking for the 1990s', *Journal of the Operational Research Society*, Vol. 36: 757–67.

Chuma, E. (1994) 'The Contribution of Different Evaluation Methods to the Understanding of Farmers' Decision on Adoption and Adaptations of Innovations: experiences from the development of a conservation tillage system in Zimbabwe', in *Systems-Oriented Research in Agriculture and Rural Development*, International symposium held in Montpellier, 21–25 November 1994. Papers published by CIRAD-SAR, Montpellier, 161–67.

Clark, J. (1991) *Democratizing Development: The Role of Voluntary Organizations*, London: Earthscan.

181

Commonwealth Secretariat (1989) *Integrating Conservation into the Farming System*, London: Commonwealth Secretariat.

Cornwall, A. (ed.) (1992) 'Look Who's Talking', *A Report of a Training of Trainers Course in Participatory Rural Appraisal* in Dalocha, Southern Shewa, November 1992, IIED, 3 Endsleigh street, London, WC 1H 0DD.

Cornwall, A., I. Guijt and A. Welbourn (1994) 'Acknowledging Process: challenges for agricultural research and extension methodology', in I. Scoones and J. Thompson (ed.) *Beyond Farmer First: rural people's knowledge, agricultural research and extension practice*, London: Intermediate Technology Publications, Ltd., 98–117.

Cornwall, A., and S. Fleming (1995) 'Context and Complexity: anthropological reflections on PRA', in *Critical Reflections from Practice*, PLA Notes 24, London: IIED.

Cousins, B. (ed.) (1994) 'Issues and Options for Institutional Change for Rural Development, Agriculture and Land Reform', *L&APC Policy Paper*, No. 9, Johannesburg: Land and Agriculture Policy Centre.

Curtis, D. (1991) *Beyond Government*, London: Macmillan.

De los Reyes, R.P. and S.M.G. Jopillo (1988) 'The Impact of Participation: an evaluation of the NIAs communal irrigation program,' in F.F. Korten, and R.Y. Siy Jr. (ed.), *Transforming a Bureaucracy: the experience of the Philippine national irrigation administration*, West Hartford, CA: Kumarian Press, 90–116.

De los Reyes, R. (1987) 'Sociotechnical Profile: a tool for rapid rural appraisal', in Khon Kaen University (ed.), *Proceedings of the 1985 International Conference on Rapid Rural Appraisal*, Rural Systems Research and Farming Systems Research Projects, Thailand: Khon Kaen University, 225–81.

De los Reyes, R.P. and S.M.G. Jopillo (1986) *An Evaluation of the Philippine Participatory Communal Program*, Quezon City, Metro Manila: Institute of Philippine Culture.

De los Reyes, R.P. (1980) *Managing Communal Gravity Systems: farmers' approaches and implications for program planning*, Quezon City, Metro Manila: Institute of Philippine Culture.

De Toma, C. (1996) *Promoting Popular Participation in Bolivia: assessing the potential for institutional reform*, unpublished, M.Phil Dissertation, Institute of Development Studies, Sussex University, Brighton, UK.

Doon Valley 1: Government of India (GOI), Government of Uttar Pradesh (GOUP), Commission of the European Communities (CEC) (1993a) *Doon Valley Integrated Watershed Management Project: work programme 1993–4*, Dehrandun: Watershed Management Directorate.

Doon Valley 2: GOI, GOUP, CEC (1993b), *Doon Valley Integrated Watershed Management Project: Overall Workplan 1993–2001*, Dehrandun: Watershed Mangement Directorate.

Doyal, L. and I. Gough (1991) *A Theory of Human Need*, London: Macmillan Education, Ltd.

Drinkwater, M. (1994) 'Establishing a Community Development Approach in Ndola Rural District', unpublished paper, June, available from DARUDEC, Copenhagen, Denmark or the Smallholder Development Project, Mpongwe, Ndola Rural District, Zambia.

Dudley, E. (1993) *The Critical Villager: beyond community participation*, London: Routledge.

Due, J.M. (1993) 'Liberalization and Privatization in Tanzania and Zambia', *World Development*, Vol. 21, No. 12: 1981–88.

Edwards, M. and D. Hulme (1992) *Making a Difference: NGOs and development in a changing world*, London: Earthscan Publications.

Edwards, R. and M. Humera (1994) 'Ensuring Equitable Development as a Basis Towards Community Based Sustainable Development', Discussion Note, Action Aid Pakistan, June.

Edwards, R. (1994) 'Raising Expectations Through Participatory Rural Appraisals – A False Worry?', Discussion Note, Action Aid, Pakistan, January.

Fals Borda, O. (1988) *Knowledge and People's Power: lessons with peasants in Nicaragua, Mexico and Colombia*, Geneva: International Labour Office.

Farrington, J. and A.J. Bebbington (1994) 'From Research to Innovation: getting the most from interaction with NGOs', in I. Scoones and J. Thompson (ed.), London: Intermediate Technology Publications, 203–13.

Farrington, J. and A.J. Bebbington with K. Wellard, and D.I. Lewis (1993) *Reluctant Partners: non-governmental organizations, the state and sustainable agricultural development in Latin America*, London: Routledge.

Fernandez, A.P. (1994) 'The MYRADA Experience: alternate management systems for savings and credit of the rural poor', available from MYRADA, No. 2 Service Road, Domlur Layout, Bangalore 560 071, India.

Fowler, A. (1992) 'Prioritizing Institutional Development: a new role for NGO centres for study and development', *Gatekeeper Series No. 35*, Sustainable Agriculture Programme, London: International Institute for Environment and Development.

Fowler, A. (1993) *Non-Governmental Organizations and the Promotion of Democracy in Kenya*, PhD dissertation, University of Sussex, Brighton, UK.

Fowler, A. (1994) 'Assessing NGO Performance: difficulties, dilemmas and a way ahead', paper presented at the *International Workshop on NGOs and Development: Performance and accountability in the 'New World Order'*, University of Manchester, UK, 27–29 June.

Freire, P. (1982) *Education for Critical Consciousness*, New York: Continuum Books.

Freire, P. (1968) *Pedagogy of the Oppressed*, New York: The Seabury Press.

Galindo, M. (1995) 'Contradicciones que la Participación Popular Intenta Resolver', in *Participación Popular y Desarrollo Rural*, (M. Arrieta *et al.* (eds) Bolivia: Colección Debate de Políticas Agropecuarias, Club de Economía Agrícola y Sociología Rural.

Gaventa, J. (1980) *Power and Powerlessness: quiescence and rebellion in an Appalachian valley*, Clarendon Press.

Gibbon, P., K. J. Havnekik and K. Hermele (1995) *A Blighted Harvest: the World Bank and African agriculture in the 1980s*, Trenton, NJ: Africa World Press.

Gibbs, G. *et al.* (1990) 'The growth of the Philippine Social Forestry Programme', in M, Poffenberger, *Keepers of the Forest: land management alternatives in Southeast Asia*, West Harford, CA: Kumarian Press, 253–66.

Godfrey, B. (1994) 'Can Large Government Learn? The Challenge of Strategic Change in the Australian Taxation Office', in P. Senge *et al.* (ed.), *The Fifth Discipline Fieldbook: strategies and tools for building a learning organization*, London: Nicholas Brealey Publications, pp. 493–9.

Göricke, F. (1993) 'An Outline of Experiences with Community-level Planning and Development in the Framework of CARD', background paper prepared for the Arusha Conference on Assessment of New Approaches Towards Rural Development (CARD), Masvingo, Zimbabwe.

Government of India (1993) *The Constitution (73rd Amendment) Act.*

Griffin, K. (1991) 'Foreign Aid after the Cold War', *Development and Change*, Vol. 22, No. 4, 28–49.

Grounder, R. (1994) 'Empirical Results of Aid Motivation: Australia's bilateral aid program', *World Development*, Vol. 22, No. 1: 99–113.

GTZ (1995a) *Dare-to-share Fair Participatory Learning Approaches in Development Co-operation – Documentation and 1 Directory,* Yvonne Mabille.

GTZ (1995b) *Managing the Implementation of German Technical Cooperation Activities.*

GTZ (1996) *Project Cycle Management (PCM) and Objectives-oriented Project Planning* (ZOPP).

GTZ GmbH. (1987) 'ZOPP, Zielorientiertes Planen von Programmen der Technischen Zusammenarbeit', Eschborn, Germany: Einführung in die Grundlagen der Methode.

Guha, R. (1989) *The Unquiet Woods*, Oxford: Oxford University Press.

Guijt, I. and J. Thompson (1994) 'Landscapes and Livelihoods: environmental and socio-economic dimensions of small-scale irrigation', *Land Use Planning*, Vol. 11, No. 4: 294–308.

Hage, J. and K. Finsterbusch (1987) *Organizational Change as a Development Strategy: models and tactics for improving Third World organizations*, Boulder, CO: Lynn Reinner Publishers.

Hagmann, J., (1993), 'Farmer Participatory Research in Conservation Tillage; Approach, Methods and Experiences from an Adaptive Trial Programme in Zimbabwe', in M. Kronen (ed.), *Proceedings of the 4th Annual Scientific Conference of the SADC Land and Water Management Programme*, Windhoek, Namibia, 11–15 October, 1993, pp. 217–36.

Hagmann, J. and H. Loos (1995) *Soil and Water Conservation for Smallholder Farmers in Semi-arid Zimbabwe,* Proceedings of a technical workshop held 3–7 April 1995 in Masvingo, Zimbabwe, Belmont Press.

Hagmann, J. and K. Murwira (1996) 'Indigenous Soil and Water Conservation in Southern Zimbabwe: a study of techniques, historical changes and recent developments under participatory research and extension', in *Drylands Programme Issues Paper No. 63*, London: International Institute for Environment and Development (IIED).

Hagmann, J., K. Murwira and E. Chuma (1996) 'Learning Together: development and extension of soil and water conservation in Zimbabwe', in *Quaterly Journal of International Agriculture*, Vol. 35, No. 2: 142–62.

Hagmann, J., E. Chuma and K. Murwira (1997) 'Kuturaya: a new approach to participatory research, innovation and extension', in L. Van Veldhuizen, A. Waters-Bayer, R. Ramirez, D. Johnson and J. Thompson, *Research in Practice: lessons from the field*, London: IT Publications.

Hall, B. (1981) 'Participatory Research, Popular Knowledge and Power: a reflection', in *Convergence 3:* 6–19.

Handy, C. (1995) (5th edn) *Gods of Management: the changing work of organisations*, London: Arrow Books Ltd.

Handy, C. (1989) *The Age of Unreason*, London: Business Books Ltd.

Hardoy, J.E., D. Mitlin and D. Satterthwaite (1992) *Environmental Problems in Third World Cities*, London: Earthscan Publications.

Hardoy, J.E., S. Cairncross and D. Satterthwaite (1990) *The Poor Die Young: housing and health in third world cities*, London: Earthscan Publications.

Helleiner, G.K. (1992) 'The IMF, the World Bank and Africa's Adjustment and External Debt Problems: an unofficial view', *World Development*, Vol. 20, No. 6: 779–792.

Hirschman, A.O. (1995) *Development Projects Observed* (4th edn), Washington DC: The Brookings Institution.

Holland, J. (forthcoming) *Whose Voice? Participatory research and policy change*, London: Intermediate Technology Publications.

Holland, J. with J. Blackburn (eds), (1997) *Participatory Research and Policy Change*, London: Intermediate Technology Publications.

Honadle, G. and J. VanSant (1987) *Implementation for Sustainability: lessons from integrated rural development*, West Hartford, CT: Kumarian Press.

Hope and Timmel (1984) *Training for Transformation: a handbook for community workers*, Gweru, Zimbabwe: Mambo Press,

Howes, M. and C. Roche (1995) 'A Participatory Organisational Appraisal of ACORD', *PLA Notes 22*, London: International Institute for the Environment and Development.

Hulme, D. (1994) 'Social Development Research and the Third Sector: NGOs as users and subjects of social inquiry', in D. Booth (ed.), *Rethinking Social Development: theory, research and practice*, Harlow, UK: Longman Scientific and Technical, pp. 251–75.

ILDIS (Instituto Latinoamericano de Investigaciones Sociales) (1992) *La Relación entre Estado y ONGs*, La Paz, Bolivia: Cooperación Holandesa y COTESU.

Illich, I. (1971) *A Celebration of Awareness: a call for institutional revolution*, Harmondsworth: Penguin Education.

Illo, J.F.I. (1988) 'Farmers, Engineers and Organizers: the Taisan Project', in F.F. Korten and R.Y. Siy, Jr. (ed.) (1988): 31–60.

Ison, R.L. (1990) 'Teaching Threatens Sustainable Agriculture', *Gatekeeper Series No. 21*, London: Sustainable Agriculture Programme, International Institute for Environment and Development.

Jamieson, N. (1987) 'The Paradigmatic Significance of Rapid Rural Appraisal', Khon Kaen University, Proceedings of the 1985 International Conference on Rapid Rural Appraisal, Khon Kaen, Thailand, available from Dr Terd Charoenwatana, Faculty of Agriculture, Khon Kaen University, Khon Kaen 40002, Thailand.

Johnston, B.F. and Clark, W. (1982) *Redesigning Rural Development: a strategic perspective*, Baltimore: Johns Hopkins University Press.

Kahandawa, K.A.J. (1994) 'Participatory Planning and Implementation:

experiences of the Badulla Integrated Rural Development Project', paper presented at the Asia Regional Participatory Rural Appraisal Workshop, Colombo, Sri Lanka, 3–18 December 1994.

Kahane, A. (1994) *Scenarios for Building Community*, Emeryville, CA: Global Business Network.

Kaimowitz, D. (1993) 'The Role of Nongovernmental Organizations in Agricultural Research and Technology Transfer in Latin America', *World Development*, Vol. 21, No. 7: 1139–50.

Kaplinski, R. (1994) *Easternisation: the spread of Japanese management techniques to developing countries*, London: Frank Cass.

Kar, K. and C. Backhaus (1994) 'Old Wine in New Bottles? Experiences with the application of PRA and participatory approaches in a large-scale foreign-funded government-development programme in Sri Lanka', unpublished paper available from the Institute of Development Studies, University of Sussex, UK: Falmer, Brighton.

Kates, R.W. and V. Haarmann (1992) 'Where the Poor Live: are the assumptions correct?' *Environment*, Vol. 34, No. 4: 4–28.

Kiara, J.K., M. Segerros, J. Pretty and J. McCracken (1990) *Rapid Catchment Analysis in Murang'a District, Kenya*, Nairobi, Kenya: Soil and Water Conservation Branch, Ministry of Agriculture.

Kievelitz, U. and R.D. Reineke, 'Rapid Appraisal of Organisational Cultures: a challenge for field work', unpublished and undated paper, available from the authors at GTZ, Postfach 5180, D-6236, Eschborn, Germany.

Kishor, V. and R.K. Gupta (nd) *Socio-economic Studies for Land-use Planning and Eco-development in Garhwal Himalaya*, New Delhi: Indian National Trust for Art and Cultural Heritage.

Kitching, G. (1982) *Development and Underdevelopment in Comparative Perspective*, London: Methuen.

Klitgaard, R. (1991) *Adjusting to Reality: beyond 'state and market' in economic development*, San Francisco, CA: ICE Press.

Kolb, D. (1984) *Experiential Learning: experience as the source of learning and development*, Newark, NJ: Prentice-Hall.

Korten, D.C. (1980) 'Community Organization and Rural Development: a learning process approach', *Public Administration Review*, Vol. 40, No. 5: 480–511.

Korten, D.C. (1984) 'Strategic Organization for People-centered Development', *Public Administration Review*, Vol. 44, No. 4: 341–52.

Korten, D. (1988) 'From Bureaucratic to Strategic Organization', in F.F. Korten and R.Y. Siy, Jr. (ed.) (1985), pp. 117–44.

Korten, D.C. (1990) *Getting to the 21st Century: voluntary action and the global agenda*, West Hartford, CT: Kumarian Press.

Korten, D.C. and F.B. Alfonso (ed.) (1983) *Bureaucracy and the Poor: closing the gap*, West Hartford, CT: Kumarian Press.

Korten, F.F. (1982) 'Building National Capacity to Develop Water Users' Associations: Experiences from the Philippines', *World Bank Staff Working Paper*, No. 528, Washington D.C: The World Bank.

Korten, F.F. (1988) 'The Working group as a Catalyst for Organizational Change', in F.F. Korten and R.Y. Siy, Jr. (ed.) (1988) pp. 61–89.

Korten, F.F. and R.Y. Siy, Jr. (1988) *Transforming a Bureaucracy: the experi-*

ence of the Philippine National Irrigation Administration, West Hartford, CT: Kumarian Press.

Kumar, S. (ed.) (1996) 'ABC of PRA: attitude and behaviour change', in *Participation, Policy and Institutionalisation, PLA Notes 27*, London: IIED.

Leurs, R. (1994) 'Reflections on PRA', paper presented at the 'Dare-to-Share Fair' Conference, organised by GTZ in Eschborn in September 1994; available from the author at the Development Administration Group, University of Birmingham.

Leurs, R. (1995) 'Reflections on the Perceived Impact, Quality and Contextual Challenges of Participatory Rural Appraisal in South Asia', DAG publication, available from the author at the Development Administration Group, University of Birmingham.

Lincoln, Y. (1985) *Organizational Theory and Inquiry: the paradigm revolution*, Beverley Hills, CA: Sage Publications.

Macadam, R.D. and R.G. Packham (1989) 'A Case Study of the Use of Soft Systems Methodology: restructuring an academic organization to facilitate the education of systems agriculturalists', *Agricultural Systems*, Vol. 30: 351–67.

Madondo, B. (1992) *Technology Generation and Transfer Systems for Communal Areas of Zimbabwe after Independence (1981–1991): a decade of institutional adaptation*, Harare, Zimbabwe: Regional Research Cooperation Office, SAREC.

Madondo, B. (1993) 'Extension Strategies from 1993 and Beyond', paper presented at a workshop of AGRITEX, Manicaland Province, held at Kyle View (Masvingo), 1993 September, Mutare, Zimbabwe: AGRITEX.

Madondo, B. (1995) 'Agricultural Transfer Systems of the Past and Present', in S. Twomlow, J. Ellis-Jones, J. Hagmann and H. Loos, *Soil and Water Conservation for Smallholder Farmers in Semi-arid Zimbabwe*, Proceedings of a technical workshop held 3–7 April 1995 in Masvingo, Zimbabwe, Belmont Press.

Manor, J. (1995) 'Democratic Decentralization in Africa and Asia', in *Towards Democratic Governance*, IDS Bulletin, Vol. 26, No. 2.

Mitlin, D. and J. Thompson (1995) 'Participatory Approaches in Urban Areas: experiences, issues and opportunities', *Environment and Urbanization*.

Moris, J. (1981) *Managing Induced Rural Development*, Boomington, IN: International Development Institute, Indiana University.

Mosse, D. and the KRIB Project Team, (1995) ' "People's Knowledge" in Project Planning: the limits and social conditions of participation in planning agricultural development', ODI Network Paper 58 (Agricultural Administration – Research and Extension), London, July 1995.

Mosse, D. (1993) 'Authority, Gender and Knowledge: theoretical reflections on the practice of participatory rural appraisal', Agricultural Administration (Research and Extension) Network Paper 44, London: Overseas Development Institute.

Mouzelis, N. (1994) 'The State in Late Development: historical and comparative perspectives,' in D. Booth (ed.), *Rethinking Social Development: theory, research and practice*, Harlow, UK: Longman Scientific and Technical, pp. 126–51.

Mwenda, E. (1991) *Soil and Water Conservation. Field Notes for Catchment*

Planning, Nairobi: Soil and Water Conservation Branch, Ministry of Agriculture, Government of Kenya.

Nelson, N. and S. Wright (1995) *Power and Participatory Development: theory and practice,* London: Intermediate Technology Publications.

NIACONSULT (1993) *Farmer's Participation in National Irrigation Systems in the Philippines: lessons learned,* NIACONSULT, Inc., a subsidiary of the National Irrigation Administration, Manila, Philippines, December 1993.

Nott, G.A., (1992) 'Project Implementation Workshops on Participatory Village Planning (PVP)', aide memoire to the Regional Development Division, Ministry of Policy, Planning and Implementation, Sri Lanka, the United Nations Development Programme, Colombo, and the Institute for Agricultural Development, Rome, 25 June 1992.

Nyagumbo, I. (1995) 'Socio-cultural Constraints to Development Projects in Communal Areas of Zimbabwe: a review of experiences from farmer participatory research in conservation tillage', Research Report 14, Conservation Tillage Project, Institute of Agricultural Engineering, Harare, Zimbabwe.

Ostrom, E. (1986) 'An Agenda for the Study of Institutions', *Public Choice,* Vol. 48: 3–25.

Ostrom, E. (1990) *Governing the Commons: the evolution of institutions for collective action,* New York: Cambridge University Press.

Osuga, B. and D. Mutayisa, (1994) 'PRA Lessons and Concerns: experiences in Uganda', unpublished paper available from the Institute of Development Studies, University of Sussex, Brighton.

Pedler, M., J. Burgoyne and T. Boydell (1991) *The Learning Company* London: McGraw Hill.

Peres Arenas, J. 'Bolivia: reformas, actores y participación popular en la coyuntura actual', in J. Blauert (ed.) *Making sustainable development,* forthcoming.

Peters, T. (1987) *Thriving on Chaos: handbook for a management revolution,* New York: Alfred A. Knopf.

Peters, T. (1994) *The Tom Peters Seminar: crazy times call for crazy organizations,* London: Macmillan.

Peters, T. and R.H. Waterman, Jr. (1982) *In Search of Excellence: lessons from America's best-run companies,* New York: Harper and Row.

Poffenberger, M. (1990) 'Facilitating Change in Forestry Bureaucracies', in M. Poffenberger, (ed.) *Keepers of the Forest: land management alternatives in Southeast Asia,* West Hartford, CT: Kumarian Press, pp. 101–18.

Pretty, J.N. (1990) *Rapid Catchment Analysis for Extension Agents: Notes on the 1990 Kericho Training Workshop for the Ministry of Agriculture, Kenya,* London: Sustainable Agriculture Programme, International Institute for Environment and Development.

Pretty, J.N. (1994) 'Alternative Systems of Enquiry for Sustainable Agriculture', *IDS Bulletin,* 25, Vol. 2, Brighton: IDS, University of Sussex, pp. 37–48.

Pretty, J.N. and R. Chambers, (1994) 'Towards a Learning Paradigm: new professionalism and institutions for agriculture', in I. Scoones and J. Thompson (ed.), pp. 182-203.

Pretty, J.N., J. Thompson and J.K. Kiara (1995) 'Agricultural Regeneration in

Kenya: the catchment approach to soil and water conservation', *Ambio: A Journal of the Human Environment*, Vol. 24, No. 1.

Raintree, J. (1987) *D&D User's Manual. An Introduction to Agroforestry Diagnosis and Design,* Nairobi, Kenya: ICRAF.

Reusen, R. and J. Johnson (1994) 'Linking Government Agents and Local Users: participatory urban appraisal for artisanal fishing-port development', *RRA Notes*, Vol. 21: 57–69.

Richards, P. (1995) 'Participatory Rural Appraisal: a quick and dirty critique', in *Critical Reflections from Practice, PLA Notes 24*, London: IIED.

Rocheleau, D. (1994) 'Participatory Research and the Race to Save the Planet: questions, critique and lessons from the field', *Agriculture and Human Values*, Vol. 11, No. 2–3: 4–25.

Rojas Ortuste, G. (1996) 'La Participación Popular y el Modelo Boliviano de Descentralización Administrativa', from the Bolivian Ministry of Social Communication's HomePage on Internet.

Röling, N. (1994) 'Facilitating Sustainable Agriculture: turning policy models upside down', in I. Scoones and J. Thompson (ed.) (1994), pp. 245–48.

Rondenelli, D.A. (1983) *Development Projects as Policy Experiments: an adaptive approach to development administration*, London: Methuen.

Schein, E.H. (1992) *Organizational Culture and Leadership*, San Francisco, CA: Jossey-Bass.

Schoonmaker Freudenberger, K. (1994) 'Challenges in the Collection and Use of Information on Local Livelihood Strategies and Natural Resource Management', in I. Scoones and J. Thompson (1994) pp. 124–32.

Scoones, I. and J. Thompson (ed.) (1994) *Beyond Farmer First: rural people's knowledge, agricultural research and extension practice*, London: Intermediate Technology Publications, Ltd.

Senge, P.M. (1990) *The Fifth Discipline: the art and practice of the learning organization*, New York: Currency, Doubleday.

Senge, P.M., C. Roberts, R.B. Ross, B.J. Smith and A. Kleiner (1994) *The Fifth Discipline Fieldbook: strategies and tools for building a learning organization*, London: Nicholas Brealey Publishing.

Shah, P. and M.K. Shah (1994) *Training of Village Analysts: from PRA methods to process*. PLA Notes 19, london: IIED.

Shah, P. (1993) 'Participatory Watershed Management Programmes in India: reversing our roles and revising our theories', in Asia *Rural Peoples Knowledge, Agricultural Research and Extension Practice: Asia Papers*, IIED Research Series, Vol. 1, No. 3.

Shaxson, T.F. and D.M. Sehlolo (1993) *Production Through Conservation: the PTC II programme – Mafeteng, Mohale's Hoek, Quthing Districts, Lesotho*, draft report of the informal mission, 5 September to 1 October, 1993, Swedforest and the Swedish International Development Authority, Stockolm, and Government of Lesotho, Maseru.

Siy, R.Y., Jr. (1987) 'Averting Bureaucratization of a Community-managed Resource: the case of the Zanjeras', in E.D. Martin and R. Yoder (ed.), *Public Intervention in Farmer-managed Irrigation Systems*, International Irrigation Management Institute, Colombo, pp. 35–48.

Someshwar, S. (1993) 'People Versus the State? Social Forestry in Kolar, India', in J. Friedmann and H. Rangan (ed.) *In Defense of Livelihood:*

comparative studies on environmental action, West Hatford, CT: Kumarian Press, pp. 182–208.

Stiefel, Matthias and Marshall, Wolfe (1994) *A Voice for the Excluded: popular participation in development*, Zed Books: London.

Svendsen, M. (1993) 'The Impact of Financial Autonomy on Irrigation System Performance in the Philippines', *World Development*, Vol. 21, No. 6: 989–1006.

Svendsen, M. (1992) 'Assessing Effects of Policy on Philippine Irrigation Performance', *Working Papers on Irrigation Performance*, No. 2, Washington D.C: International Food Policy Research Institute.

Talagune, A.B. (1982) 'Change Agents to Promote Participatory Village Development in Sri Lanka', *Rural Development Participation Review*, Vol. 3, No. 3: 21–4.

Tamang, D. (1994) 'The Use of PRA/RRA Methods in Policy Research and Analysis', unpublished paper, available from the Institute of Development Studies, University of Sussex, Brighton, UK.

Theis, J. (1994) 'Assessing Needs, Analysing Problems and Negotiating Solutions: reflections on PRA Experiences in Vietnam', unpublished paper, available from Loisa Gosling, Research and Information Officer at Save the Children Fund office in London.

Theis, J. and H. Grady (1991) *Participatory Rapid Appraisal for Community Development: a training manual based on experiences in the Middle East and North Africa*, London: International Institute for Environment and Development (IIED).

Thomas-Slayter, B. (1992) 'Implementing Effective Local Management of Natural Resources: new roles for NGOs in Africa', *Human Organisation*, Vol. 51, No.2: 136–143.

Thompson, J. (1991) 'Combining Local Knowledge with Expert Assistance in Natural Resources Management: small-scale irrigation in Kenya', *'From the Ground Up' Case Study No.2*, Washington DC: Center for International Development and Environment, World Resources Institute.

Thompson, J. (1993) 'Process Notes on the Training of Trainers and National PRA Training Workshop, Hambantota, Sri Lanka, 3–18 August 1993', Sustainable Agriculture Programme, International Institute for Environment and Development, London, and Self-help Support Programme, Intercooperation, Colombo, Sri Lanka.

Thompson, J. (1994a) 'From Participatory Appraisal to Participatory Practice: viewing training as part of a broader process of institutional development', *PLA Notes 19*, London: IIED.

Thompson, J. (1994b) 'From Participatory Rhetoric to Participatory Reality: training for institutional transformation', *RRA Notes*, No. 19: 56–60.

Thompson, J. (1994c) 'Participatory Rural Appraisal and the Catchment Approach', an *aide mémoire* to the Soil and Water Conservation Branch, Ministry of Agriculture, Marketing and Livestock Development, Kenya, 2 August, 1994, London: Sustainable Agriculture Programme, IIED.

Thompson, J. (1995) 'Participatory Approaches in Government Bureaucracies: facilitating the process of institutional change', *World Development*, Vol. 23, No. 9: 1521–54.

Thompson, J. and G.A. Nott (1992) *Promoting the Process: report on the first*

PRA workshop for participatory village planning, final report prepared for the Rural Development Division, Ministry of Planning, Policy and Implementation, Sri Lanka, Rural Development Division, Ministry of Planning, Policy and Implementation, Colombo.

Thompson, J. and I. Scoones (1994) 'Challenging the Populist Perspective: rural people's knowledge, agricultural research and extension practice', *Agriculture and Human Values*, Vol. 11, Nos 2–3: 58–76.

Thrupp, L.A., B. Cabarle and A. Zazueta (1994) 'Linking Grassroots Actions to Policy-making for Sustainable Development in Latin America', in I. Scoones, and J. Thompson, (ed.) (1994), pp. 170–7.

Tilakaratna, S. (1982) 'Grassroots Self-Reliance in Sri Lanka: organization of Betel and Coir Yarn producers', *WEP Working Paper*, No. 24, Geneva: World Employment Program, International Labour Office.

Uphoff, N. (1986) *Improving International Irrigation Management with Farmer Participation: getting the process right*, Boulder, CO: Westview Press, pp. 59–75.

Uphoff, N. (1991) *Learning from Gal Oya: possibilities for participatory development and post-Newtonian social science*, Ithaca, New York: Cornell University Press.

Uphoff, N. (1992) 'Local Institutions and Participation for Sustainable Development', *Gatekeeper Series*, No. 31, London: Sustainable Agriculture Programme, International Institute for Environment and Development.

Uphoff, N. (1993) 'Grassroots Organizations and NGOs in Rural Development: opportunities with diminishing states and expanding markets', *World Development*, Vol. 21, No. 4: 607–22.

Uphoff, N. (1994) 'Local Organisation for Supporting People-based Research and Extension: lessons from Gal Oya, Sri Lanka', in I. Scoones and J. Thompson (ed.), pp. 213–19.

Uvin, P. (1995) 'Fighting Hunger at the Grassroots: paths to scaling-up', *World Development*, Vol. 23, No. 6: 927–39.

Wallace, T. (1994) 'PRA: some issues raised by experience in the North', Paper for DSA Conference, Lancaster, September 1994, available from Dr Robert Leurs at the Development Administration Group, University of Birmingham.

Webber, L.M. and R.L. Ison (1995) 'Participatory Rural Appraisal Design: conceptual and process issues', *Agricultural Systems*, Vol. 47: 107–31.

Weisbord, M. (1992) (ed.), *Discovering Common Ground*, San Francisco, CA: Berrett-Koehler,

Welbourne, A. (1993) 'PRA, Gender and Conflict Resolution: some problems and possibilities', paper for the PRA and Gender Workshop, December 1993, IDS, Sussex, available from the Institute of Development Studies, Sussex University, Brighton, UK.

Wijayaratna, C.M. and D.L. Vermillion (1994) 'Irrigation Management Turnover in the Philippines: strategy of the National Irrigation Administration', *Short Report Series on Locally Managed Irrigation No.4*, Colombo, Sri Lanka: International Irrigation Management Institute.

Wisner, B. (1988) *Power and Need in Africa: basic human needs and development policies*, London: Earthscan Publications.

Wisner, B. and L.S. Yapa (1992) *Building a Case Against Economic*

Development, Manuscript, Hampshire College, MA, and State College, PA, Pennsylvania State University.

Womack, J., D. Jones and D. Roos (1990) *The Machine That Changed the World*, New York: Rawson Associates.

World Bank (1994a) *The World Bank and Participation: report of the learning group on participatory development*, fourth draft (revised), Washington, D.C: World Bank.

World Bank (1994b) *World Bank Sourcebook on Participation*, draft, Environment Department, Washington, D.C: World Bank.

World Bank (1989) *Sub-Saharan Africa, From Crisis to Sustainable Growth: a long-term perspective*, Washington, D.C: World Bank.

Wright, Keith (1995) 'Community-based Health Care and its Role in the development of Community Participation for Primary Health Care', MSC dissertation, University of Birmingham.

Wunsch, J.S. and D. Olowu (1990) *The Failures of the Centralized State: institutions and self-governance in Africa*, Boulder, CO: Westview Press.

Index

195

197